PRIMA'S OFFICIAL COMPANION TO

Family Tree Maker

VERSION 5

Send Us Your Comments:

To comment on this book or any other Prima Tech title, visit Prima's reader response page on the Web at www.primapublishing.com/comments.

How to Order:

For information on quantity discounts, contact the publisher: Prima Publishing, P.O. Box 1260BK, Rocklin, CA 95677-1260; (916) 632-4400. On your letterhead, include information concerning the intended use of the books and the number of books you wish to purchase. For individual orders, turn to the back of this book for more information, or visit Prima's Web site at www.primapublishing.com.

PRIMA'S OFFICIAL COMPANION TO

Family Tree Maker

VERSION
5

Myra Vanderpool Gormley

CERTIFIED GENEALOGIST

To Leo and Julie

A Division of Prima Publishing

Prima Publishing and colophon are registered trademarks of Prima Communications, Inc., Rocklin, California 95677.

Publisher: Matthew H. Carleson

Managing Editor: Dan J. Foster

Acquisitions Editor: Deborah F. Abshier

Senior Editor: Kelli R. Crump

Development Editor: Jan Snyder

Copy Editor: Hilary Powers

Technical Reviewers: Paul F. Burchfield II and Marthe Arends

Project Editor: Kevin W. Ferns

Assistant Project Editor: Kim V. Benbow

Editorial Assistant: Rebecca Fong

Interior Design and Layout: Danielle Foster

Cover Design: Prima Design Team

Indexer: Katherine Stimson

Brøderbund, Family Tree Maker, FamilyFinder, Genealogy "How-To" Guide, Genealogy SiteFinder, GenealogyLibrary.com are trademarks or registered trademarks of Brøderbund Software, Inc.

Wyatt Earp's picture courtesy of the Arizona Historical Society/Tuscon AHS#1447.

IMPORTANT: If you have problems installing or running Family Tree Maker 5, please contact Brøderbund at 510-794-6850 or on the Web at www.familytreemaker.com. Prima Publishing cannot provide software support.

Prima Publishing and the author have attempted throughout this book to distinguish proprietary trademarks from descriptive terms by following the capitalization style used by the manufacturers.

Information contained in this book has been obtained by Prima Publishing from sources believed to be reliable. However, because of the possibility of human or mechanical error by our sources, Prima Publishing, or others, the Publisher does not guarantee the accuracy, adequacy, or completeness of any information and is not responsible for any errors or omissions or the results obtained from the use of such information. Readers should be particularly aware of the fact that the Internet is an ever-changing entity. Some facts may have changed since this book went to press.

ISBN: 0-7615-1677-8

Library of Congress Catalog Card Number: 98-66015

Printed in the United States of America

98 99 00 01 BB 10 9 8 7 6 5 4 3 2 1

Contents at a Glance

❖ v ❖

Contents

Contents

Contents

Foreword

Dear family history enthusiasts,

First of all, thank you for choosing Family Tree Maker. We're sure you will find it to be the easiest and most complete resource for building your family tree.

It gives me a great deal of pleasure to finally present *Prima's Official Companion to Family Tree Maker* to you and our many loyal customers. This book is a result of your many letters of thanks and suggestions. We hope it serves to guide, educate, and inspire you while bringing your own family history to life.

Also, after a decade of working with the genealogy community—from beginners to experts—we want to pass along some ideas, tips, and insights to make your journey as successful and productive as possible.

Myra Vanderpool Gormley was chosen to write this book for you. A syndicated columnist and feature writer for the *Los Angeles Times Syndicate*, she is also a certified genealogist who in her spare time, searches for her own elusive family history. She has written dozens of articles for major genealogy publications, and is the author of two books, *Family Diseases: Are You at Risk?* and *Cherokee Connections*.

As you read *Prima's Official Companion to Family Tree Maker*, you will learn how to get the most out of Family Tree Maker. Plus, you'll benefit from expert genealogical tips and short cuts, avoiding many of the pitfalls that lie in wait for the unprepared. Best of all, you will learn the *right* way to get started, to effectively communicate with other genealogists, and to make the most of every resource available to you.

From all of us at Brøderbund Software, we wish you great success on your journey into your family's past.

Doug Mack
General Manager
Brøderbund Software
Banner Blue Division

Acknowledgments

Writers get the recognition, but it is the editors who deserve the praise for we would never succeed without them. Having been both, I appreciate the outstanding work of my editors at Prima Publishing, and wish to give special thanks and recognition particularly to Debbie Abshier, the acquisitions editor--the best in the business, and to Kelli Crump and Hilary Powers, who labored in the trenches, keeping track of everything, making helpful suggestions, and providing feedback. I also appreciate the assistance of Paul Burchfield, the tech editor from Brøderbund, and a special thanks goes to Jan Snyder, a great development editor, and to Marthe Arends, for her invaluable and timely contributions to this book.

About the Author

Myra Vanderpool Gormley, a certified genealogist, is a syndicated columnist and feature writer for the *Los Angeles Times Syndicate*. She is the online genealogy expert for Prodigy Services and co-editor of *Missing Links* and *RootsWeb Review*, weekly online newsletters. Additionally, Myra writes articles for *Colonial Homes* magazine and is contributing editor for *Heritage Quest* and *American Genealogy Magazine*. She is author of more than a thousand articles and two books on the subject of genealogy.

Myra is a member of many genealogical and historical societies, has been a guest on dozens of television and radio programs throughout the United States and Canada, and has addressed numerous genealogical and historical groups and seminars. Among her awards are the National Society Daughters of American Revolution's Continental Congress Special Recognition Award and the National Genealogical Society's Award of Merit for distinguished work in genealogy. She currently is the webmaster for several counties for the U.S. GenWeb project on the Web. In her spare time, she traces her own colorful and elusive ancestors.

Introduction

Genealogy is fun and easy to learn—perhaps deceptively easy. Computers, software, and the Internet help people find out things about their families, but it soon becomes clear that genealogical research involves much more than just gathering names and compiling them in a database. Ancestors aren't just names; they were real people who led fascinating lives—and their history is part of the family legacy they left for their descendants, if their descendants only think to look.

Each family is unique. The further back in time you go, the more difficult it can be to find, access, and understand records about family members. Having found genealogical material, you must sift through the tidbits to figure out if the information pertains to your own ancestors—and if it's accurate. How do you organize it and use it? How do you know you really have the right William Brown? If genealogy were simply a matter of collecting all the information about the Brown, Jones, Vanderpool, or Case families, and then sorting it into generations or family groups, one could just feed raw data into the computer and let it do the sorting and analyzing. But genealogy is much more. It is the tracing of historical bits and pieces buried in old records about possible ancestors—most of them quite ordinary people, the sort seldom mentioned by historians—that presents the challenge and the thrill. It takes no genius or particular skills to find information about well-known personalities. Type in those names in any search engine on the Web, and voilà! But try to find information about your ancestor Alain O'Brien who supposedly came through Ellis Island in 1895, or learn if your John Utley (the one who shows up in the 1860 California census) is the same one who left Wake County, North Carolina, in 1849. Then you begin to discover what genealogical research is all about.

As you delve into your family genealogy, you need a method of collecting, recording, and presenting the vast array of historical facts and artifacts. That's where Family Tree Maker comes in. It's not just a database, it's an excellent tool both for enhancing your research and for pulling together your valuable information into trees, reports, electronic scrapbooks, multimedia presentations, and more.

Who Should Read This Book

This book is designed for genealogists and aspiring family historians who are using Family Tree Maker software. You don't have to be a computer guru, nor do you have to be a professional or experienced genealogist to use it. Most genealogists are so involved with their research that their main wish is for their software program to work, and quickly, with a minimum of hassle or learning curve.

Whether you are a first-time user of Family Tree Maker or have been familiar with the program since it first came out, whether you're a beginning or experienced genealogist, this book is for you. Like tracing ancestors, this hobby—or obsession—is a constant learning process, and the more you learn, the more fun it is.

This book tells you much more than how to use the Family Tree Maker software—it teaches you some shortcuts pertaining to genealogical research and answers some questions you've always wanted to ask. It also shows you how genealogists use the software to accomplish their research goals. Whether the information you need is on the Family Tree Maker Archive CDs, accessible on the Internet, hidden in family records, or stored in some distant library or collection, this book is your guide to researching more information and managing it effectively. Ultimately, you'll be proud of the way Family Tree Maker allows you to present the product of your research.

Overview of Contents

Whether you review the chapters here from start to finish or browse around to review specific subjects, *Prima's Official Companion to Family Tree Maker* is structured for easy use. Here's a brief review of what you'll find in each part of the book:

Part I, "Where to Start," introduces you to the world of genealogy and tells you just what's involved in tracing your family. You set some goals, get ideas for projects, and learn what you can do with Family Tree Maker to accomplish those goals. Then you explore what information to collect, how to collect it, and how to document your sources. Finally, you start to enter data into Family Tree Maker and see how that data automatically shows up in family trees.

Part II, "Exploring Your Family Tree," puts you on track, searching the Family Tree Maker CDs, including the FamilyFinder Index and the World Family Tree. Then it's time to hit the Web with Family Tree Maker Online, learning to use Internet FamilyFinder, Genealogy SiteFinder, Genealogy ResourceFinder, and putting Agents to work for you. Beyond the Family Tree Maker Online Web site, you'll learn what's out there of interest to genealogists all over the World Wide Web—finding vital records, national archives, favorite sites of genealogists, and how to use search engines.

Part III, "Shaping Your Family Tree," shows you all the other places where you can enter data in Family Tree Maker using the More About features. In the More About windows, you can enter narrative text and biographical details that you can include in Genealogy Reports and your family tree. Learn to locate anyone in your Family File by using the Index of Individuals and Find Individual features. Next you can prune your family tree—just in case you've made any errors in your Family File. You can run the Spell Checker and the Data Errors report, to help locate potential errors. You'll also learn to fix relationship links and duplicate entries. With your family tree all cleaned up, you're ready to run all sorts of Genealogy Reports, create several kinds of family trees, and learn to customize those reports and trees.

Part IV, "Computerizing Your Family Tree," shows you the great advantages of computerized family records over strictly paper collections. Creating an electronic Scrapbook is easy, giving you a place to arrange and display artwork, Kodak Photo CD pictures, scanned pictures and memorabilia, sound clips, and video clips. You'll learn to play your Family Tree Maker Scrapbook on a computer screen like a video slide show—always a winner at family reunions—and you can make printed copies too. Next you learn how to run the more advanced genealogy reports, including a bibliography of your sources. Then, using the Book feature, you learn to create an extensive family history book that can include almost any Family Tree Maker item you select—trees, reports, photographs, as well as a calendar and timeline. There are projects that give you examples of how to set up your own book. For exchanging your completed work, you learn how to export your Family Tree Maker file to a GEDCOM file, and how to join the World Family Tree Project. Finally, you can create your own Web page at Family Tree Maker Online with links to reports, the InterneTree, and your family Book.

Glossary. Here's where you can go to remind yourself of Family Tree Maker terms, genealogical terms, and even some computer terms used in this book. If you run across a new word you missed when it was first introduced, check the glossary to find out what it means.

Conventions Used in This Book

To make it easier for you to use this book the following conventions are used for presenting different kinds of information. You should review these conventions before moving on in the book:

- **Clicking.** Toolbar buttons or buttons in dialog boxes are typically chosen by clicking on a button with your mouse pointer. *Click* or *click on* refer to the left mouse button unless the text specifies using the right mouse button. Double-clicking refers to clicking the left mouse button twice in quick succession. Menus and menu commands can also be chosen by clicking on them, even when the instructions say things like, "From the File menu, choose Preferences." Frequently, when you need to select an option from a list box in a dialog box, you do so by clicking on the specified item.

- **Key combinations.** Pressing and holding one key, then pressing another key is called a *key combination.* In this book, key combinations are indicated by a plus sign (+) separating the keys you have to press. For example, Ctrl+P is a key combination that requires you to press and hold the Ctrl key, and then press the P key.

- **Menu names, commands, and dialog box options.** In virtually all Windows programs, each menu name, command name, and dialog box option contains an underlined letter called a *selection letter.* The selection letter is used to make that particular selection via the keyboard, sometimes as part of a key combination. In this book, all selection letters are indicated as an underlined letter, as in View.

- **Text you type.** When you need to type some text to complete a procedure, or when provided with an example of text you can type in, the text you need to type appears in boldface, as in the following: In the Date Born field, type **September 6, 1813**.

Special Elements

You'll find several elements throughout the book that call attention to specialized information. Here's how they look:

NOTE *Notes provide supplemental information that is a bit more technical or that describes special situations you might encounter. Some notes just give you interesting highlights about genealogy.*

TIP *Tips provide shortcuts to make your job easier, better ways to accomplish tasks, or even tricks the experts use.*

CAUTION *Cautions warn you about steps where you might make a mistake that could cause you to lose some of your work. They also tell you how to get out of trouble if you have difficulty.*

Sidebars Take You Aside

Sidebars give you information that is slightly outside the flow of the chapter discussion, or give more detail for a procedure some readers may not know how to perform. You can stop and read them, or continue on with the chapter material.

Contacting Prima Publishing

We welcome your feedback, and would like to hear more about the kind of help you need, other computing topics you'd like to read about, or any other questions you have. Please visit our Web site at **www.primapublishing.com/comments** to get in touch with us.

For a catalog, call 1-800-632-8676 ext. 4444 or visit our Web site at **http://www. primapublishing.com**.

PART I

Where to Start?

CHAPTER ONE

What Is Genealogy?

enealogy has fascinated people as far back as biblical times, and probably beyond. In fact, that's what all those *begats* are in the Bible—the genealogies of notable people of their age. But genealogy is much more than just a monotonous list of names of fathers, mothers, sons, and daughters. It is the story of real people, your ancestors—where they came from, what happened to them along the way, and how you connect to them. It is a story of heroes and cowards. It is about love, pain, joy, deaths, and births. It includes adventure, drudgery, violence, tenderness, and thousands of yet-to-be-written stories of the unconquerable human spirit. These tales are not about fictional characters in movies, books, or made-for-TV plots, but real people—your people and my people and their lives.

Most of my ancestors were rather ordinary people, but they played a role, albeit obscure, in American history and in the histories of the Old World countries from which they emigrated. And so probably did yours. Few references to my ancestors appear in the history books—historians seldom write about ordinary people. Yet my genealogical research has uncovered hundreds of stories about my ancestors and the part they took in everyday, as well as historical, events. Upon my family tree hang—figuratively speaking, of course—many characters about whom I have been able to learn more than just their names and when and where they were born, married, and died. They include rich men, poor men, midwives, wicked stepmothers, accused witches, church clerks, ministers, spies, military heroes, deserters, indentured servants, bigamists, and moonshiners. Historian John Fiske once noted, "Without genealogy, the study of history is lifeless and incomplete." How true.

Testing the Genealogical Waters

According to a 1997 *Newsweek* article, "47 million Americans have started to trace their heritage." An earlier poll by *USA Today* revealed that 74.4 percent of those responding were "extremely/very interested" in learning more about their family trees. Genealogy is a personal and often lifetime hobby. Drop by a library with a genealogical collection, the National Archives or one of its regional repositories, and you are likely to discover there is standing room only to access a microfilm or microfiche reader or check out the computerized records. The desks near the books are often packed elbow-to-elbow with eager family historians trying to dig up their roots.

Technology Opens Windows

Technology, particularly computers and software has been an enormous help to people tracking their family trees, and has made genealogical research much easier than it was a few decades ago. Family Tree Maker was first released by Brøderbund as a DOS product back in 1989. Today Family Tree Maker not only stores family information and prints beautiful family trees, but it helps you find your ancestors. Also, object Linking and Embedding (OLE) technology is used so users can create electronic Scrapbooks, which include multimedia elements.

Technology has brought other benefits to genealogists. The explosion of genealogical data on the Internet and the World Wide Web has opened the way for many researchers. Virtual libraries are open 24 hours a day. You can search files and exchange information with your cousins around the world at 5 A.M. or 11 P.M. The Internet is always open.

It's fun to create family tree charts on a computer. Family Tree Maker takes the guesswork out of figuring out what a third cousin once removed is and makes it easy to count back the generations of your family that you are able to identify and link together.

It can help tie living generations of your family together, too. When my grandson asked if he was really related to the American pilgrims John Alden and Priscilla Mullins, who arrived on the *Mayflower* in 1620, we were able to create an attractive chart on the computer using Family Tree Maker that graphically revealed his connection to these historical figures.

Reasons to Search

Most people start seriously studying their family history later in life than my grandson, however. Often it is the loss of a family member, especially a parent or grandparent that makes you realize that time is flying by and loved ones are not around forever. Midlife is also a time when more people discover they have the time to devote to a hobby. The Baby Boomers are now passing 50, and because of the sheer numbers of this generation, their increasing interest in the genealogy hobby is having a major impact on repositories throughout the country. Baby Boomers are also pioneers of Internet genealogical research, making contact with cousins around the world in ways never dreamed possible just a short time ago.

What makes genealogy such a popular pursuit? Ask a dozen genealogists and you will get a dozen different answers because there is no definitive answer. Genealogy has wide appeal because everyone has ancestors, even if you don't know their names. Most North Americans know their ancestors came from other countries but are vague on the details, and curiosity about exactly where and when are popular motives to begin digging up the family roots. People with fragmented families and lost family histories often decide to research family members that no one will talk or admit knowing anything about. Adoptees are often curious about their biological families. And it's often much more than simple curiosity—many family historians began with a search to learn more about ways their genetic history may affect current health problems or to prepare a family health history in response to a doctor's request. Still others wish to join a lineage society, such as the Society of the Daughters of the American Revolution, the Mayflower Society, or the First Families of Oklahoma. Also, some people like to join genealogical societies to learn how to research their family tree and meet others who share their interest. Most counties and states have local societies. Yet others, like myself, embark upon this hobby in an attempt to learn the truth about some family legends. Little did I know when I began this quest that I would discover more about myself. History becomes alive, personal, and more meaningful when you discover who your ancestors were that actually took part in or were affected by events.

Genealogy has many uses:

- Trace your biological family lines
- Determine your surname's meaning and origin

- ☀ Fulfill religious requirements

- ☀ Learn your medical and health history

- ☀ Track down family legends

- ☀ Join a hereditary society

- ☀ Explore history on a more personal level

- ☀ Determine your ethnic origins

- ☀ Prove or disprove your relationship to a famous (or infamous) personality

- ☀ Find a lost family fortune

- ☀ Leave a written legacy for your descendants

Beyond Legend

To be successful in finding your ancestors, you need to look at those treasured family legends with the cold eye of an investigative reporter. Legends can lead you astray, and yet many people—including your relatives—will cling to them like favorite toys.

You may be surprised to discover that other families have the same or similar legends as yours does. In fact, some legends are so common that you should be alert to them right from the beginning of your research. When you begin your research you will talk to your relatives and they probably will pass along some family stories. Record what they tell you, but keep an open mind about the tales. Some common legends that have been handed down in many families include:

- ☀ We've always spelled our surname this way. . . .

- ☀ Our immigrant ancestor changed his name at Ellis Island. . . .

- ☀ There's a town in England (Norway, Germany, or wherever) named for our family. . . .

- ☀ We've got a relationship to someone rich or famous, or are descended from nobility or royalty. . . .

- Great-great-grandfather was one of three brothers who came to Australia, Canada, or America from. . . .

- Great-great-grandmother was an Indian princess. . . .

- An ancestor disappeared and was never heard from again, or was shipwrecked. . . .

SPELLING OF YOUR SURNAME

The minute you insist your surname has always been spelled a particular way you label yourself a neophyte researcher. Yet grandpa may tell you that "our name has always been spelled Readdy—with two d's." Perhaps his grandpa told him that. And great-grandpa should know how his name was spelled, right? However, what you find as you examine census records, deeds, wills, and church records is the name recorded as Ready, Readey, Readdy, Readdye, and Readie, for example. Spelling, particularly as applied to surnames, was never rigid until the late 19th century. Most of the records in which you will find your ancestors were written down by someone else—a court clerk, enumerator (census taker), or a minister or rabbi—few of whom paid a lot of attention to any strict spelling rules. Indeed, when you look at the original document, you may find that your own ancestor spelled his name three different ways in his holographic will (a will believed to have been written by a person entirely in his or her own handwriting) and signed it with a fourth version. Get over the surname-spelling hump. Listen to how your name sounds. Think how often you have had to spell your name for someone. Think of the many ways you have seen it misspelled. Learn to look for all possible variants of your names or you will overlook your ancestors in the records. The particular spelling of a surname will not identify your ancestor in those old records. If you search only for O'Kelly, you'll miss your great-grandpa hiding in a deed under the name of Kelley or Kelly.

CHANGED AT ELLIS ISLAND

This myth is widespread, even though surnames were rarely changed intentionally at Ellis Island. But Uncle Joe may insist it was. Most passengers were listed on the ship's manifest before the ship left its port of departure. On arrival in the port of New York, the U.S. inspectors boarded each ship and examined the manifest and tickets of all passengers. For those who were taken to Ellis

Island, immigration officials reviewed the questions and answers with each person, and the inspectors developed systems to prevent the misspelling of names. To handle language problems interpreters were on hand who could understand dozens of languages. Researchers often discover that name changes occurred during the naturalization process, years after the encounter with immigration officials at Ellis Island.

> ❊ **TIP** ❊   *If someone in your family claims your immigrant ancestor arrived at Ellis Island prior to 1892, just smile. Ellis Island did not open until January 1, 1892.*

NAMED FOR YOUR FAMILY

It is much more likely that your ancestors took the name of a locality (town or village) or from a castle than vice versa. Almost every town and village in existence during the Middle Ages has served to name one or more families. While a person lived in a town the name of the town would not have been a means of identification, but when he left his hometown, then people in the new town might refer to him as John of Oldham, later shortening it to John Oldham. Of course, John Oldham's son, William, might have been born in Middleton, but the surname of Oldham had by this time become a hereditary one—meaning it was passed along to each succeeding generation. Hereditary names are how a blacksmith or a stonemason might have come to have Carpenter for a surname instead of Smith or Mason.

Did the Drum Castle in Scotland once belong to your family? You might be inclined to think so, if your surname is Drum. However, it was the Irvine family who were lairds (proprietors of a landed estate) there for 24 generations before giving the property to the National Trust for Scotland. Known as the Irvines of Drum, it is the locality name of Drum (located in the parish of Drumoak, Aberdeenshire in Scotland) that is attached to the castle rather than the surname of the longtime owners.

Most surnames have ancient roots. Your ancestor who *first* passed along your surname as a hereditary one may have lived in the 13th or 14th century, and you will be lucky to ever identify him. Use surnames as clues to, not proof of, origins. Surnames have histories of their own, and the histories are not necessarily the same as your family's history. Moreover, an ancestor long, long ago might simply have taken the name of Oldham, for whatever reason, somewhere along the way. Genealogy is full of surprises. You'll encounter many as you search for your roots. Learning about the history of your family name and name changes are part of the fun of the research and some of the challenges of this hobby.

RICH AND FAMOUS KIN

You may be related to someone rich and famous of the same surname, but don't bet the farm on it. Most of us descend from ordinary people. Now and then you will find a famous personality or even an infamous character hanging on your family tree. They are nice decorations and add color to your pedigree, but the real challenge is to trace those undistinguished folks who left few records and moved frequently.

My Uncle Teck told a story—to anyone who would listen—about how his father (my grandfather) once encountered the outlaw Jesse James hiding some bank-robbery loot in the Cookson Hills of Oklahoma and how that money had never been found. As a child I thought that was a wonderful tale—*my grandpa met Jesse James*. For a school theme assignment I decided to write about how grandpa came to make the acquaintance of this notorious character. However, some basic biographical research at the local library crushed my theme topic and ripped apart the family lore. There were some glaring problems with Uncle Teck's story. Jesse James died in 1882 in St. Joseph, Missouri. Grandpa was born in 1873 in Georgia. He came to Oklahoma as a young man in 1892, which was 10 years after Jesse James died. Anyone with basic math skills can figure out that in 1882 my grandpa was only nine years old—unlikely to be wandering alone in the Cookson Hills thousands of miles from his family's Georgia home. When I told my uncle about what I learned at the library, he shrugged it off with, "Well, that's what Papa told me."

Some family legends are impossible to squelch. It isn't necessary to offend relatives by pointing out the gaping holes in the cherished family legends, but don't believe everything they tell you. Like gossip, the stories probably have changed with each retelling. Some families are blessed (or cursed, as the case may be) with wonderful storytellers. But there might not be any truth to the tales. Half the fun of genealogy is finding out the truth. Be wary of noble and royal lineages. Many of these are false and some have been fabricated.

THREE BROTHERS

The three brothers myth probably arose when early-day researchers were unable to find links between men of the same surname in different localities and just assumed they must be related—somehow. No doubt there are instances of three (or four, or five) brothers immigrating to America, Australia, or Canada but don't make such assumptions based simply on the same surname. Like the virus hoaxes flooding our e-mail boxes, the "three brothers came to America (or wherever)" myth is difficult to trace to its origins and almost impossible to eradicate from family stories.

INDIAN PRINCESS

The "princess" designation was used by the English and colonial Americans, and probably originated from stories pertaining to the famous daughter of a chief of the Powhatans—Pocahontas. However, it is inaccurate in most instances, and, of course, common sense will tell you that not everyone descends from a chieftain's daughter.

DISAPPEARING OR SHIPWRECKED RELATIVES

Stories abound about lost relatives or those who disappeared, often into the frontier. Families did lose track of each other in the days when communication was primitive, but with all the sources at your fingertips now you may be able to learn what happened to Aunt Violet, who didn't necessarily die when family legend says she vanished. Perhaps she really did become a dancer who appeared in early movies. Uncle Aaron may turn up on the 1900 census in Alaska, where he went to search for gold (that's where you'll find Wyatt Earp, the famous law officer of Kansas and Arizona, who wandered throughout the mining towns of the American West).

Many ships and boats were wrecked along the coasts and in the rivers, and many people survived these disasters. If such a legend has been handed down in your family—investigate it. It just might be true, albeit embellished somewhat along the way.

TRUE STORIES ARE BETTER

Accept no family legends at face value and do not allow them to blind you to possibilities that contradict the family tales. Actually, the real stories about your ancestors are much better than these tired old legends. Discovering true tales about your ancestors is the real joy of genealogy.

Basics of Research

North Americans descend mostly from people who left other lands because of discontent with conditions—economic, religious, or political. They were impatient and eager to change things. While we like to brag about our ingenuity, most of us don't like to admit we hate to follow guidelines and rules, and that we are terribly impatient people. It is as though we inherited restless, impatient, rules-do-not-apply-to-me genes. While these traits might produce positive results in some areas, they are not good ones for genealogists. No matter how much you hate to follow rules or read instructions, you need to learn some methodology for researching and compiling your family tree to be a good and successful genealogist. It will make your role as the family detective much easier and more enjoyable. Any job worth doing is worth doing right, right?

Avoid the Shotgun Approach

Technology—the Internet particularly—is changing the genealogist's world. For the good in many areas, but the great majority of the records genealogists need and use are not, and may never be, accessible online. The recent explosion of online "shotgun approach" genealogical research requests by eager, new researchers is not the way to go. This approach to family history is a lot like the way junk mailers operate: send a request about some family name to hundreds or thousands of people, the theory goes, and you're bound to find somebody who has all the answers. You will get requests online like, "Send me all you have on the Blakely family!" You needn't bother to answer—and you shouldn't send that sort of request yourself. Keep in mind not everyone of the same name belongs on your family tree, and name collecting is not genealogy. You'll learn how to unlock the secrets of your family's history—how to collect your ancestors and enter information about them into Family Tree Maker—as you go.

What's Involved?

Genealogical research requires three ingredients:

- 👟 Names (including maiden names of females)
- 👟 Dates
- 👟 Places

Those are the necessary components. To find information about anyone you must know his or her name. Your grandmother is not going to be listed as "Grandma Jones" on her marriage license. You will find her recorded as Mary Grant, or perhaps Polly (if that was her nickname) Grant.

Dates, or rather time frames, are important because they often determine what kinds of records you'll find. The records of your ancestors were generated at different times and in different localities for various reasons. You won't know what to look for (or what to ignore as a waste of effort) until you know when and where your ancestors were. If your father or grandfather was born before 1900 in Oklahoma, for example, that state will not have a record of the birth; it did not begin keeping such records until 1908. Moreover, Oklahoma did not become a state until the latter part of 1907. (So what do you do? See the discussion of Oklahoma as a place a few paragraphs down.)

Time frames also help you approximate when your ancestors probably married. They enable you to know what wars they might have served in, and of course, they provide a basis for approximating when they died—all information that you might not have when you begin your research.

Places—or *localities* as they are commonly called in genealogical references—are critical pieces of the puzzle. You must determine where your ancestors were at particular times of their lives so you know where to look for the records. The United States is a large country. There is no database that contains all the births, marriages, and deaths that have occurred in the U.S. in the past 300-plus years. Even the Social Security Death Index (SSDI), huge as it is, goes as far back as 1937 but mostly reports deaths only from 1962 onward. To find information about an ancestor who died prior to 1962, you will need to know the state, county, or city in which that person died.

Also, localities and their histories are important to your research in other ways. To find someone who was born in what is now Oklahoma in 1900, for example, you will need to know whether he or she was born in Oklahoma Territory or Indian Territory. Oklahoma did not become a state until 1907 and the 1900 federal census for this area is arranged by the territorial divisions.

If your great-great-grandfather said he was born in Canada, about 1840, you need to know that Canada was not a country until 1867. What is known as Canada today has been called by many different names over the last four centuries and the dates when the names change are important to researchers.

COLLECTING INFORMATION ABOUT TIMES AND PLACES

Gather information from your family; talk to your parents, grandparents, and relatives; and write down or record their oral histories. Remember the three necessary components of genealogical research: names, dates and places. Also:

- Search for family documents (birth, marriage, and death certificates and military service records), Bibles, photographs, baby books, and high school and college yearbooks.

- Put the basic information (names, dates, and places) about each individual on charts—pedigree and Family Group Sheet (see Chapter Four for details about entering information in Family Tree Maker). Most genealogists use both paper and computer forms to record this information. Cite the sources (where you found or learned the information) properly for each one. If you do not know how, use *Evidence!* by Elizabeth Shown Mills. Tips on citing sources will be covered in more detail in Chapter Four.

- Work in the reverse order of life's events. Start with when and where your parents or grandparents died; work backward in your research to when and where they were married, and then when and where they were born.

- Try to obtain copies of all extant civil and/or church vital records (death, marriage, and birth) for your parents, grandparents, and great-grandparents.

❧ For American researchers, once you have information that takes you back into a time frame of 1920 and earlier, the federal census records can be utilized to trace each line back as far as you can go. These particular records exist back to 1790. Don't skip census years. Start with 1920 (if applicable), then 1910, 1900, 1880 (most of the 1890 census was destroyed in a fire), 1870, 1860, 1850, 1840, 1830, 1820, 1810, 1800, and 1790. The years 1790 to 1840 recorded only the head of household by given name, but these records are still valuable.

❧ Use the Internet to find others researching the same families in a particular locality and time frame. Don't try to collect or compile information about all the Zimmerman families in the world at first. Go to Family Tree Maker Online (**http://www.familytreemaker.com**) to find information. Join mailing lists for specific surnames. Use the online services' forums and bulletin boards to find others working on the same family lines or in the same area.

❧ **TIP** ❧   *Remember neighbors' children often married each other.*

❧ Visit your local public library and any nearby university libraries to explore their genealogical and historical collections. Use their collection of Family Tree Maker CDs. Go to Family History Centers (branches of the Family History Library, the famed genealogy library of Salt Lake City). They are accessible to all researchers throughout the world. Use the databases there, such as the International Genealogical Index (IGI) and Ancestral File, as aids to finding additional records and previous research that has been done on your families.

❧ Study the local histories of the places where your families resided. Comb through every available record, particularly probate and land for American researchers, in those localities, starting with the one where your ancestors died. Don't even think about doing research in the "old countries" until you have exhausted every record your ancestors generated in North America, or wherever they immigrated to or later lived.

❧ Your local libraries and bookstores have how-to books on genealogical research. Read them all. You can never learn too much. Also

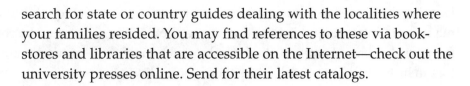

search for state or country guides dealing with the localities where your families resided. You may find references to these via bookstores and libraries that are accessible on the Internet—check out the university presses online. Send for their latest catalogs.

TIP The Researcher's Guide to American Genealogy *by Val Greenwood—published by Genealogical Publishing Company (**http://www.genealogical.com**)—is a good source.*

- Subscribe to the scholarly genealogy periodicals or read them at your library—two that are widely available are the National Genealogical Society's *Quarterly* and the New England Historic Genealogical Society's *Register*.
- Join your local genealogical society. Most of these organizations offer classes for beginners and ongoing educational workshops, seminars, and genealogy conferences. In addition to learning a lot of useful tips, you will make new friends with fellow enthusiasts.
- Family Tree Maker has an online university and offers a series of free, self-paced genealogy classes (**http://www.familytreemaker.com/university.html**). Also, consider signing up for the National Genealogical Society's Home Study Course (**http://www.genealogy.org/~ngs/**). You can learn as you dig.
- Take genealogy lessons online through virtual universities (**http://www.vu.org**).
- Harness the power of the Internet. How-to articles abound and are widely available free online at Family Tree Maker (**http://www.familytreemaker.com**), Board for Certification of Genealogists (**http://www.genealogy.org/~bcg**), and Everton's Publishers (**http://www.everton.com**). Download them for study at your convenience.

Putting Flesh on Bare-Bones Genealogies

Most genealogists wind up with names, dates, and places, but not much biographical information about their ancestors. It's possible to content yourself with learning the names of your ancestors and a few bare-bones facts, but there are many more interesting things to do than see how many names can be collected for your database. Family history can be much more, and putting your ancestors in historical context will make them come alive.

Most of your ancestors were probably ordinary people, unlikely to be mentioned by name in history books. However, you can pick up a great deal of local and social history from various sources and use it to enhance your family history. While you do not want to fictionalize your genealogy, you can include relevant details about the times and places in which your ancestors lived, along with information gleaned from biographies of others who lived in the same time period and location—who probably shared similar experiences with your ancestors.

> ❧ **NOTE** ❧ *It is not necessary to include large amounts of historical facts to make your family history interesting. A light brush paints a better picture.*

To find historical information about your ancestors, you need to know the following:

- ⚘ Ethnic origins.
- ⚘ Religious preference.
- ⚘ Date of immigration to North or South America, Australia, New Zealand, or wherever they roamed, and dates of when they resided at various localities.
- ⚘ Social status (rich, poor, or middle class) and occupation—farmers, merchants, professionals, ministers, horse thieves, politicians, miners, teamsters, indentured servants, or river boat captains?

City, town, and county biographical compilations usually include information about those who were responsible for building a community and establishing its services and institutions. These records can be used to provide you with some background information. Local histories are a must-read for any serious genealogist. Be sure to check the latest edition of *Genealogical and Local History Books in Print*, edited by Marian Hoffman and published by Genealogical Publishing Company (**http://www.genealogical.com**).

Soaking Up the Background

How can you really know your ancestors if you don't know about the times and places in which they lived? Consult *The Subject Guide to Books in Print* (SGBIP) for ideas—you can find it in most libraries. SGBIP is a reference book showing countless local histories that are available, many of them in reprint editions. By following the "see also" listings you can discover other subjects to explore. These include such categories as education, costumes, transportation, social life, and customs.

To get a sense of the history and details about the town, city, state, region, or country your ancestors came from, check old encyclopedias. For example, the 12-volume *Jewish Encyclopedia,* published about the turn of the 20th century, gives specific information on many towns and villages in Europe, revealing facts about Jewish history that probably cannot be found in general history books.

The personal papers of individuals who influenced history and social events can give us a better understanding of these events. For ancestors in the United States, check out the National Union Catalog of Manuscript Collections—known as NUCMC—which lists the photographs, diaries, account books and receipts, genealogies, correspondence, and other personal papers acquired by the country's several hundred archives, historical societies, and special collections. NUCMC covers nationally and locally known personalities; also governors, legislators, inventors, farmers, surgeons, landowners, journalists, authors, merchants, playwrights, actors, soldiers, and others—representing all walks of life. Get your local reference librarian to show you the treasures that can be accessed via NUCMC.

The Internet makes research, especially for genealogical historical material, easy and exciting. There is no excuse for bare-boned ancestors. Put some flesh on them. A great starting place is the History Net (**http://www.thehistorynet.com/ home.htm**). It will lead you to many elements of social history. Explore such subjects as:

- Architecture
- Language
- Marriage, sex, and intimacy

- Naming patterns (choosing given names)
- Child raising
- Dress and costumes
- Health, medicine, and remedies
- Old age
- Death and burial customs
- Food (growing, cooking, and preserving it)
- Migration patterns and methods
- Work and occupations
- Leisure time, sports, theater, and movies
- Superstitions
- Education

What Do I Need to Know?

Work from the known to the unknown—always. Start with yourself, your parents, and your four grandparents, and write down what you know. Don't worry if you don't know everything at this point. Record for each person, to the best of your ability:

- When and where were they born?
- When and where were they married?
- If your parents and grandparents are deceased, when and where did they die?
- What is the maiden name of your mother and both your grandmothers?

Include dates and places of births, marriages, and deaths. These are the major events of our lives. Then include other information such as military service and occupations. If you don't know for sure, and it is not unusual to not know all these facts, simply put a question mark by the information. For example, you think your paternal grandfather (your father's father) died in Michigan right after World War II, but you are not sure. Put down Michigan? (note the question mark) and ca 1946. (*Ca* stands for the Latin *circa,* and means approximately—an abbreviation used frequently in genealogy. Did I mention you would be learning foreign languages too?) Genealogy is a many-faceted hobby—that's what makes it so fascinating.

When you get stuck and your parents say they have told you all they remember, figure out who in the family might know something more. Does your father have an older brother? Perhaps Uncle John remembers when his parents were married. Someone in the family usually knows a little bit about the family—or may have the family Bible or old photographs that will provide the answers. If you don't ask, you'll never know.

Interview your relatives. You'll discover this is one of the great joys of genealogy. Older family members are often delighted to find someone who takes an interest in them and the family. You can conduct interviews in person, or by phone, e-mail, or regular mail. I can hardly wait until I'm old enough to be interviewed for my family history!

Among my treasures from interviews are letters from a cousin in Arkansas—written when he was in his late 80s. He remembered my great-grandfather and shared those memories with me. Always ask about photographs, diaries, letters, and other documents that may give answers or clues about your ancestors. For example, Aunt Helen may have saved all the obituaries or funeral notices of her siblings, her parents, and her grandparents (your great-grandparents). Those documents will provide you with valuable information.

> ❊ **TIP** ❊   *Biography Assistant at Family Tree Maker Online (**http://www.familytreemaker.com/bio/index.html**) provides more than 5,000 writing ideas. You can use it to create a set of questions to help you with your interviews.*

Record the information. Most of us use paper and pencil initially until we can verify the basic information. Then you will be ready to enter it into Family Tree Maker.

Genealogists use two basic forms—understood throughout the world. Until the advent of computer software, these paper forms or charts were completed by hand or on a typewriter:

- Pedigree Chart
- Family Group Sheet

Pedigree charts are like road maps (see Figure 1-1). They give an overview of family lines, showing the basic data about each individual and their connection to you. Notice Family Tree Maker uses two different box styles for each gender.

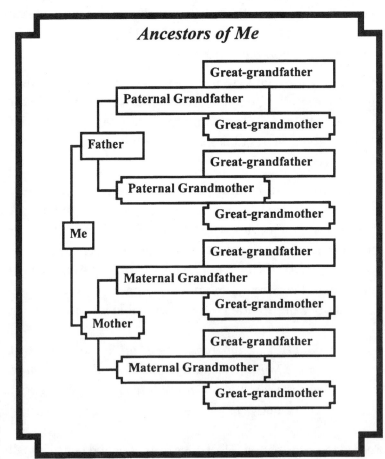

Figure 1-1

Pedigree charts show ancestors from whom you are directly descended.

Earp Genealogy | 3 June 1998

Husband: Nicholas Porter Earp	
Born: September 06, 1813	in: Lincoln County, North Carolina
Married: July 27, 1840	in: Hartford, Ohio County, KY
Died: November 12, 1907	in: Los Angeles County, California
Father: Walter Earp	
Mother: Martha Ann Early	
Other Spouses: Abigail Storm, Annie Alexander	

Wife: Virginia Ann Cooksey	
Born: February 02, 1821	in: Kentucky
Died: January 14, 1893	in: San Bernardino County, California

CHILDREN

1 M	Name: James Cooksey Earp	
	Born: June 28, 1841	in: Hartford County, Kentucky
	Married: April 18, 1873	in: Illinois
	Died: January 25, 1926	in: Los Angeles County, California
	Spouse: Nellie "Bessie" Bartlett Ketchum	
2 M	Name: Virgil Walter Earp	
	Born: July 18, 1843	in: Hartford County, Kentucky
	Married: September 21, 1861	in: Knoxville, Marion County, IA
	Died: October 20, 1905	in: Goldfield, Esmeralda County, Nevada
	Spouses: Magdelana C. "Ellen" Rysdam, Rosella Dragoo, Alvira Packingham Sullivan	
3 F	Name: Martha Elizabeth Earp	
	Born: September 25, 1845	in: Kentucky
	Died: May 26, 1856	in: Monmouth, Warren County, Illinois
4 M	Name: Wyatt Berry Stapp Earp	
	Born: March 19, 1848	in: Monmouth, Warren County, Illinois
	Married: Abt. 1883	in: CA?
	Died: January 13, 1929	in: Los Angeles County, California
	Spouses: Urilla Sutherland, Celia Ann Blaylock, Josephine Sarah Marcus	
5 M	Name: Morgan S. Earp	
	Born: April 24, 1851	in: Pella, Marion County, Iowa
	Met: Abt. 1875	
	Died: March 18, 1882	in: Tombstone, Cochise County, Arizona
	Spouse: Louise Houston	
6 M	Name: Warren Baxter Earp	
	Born: March 09, 1855	in: Pella, Marion County, Iowa
	Died: July 08, 1900	in: Willcox, Cochise County, Arizona
7 F	Name: Virginia A. Earp	
	Born: February 28, 1858	in: Iowa?
	Died: October 26, 1861	in: Pella, Marion County, Iowa
8 F	Name: Adelia Douglas Earp	
	Born: June 16, 1861	in: Pella, Marion County, Iowa
	Died: January 16, 1941	in: San Bernardino County, California
	Spouse: William Thomas Edwards	

Figure 1-2

Family Group Sheets show the father, mother, and all their children with basic information about each one.

Family Group Sheets contain information about one family (see Figure 1-2). A *family* consists of the two biological parents, whether married or not, and their birth children. A Family Group Sheet is where you identify and list all the children of a particular couple. If your mother had children by a former marriage, for example, prepare a separate Family Group Sheet for her, naming her husband at the time and those children born to them.

This book will help you figure out your personal goals, and will discuss what you can do with your genealogical data and how to find more information about your ancestors. In the process you'll learn how to use Family Tree Maker to create beautiful charts and scrapbooks and to compile valuable family histories for your loved ones. Genealogy is a journey into the past that creates treasures for future generations.

CHAPTER TWO

What Are Your Goals?

on't let the question of goals intimidate you. It's useful to think about what you want, of course—but don't worry about figuring it out with any precision. People may tell you to set goals for your genealogical research before you get started, but that's just a variant on the standard advice about shopping: figure out what you want to do first and then buy what you need to get it done. In practice, that's a lot easier said than done. Think of something as basic as an automobile. Well, you want it to run—to get you from one place to another. However, if you've never ridden in a car before, let alone owned one, how can you know what all you might use one for?

It is the same with genealogical research. How do I know what all I can do or might want to do? You probably feel the same way. This hobby, which often becomes a lifetime avocation, has myriad options. You may choose one or two goals now and add others later as your research progresses. Whatever your initial goals for your genealogy, be prepared to change your mind along the way.

How Many Ancestors?

Many people find their goals reshaping themselves as they get further into the hobby of genealogy. When I first started, what I wanted was to trace *all* my ancestors. I soon discovered I was dealing with a lot of people. I had no idea how large a family tree really can be. Everyone has two parents, four grandparents, eight great-grandparents, 16 great-great-grandparents, and so forth. See how those numbers double each generation back? In 10 generations (that's about 300 to 350 years) there are 1,024 ancestors hanging on your family tree.

Collecting and organizing information about more than a thousand people would certainly keep you occupied. And this is just the direct ancestors and an average family tree project—never mind the siblings and cousins in each generation. If you are compiling a family tree for your children, there are just as many ancestors on your spouse's side—so going back 10 generations for each parent means more than 2,000 ancestors to track down. Whew…that seems like hard work.

No matter what you do, you'll be dealing with many more names than most of us can keep straight. Thank goodness for computers and Family Tree Maker. While the numbers seem huge, however, you can manage the project—like any large project—by breaking it down into smaller sections.

After you have done some work, you may decide to focus—at least for a while— just on your father's *father line* (your surname) or on someone on your mother's side who is a particularly engaging character that you'd like to know more about. What about your great-great-grandmother—was she really a beautiful red-haired Irish gal who eloped with a dashing Frenchman and sailed to Australia? Is the story really true—or just a family legend? Families are endlessly fascinating and you will discover there is always one more branch you simply have to explore. Genealogists often spend their lifetimes researching their family trees.

A Whole World of Goals

Genealogy consists of many components. It is more than just tracing your direct line of ancestors back as far as possible. Perhaps you have inherited Grandaunt Elizabeth's research notes and her hand-drawn pedigree charts, which need to be organized, or your father wants some help scanning and organizing his collection of family photos. Is your family having a reunion soon and the genealogy committee wants you to prepare charts to show how everyone is related? Or you've been asked to do the mailing lists and name tags. Once you have Family Tree Maker, it is not necessary to buy additional software to do these projects— the program works great and produces fantastic results.

Charts and stories about your ancestors make wonderful presents, too. Surprise your sister with a specially prepared genealogical scrapbook about your grandparents. She'll love it. Mine did. Or perchance you share my fascination with learning the truth about those family legends and need a way to keep all your research notes and data organized.

Genealogy can be an education in itself—and a way to get more education. For example, it's worth exploring the hereditary societies. You may find that you, or your children or grandchildren, are eligible for one of the university scholarships open only to members of a certain ethnic group or to people who can prove descent from a person who served during a particular war.

> ❋ **TIP** ❋   *Grandaunt—"Grand" aunts and uncles technically are the siblings of your grandparents. You may often hear these relatives referred to as great-uncles and great-aunts—but that's easily confused with the proper term for the siblings of your great-grandparents: great-grandaunts and great-granduncles. To keep them all straight, just remember, after the "grands" come the "great-grands."*

Family Tree Maker makes all these goals (and many others) easy to pursue—or at least much easier than they would be if you had to make up your own forms and keep track of the data by hand. I'll introduce some smaller projects first and then take you step-by-step through creating and compiling more complex projects pertaining to your family tree. Here are some interesting projects to start with:

- Creating scrapbooks
- Converting paper documents to digital records
- Completing a school assignment
- Preparing material for a family reunion
- Compiling calendars of family birthdays and anniversaries
- Assembling special customized reports
- Joining a hereditary society
- Exploring family legends

Designing Up-to-Date Scrapbooks

Paper scrapbooks have been popular for generations. People use them as treasure chests in which to paste pictures and clippings and capture memories of fleeting events. Do you have a few of your own crammed in a box somewhere or in the back of a closet? I worked in Europe for several years and collected postcards of castles I visited, each one with a unique and fascinating history. However, my old scrapbooks are crumbling—how about yours?

Family Tree Maker makes it easy to produce scrapbooks. You can store almost any type of memorabilia or family information in these Scrapbooks, including photographs, certificates of achievement, or original artwork—your own sketches, or those of your children and grandchildren. Anything that will fit in a scanner can go into a Scrapbook. Additionally, technology enables us to add sound clips, video clips, and other OLE objects, Kodak Photo CD pictures and text, and non-OLE picture files such as bitmaps and TIFF files. Figure 2-1 shows an old photo on a Family Tree Maker Scrapbook page.

> ❧ **NOTE** ❧   *Object linking and embedding (OLE) is a method of sharing information between applications within an operating system. Objects can be most any type of data, such as a graphic or a text document.*

> ❧ **TIP** ❧   *You can have your undeveloped film, old negatives, or even old photos put onto a Kodak Photo CD to preserve them and make them easy to include in a computerized Scrapbook.*

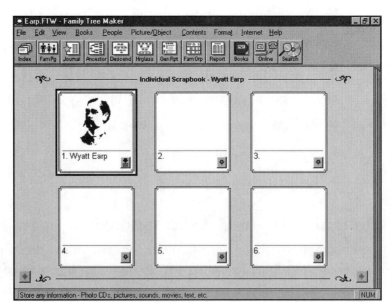

Figure 2-1

Scrapbooks are ideal places for your ancestors' pictures.

Are there artists or photographers in the family? Gather and organize Scrapbooks featuring their artwork. My father loved automobiles; his old photo albums were full of pictures of him and various relatives proudly posed beside or perched upon their cars. I scanned many of these pictures and made them into a Scrapbook that the whole family can enjoy. Do you have any similar treasures around the house? What about pictures and stories of the family pets, or a collection of places you have lived—the houses and the cities?

You have a great deal of leeway when it comes to working out exactly how you want your Scrapbook to look. Figure 2-2 illustrates some of the choices Family Tree Maker gives you for the overall appearance of the pages, and Figure 2-3 shows some refinements for individual entries.

Family Tree Maker automatically sets up a Scrapbook for each individual and each marriage in a Family File. However, you can create a computerized Scrapbook for anyone—no need to limit yourself to family members. You could create a Scrapbook for Rex, your German shepherd, or Tinker Belle, your daughter's favorite cat, if you wanted to.

> ❀ **NOTE** ❀   Family File *is the name given to the databases that you create in Family Tree Maker. You'll assign each database a unique name. See Chapter Three to learn how to create your first Family File.*

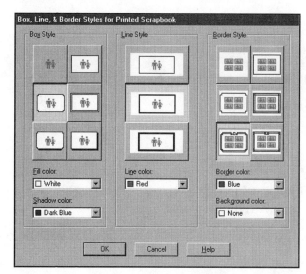

Figure 2-2

Choose from several styles, borders, and colors for your Scrapbook.

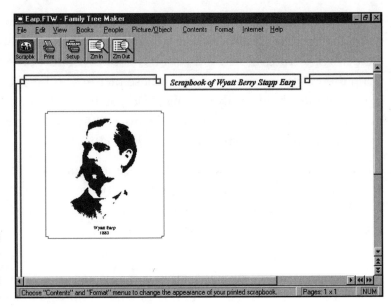

Figure 2-3

Different colors, fonts, and lines can be used in Scrapbooks.

Protecting Old Papers

Think about all the paper documents you have scattered about, tucked here and there in books, albums, and nooks and crannies:

- ✻ Old letters
- ✻ Postcards
- ✻ Diaries and journals
- ✻ Military discharge records
- ✻ School diplomas
- ✻ Marriage certificates
- ✻ Birth certificates
- ✻ Limericks or poetry you scribbled when you were 12 years old and in love with the boy next door
- ✻ That award-winning article you wrote for your high school newspaper

- 🏃 Cherished family recipes

- 🏃 Newspaper clippings of events that touched your life

- 🏃 Obituaries your mother tucked away inside the family Bible

How long would it take you to find any one of these treasures? Would the mice and silverfish have found it first? You can preserve your personal and family history much more easily if you convert these documents to digital format and let Family Tree Maker keep track of them for you.

By converting paper documents to digital you can also share family material via e-mail or a Web site. A cousin of mine in Kentucky discovered letters exchanged between our ancestors in the early 1890s. She scanned some of them and also typed them up (to make them easier to read) and shipped them to me via e-mail. One of them mentions my grandfather doing well in reading and arithmetic at school; it opens a window on a piece of his life. Another mentions one of his siblings—a child who died young of scarlet fever. This child was born in the 1880s and the birth was not recorded in official documents because of the destruction of most of the 1890 federal census. Since she died before the 1900 census, I never knew about her existence. I promptly added her to that branch of my family tree. The same letter also talked about the Kentucky relative for whom the child was named, providing additional evidence of the connection to that family.

Acing School Projects

If your child or grandchild comes home from school with a "family tree" project, you can help find and organize the information for it. Preparing attractive charts showing a child's ancestors or the ancestors of a historical figure is easy with Family Tree Maker. Today's students are familiar with the Internet, CDs, audio recordings, and scanners, and together you and the child can prepare interesting and creative family trees. Chapter Four goes into detail on how to create and build attractive family tree charts.

Wowing the Family Reunion

If your family reunion committee drafts you to help out with mailing lists or identification badges and asks you to prepare charts showing how everyone is

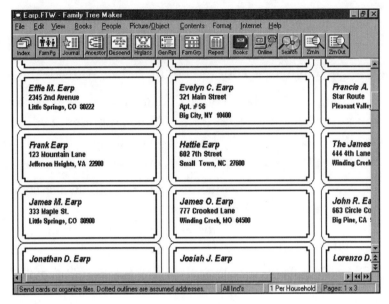

Figure 2-4

These automated
file cards help you
create mailing lists
and name tags for
family reunions.

related to your immigrant ancestors or to each other, say okay. You can do it with Family Tree Maker.

Mailings are easy. You simply give Family Tree Maker each individual's address and phone number and then print directly onto postcards or envelopes. Figure 2-4 shows you the sort of automated card file Family Tree Maker keeps for you. You can also use the same file to create introduction stickers for the reunion. You know, those stickers that say, "Hello, my name is Julie," that are popular for gatherings of any size to help you keep track of who is who.

Family Tree Maker gives you several options for printing out your family tree. If you have access to a large plotter, you can print a tree on a poster-size piece of paper—perfect for family reunions. However, Family Tree Maker also prints trees that contain as much information as you want on as many pages as it takes to show the information. Then you can piece the pages together to create a huge, beautiful tree.

Keeping Social Calendars

My mother was one of the most thoughtful people in the world. She always remembered birthdays and anniversaries. Sometimes she just sent a note when

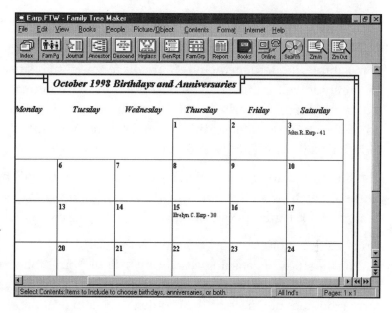

Figure 2-5

Calendars of births
and anniversaries are
easy to create.

she couldn't afford to buy a special card, but she always remembered and saw to it the notes or cards were mailed in time to arrive before the occasion. It was the remembering that meant so much to her friends and family, especially in their later years—not whether she purchased a card. I don't know how she did it—she never had a computer; she never even learned how to type. Most of her life she kept all the dates and addresses in her head, although in the last few years of her life she kept a small address book and fussed about all her friends moving so often.

My memory is not as good as my mother's—but Figure 2-5 shows how Family Tree Maker makes it a snap to keep track of friends' and family members' anniversaries as well as she did. And besides boosting your memory, Family Tree Maker calendars can provide a lot of insight and entertainment, showing you who was born or married on the same month and day. Does your family have patterns for life's major events?

Creating Customized Reports

Years of school and business give the word *report* a discouraging ring for many people—it sounds like work. But what a report really does is take information you already have and lay it out in a useful form. Pure value—and Family Tree Maker makes it easy to get.

For example, modern medicine often calls for medical histories of your immediate family as well as those of your ancestors, and such information can be difficult to track and record clearly. Family Tree Maker gives you the More About dialog box, which lets you enter additional medical and biographical information about individuals in your Family File as you come across it.

The Medical dialog box has fields for recording a person's height, weight, and cause of death, as well as other medical information that seems worthwhile to keep track of. Figure 2-6 shows how this looks onscreen.

And health histories are far from the only useful and interesting kind of information the study of genealogy can bring to light. You'll collect many biographical notes about your ancestors as you trace them through the years. Often this information does not quite fit the profile of genealogical data. Family Tree Maker provides options under its More About dialog boxes where you can enter information about an individual. One of these options is the Facts dialog box (see Figure 2-7)—or you can use the Notes option to include such biographical infor-

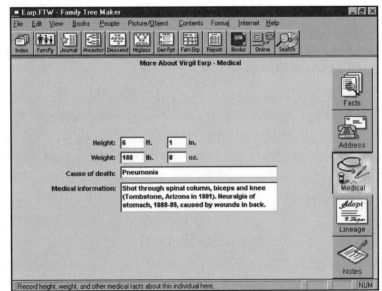

Figure 2-6

You can insert medical information in the More About dialog boxes.

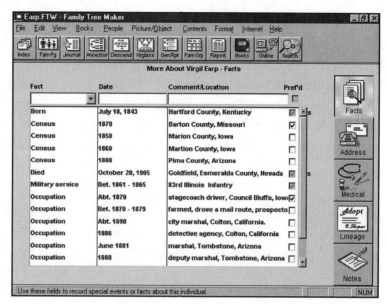

Figure 2-7

More About dialog
boxes provide
additional information
on an individual.

mation about your ancestor serving on jury in Ohio, going bankrupt, or being a
deacon in the Green Valley Baptist Church.

Joining a Hereditary Society

One of the many reasons for tracing your ancestry is to determine and prove
eligibility in a particular hereditary society. Your motive may be purely practi-
cal; as noted earlier, some societies offer scholarships to members and their
families. Alternatively, you may find a group that is interested in preserving
and publishing the histories of your families. Other societies focus on honoring
veterans who participated in various wars and marking their graves. Among
the hereditary societies are:

- ❧ National Society of the Daughters of the American Revolution
- ❧ National Society of the Sons of the American Revolution
- ❧ United Daughters of the Confederacy
- ❧ Sons of Union Veterans of the Civil War
- ❧ United Empire Loyalists' Association of Canada

↯ National Society of United States Daughters of 1812

↯ Society of Descendants of Washington's Army at Valley Forge

Some groups are based on ethnicity—Welsh, Irish, Swedish, Dutch, French, or English, for example. For Americans and Australians particularly, some organizations require proving your ancestors arrived on a particular ship, or that they were overland immigrants on the Oregon Trail or early settlers in a particular locality. Others, such as the Flagon and Trenchers, are open to descendants of owners or operators of a Colonial tavern, inn, ordinary, or other type of hostelry.

Or perhaps you have an ancestor who was an Orphan Train Rider, thereby qualifying you for the Orphan Train Heritage Society of America. In the 19th century and early 20th century thousands of children from the New York Children's Aid Society and other such institutions in the East were placed in foster homes. Groups of five to 30 children, along with an adult leader from the society, were taken by train to communities (mostly in Michigan, Ohio, Indiana, Illinois, Iowa, Missouri, and Kansas) where they found homes with families that selected them. Few of them were adopted officially. Descendants of these children are eligible for membership in the Orphan Train Heritage Society of America, which collects and preserves genealogical and historical data.

While all hereditary societies have their own forms, Family Tree Maker makes it easy to compile your links and documentation to prove your connection to a particular ancestor through whom you can join a particular organization. Once you have the information in Family Tree Maker, it is much simpler to convert it to the specific organization's required format than it would have been to work it up from scratch.

Exploring Family Legends

I come from a long line of storytellers. I'm sure some of my people could have won those "Liars" contests—hands down. I spent many childhood days sitting on the front porch in the cool of the day at my grandparents' house, listening to the old folks spin their yarns. Like Alex Haley, I heard the tales over and over and many of them stuck with me. Even my early discovery that my grandfather really couldn't have met Jesse James, the outlaw, did not dampen my enthusiasm for exploring family legends. Several family characters were only whispered about so young ears could not hear all the sordid details of their escapades and disgrace. However, there were tales of other events and relatives that I heard over and over and I asked these questions:

- Why was my grandmother's family pet dog accidentally left on the eastern bank of the Mississippi River when she moved from Alabama to Indian Territory?

- Why did Cousin Albert marry "that blonde hussy" after going West and striking it rich growing fruits and vegetables in California?

- How could Grandpa Vanderpool recite poetry that would make you cry and also be a deputy marshal that was mean as a rattlesnake?

- Uncle Buck was killed trying to hitch a ride on the railroad—what really happened to him and why did they whisper about his accident?

- What happened to great-grandpa's property that the railroad "stole?"

Then there were the questions I never asked, and should have. Fragments of stories puzzled me until I had to find the answers:

- What was the Cherokee name of my great-great-grandmother and had she walked the Trail of Tears?

- What was my great-grandmother Elizabeth (then a teenager) doing in Atlanta when Sherman came marching through?

- Was it really true that my family fought on both sides during the Civil War? Why and who were they?

So many stories; so little time. I wanted to know if any of my family tales could be historically documented, and so began a lifetime quest to learn the truth. If you share this passion, then you understand why genealogy is so enthralling and has so many facets.

Family Tree Maker gives you much more than beautiful charts and reports. You can add bits of data as you find them and let the system organize it all for you—which means that you can pursue information about your family history in your spare time for as long as it takes and never worry about losing the scraps of treasure that you gather. Most of my family legends I have proved or disproved—except for the one about the property the railroad "stole." I'm still hunting for that.

Tools for Keeping Track of Your Family Tree

Family Tree Maker allows you to do a number of different things with the same information, after you input the data just once. But you do have to get it into the system. Chapter One introduced the two basic forms used by genealogists worldwide: pedigree charts and Family Group Sheets. Take another look at Figures 1-1 and 1-2, and think about what would be involved in using these forms for hundreds and hundreds of ancestors.

Family Tree Maker calls its pedigree charts—like the one illustrated in Figure 2-8—Ancestor trees. They look rather like road maps or flow charts, showing an overview of connections between people.

Family Group Sheets are more detailed, showing genealogical data about one family unit—father and mother and all their children. Family Tree Maker uses the traditional name in this case, as shown in Figure 2-9.

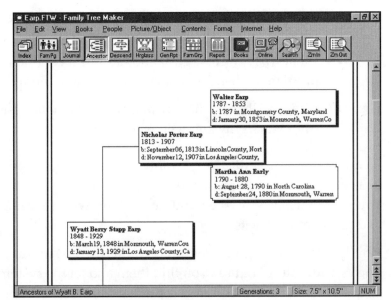

Figure 2-8

Ancestor trees (pedigree charts) show direct ancestors.

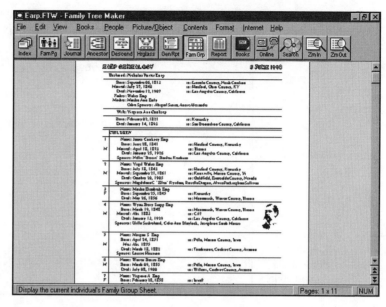

Figure 2-9

A Family Group Sheet shows information about one nuclear family.

Creating Genealogy Reports

Family Tree Maker creates several types of reports. However, the one viewed in a Genealogy Report format will probably be the one you use most. It is valuable to the beginning as well as the more experienced genealogist because it is a detailed listing of family information—in narrative form—showing all the basic genealogical facts and biographical information you have. Moreover, it presents the material in a standard format that anyone can follow. It eliminates the necessity of numbering and renumbering those legions of ancestors you'll find. You will find it handy to take these reports with you to libraries for quick and easy reference.

Family Tree Maker offers you the choice of either *Register* or *NGS Quarterly* formats—the two most popular styles and numbering systems for descending genealogies. Register (originated in 1870 by the New England Historic Genealogical Society), shown in Figure 2-10, is the oldest. The NGS Quarterly, shown in Figure 2-11, has been used by the National Genealogical Society since it started publishing its quarterly journal in 1912. The primary difference between the two is found in the numbering of children who are not "carried forward"— meaning those who do not appear later in the genealogy with more details about them in their adult lives.

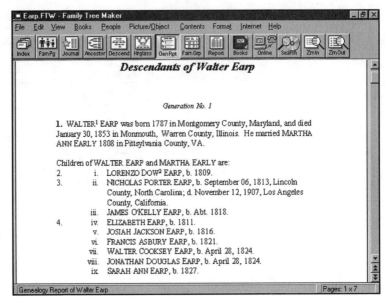

Figure 2-10

A Genealogy Report
shown in
Register format

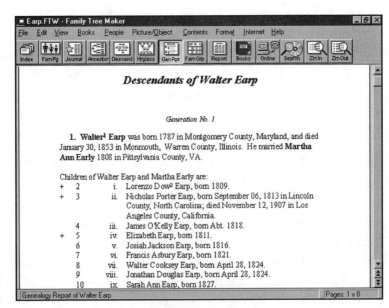

Figure 2-11

A Genealogy Report
shown in NGS
Quarterly fomat

Compiling Databases

As you consider your personal goals for your family history, take some time to learn the capabilities and limitations of your computer and scanner. Consider whether you will want to use many scanned documents and pictures and how large your genealogical database might be. Many experienced genealogists compile separate databases for their family and their spouse's family, and they often create a database that is a work in progress for a particular surname, putting it in a separate Family File while researching and checking out the links among various individuals. Large databases, especially those containing many pictures, can be unwieldy, and you'll soon discover that it looks as though your ancestors have a way of multiplying overnight.

What you're apt to discover soon after you become involved in the pursuit of your ancestors is that all your cousins suddenly turn out to be interested, too. Even your co-workers are likely to get into the act, as they discover remote connections by marriage. All these people will be eager and willing to exchange information—but only about the branches of the family they share with you. They are not interested in all of your other perfectly delightful ancestors.

> ❊ **TIP** ❊   *It is possible with Family Tree Maker to create separate Family Files and later merge or append them for specific purposes, if you wish.*

And a Word to the Wise

In your enthusiasm to discover your heritage you may tend to forget that no one has a *right* to use personal information provided by others. Most family historians are more than willing to share, but always ask first. Be considerate of your living family members' privacy and do not share their material with anyone without their permission—and written permission is best. Do not use the research notes, compiled genealogies, or other material from your cousins without their permission. That work belongs to them, whether it shows a copyright symbol or not.

Many families are fragmented. People lose track of each other, and some of them have arranged to get lost. Some of them have reasons for staying lost, at least as far as some others may be concerned. Be extra-considerate of how you handle information (especially in printed form) concerning less-than-perfect relatives, nontraditional relationships, adoptive situations, and step-relationships. Genealogy is fun—keep it that way by not stepping on anyone's toes or offending your relatives.

Ancestors of George Howard Lafferty
Samuel Lafferty
1801 - 1873
Edwin E. Lafferty
1834 - 1907
Margaret McDowell
1803 - 1861
George E. Lafferty
1867 - 1936
Erastus Fowler
1793 - 1875
Temperence Merrill
1796 - 1871
Nathan Wescott
1818 - 1900
Sarah Ann McMichael
1820 - 1901
Samuel C. Amsden
1822 - 1899
Theresa Jerusa Amsden
1845 - 1934
Clarissa Hubbard
1820 - 1870
The History of George Howard Lafferty
George Howard Lafferty was born September 2, 1894 in Lenox township, Ashtabula County, Ohio, to Amber Amelia Wescott Lafferty and George Edwin Lafferty. A sister, Maud Irene, was born May 23, 1892.
A family of farmers, the Laffertys harvested the land where they lived. On May 9, 1919, they moved to Warren, Ohio, to a house on Forest Street NE. They lived next door to their daughter Maud, her husband Jay Rood Webster, and their three beautiful daughters, Reta, Shirley, and Marion.
As a youth, Lafferty went by "Howard" rather than "George" and signed his name as G. Howard Lafferty. After graduating from Lenox Township schools in 1911, he received a Teachers Certificate and became an educator and later a high school
Principal. He then switched careers and ventured into banking just before World War I.
As a student at Ohio State University during the war, Howard Lafferty hoped to join the army but was classified 5G due to his glasses and other restrictions. In 1923 he received an L.L.B. degree and passed

CHAPTER THREE

Collecting and Documenting Information

emember those "outlines" you had to do in school before you wrote a theme paper? They could be worse chores than the actual writing. However, they were excellent teaching tools, helping you learn how to do a preliminary sketch showing the principal features of a theme—a game plan, in other words. Genealogy does not require an elaborate outline, but you will discover that a game plan for collecting information is useful. What should you collect and where should you go to get the information? In this chapter, you will learn more about interviews, sources and finding aids, libraries and collections, and ways to organize the materials you are collecting.

Developing Your Interview Strategy

Interviewing relatives, friends, and neighbors does not have to be a stiff formal event. In fact, it is best when it is conducted as though you were just chatting. Call or write your relatives first and set up a convenient time. Keep the first interview to about an hour. As my grandmother used to say, "Don't wear out your welcome." Keep your questions simple, direct, and focused on the biographical and genealogical material you need. However, this does not mean putting your relatives on the witness stand and grilling them about specific dates and times. Let Uncle Rick ramble (up to a point, of course) lest you miss some valuable information squeezed in while he tells you his "war stories."

❋ TIP ❋   *The Biography Assistant (**http://www.familytreemaker.com/ bio/index.html**) at Family Tree Maker Online is an excellent tool; it will help you come up with a list of questions to ask and inspire you with creative writing ideas.*

Beginning with Yourself

Genealogy begins with interviewing yourself. Write down what you know about yourself: When and where were you born? When and where did you marry? Where have you lived—what were the dates? Elaborate on as many of the rest of these items as you can:

- Occupation or profession.
- Education.
- Hobbies.
- Religious affiliation.
- Military service (if so, when and where, and in what capacity?).
- Spouse's name? Birth date? Place?
- Children's names and birth dates. Where were they born?

> **NOTE** *In your quest to obtain the three main ingredients of genealogy, keep in mind that you need these bits of information:*
>
> - *A full name for each family member (including maiden names of all women).*
>
> - *An approximate date (the year or at least a 10-year time span is helpful) of a vital event (birth, marriage, or death).*
>
> - *A place (locality) of a vital event—where a person was born, married, died, or resided. The more precise the locality (village, town, parish, län, förgderi, département, commune, canton, county, state, or province) the better.*

> **TIP** Vital records *are any records pertaining to births, marriages, and deaths.*

When you have exhausted your memory and recorded what you know about yourself, ask your parents the same questions. Get names, dates, and places. You're on your way to compiling a genealogy.

Interviewing Family Members

Interviewing family members may be a new experience for you (and them, too). Keep in mind you are the one asking for a favor, so be considerate of their time and feelings. No one can remember—on demand—full names or exact dates and places. If you can learn to ask gentle but specific questions, you will be rewarded. If you own a tape recorder, and if it is OK with the person being interviewed, use it. However, always take backup notes. Electronic gadgets have a way of failing at critical moments. Jot down the information in a notebook. Video cameras are splendid devices, but not everyone is comfortable with them—or with being "on stage." If you are experienced using video cameras, and if it is OK with your relative, then go ahead and videotape the interview. However, if someone is uncomfortable, don't insist. Perhaps after you have established a rapport with Uncle Harry, he will consent to do an interview on video camera.

Use family photographs as icebreakers in interviews. They are the best memory joggers around. You may well run into someone like one of my aunts, who insisted she did not know anything about the family, but regaled me with stories when I shared some old photographs of her as a beautiful young lady. (She remembered the color of the dresses and hats she was wearing; identified who her beaux were and when and where the pictures were taken; and recognized aunts and uncles, cousins, and her maternal grandparents—my great-grandparents. She added a great deal of useful information to my collection and we spent a delightful evening together in the process.) And don't stick to photos of people you know! Dig out those wonderful old pictures with no names or dates on them. So what if you haven't a clue about the people in them or the places where they were taken—your Aunt Clare might know. Take the pictures (or photocopies of them) with you when you go to interview her. Be sure to ask her if she has any old photographs, too.

Don't ask anyone for "all the information you have about the family." That's a turn-off, and a sure way to irritate your relatives, who may feel threatened by your demands. As strange as it may seem to those who are so interested in genealogy, there are people who just don't care. When you initially contact family members for interviews, explain your purpose carefully. Make it plain that:

- ❧ Your goal is to record and understand your family's history.

- ❧ There is no undistributed family inheritance that you hope to claim.

- ❧ You are not trying to expose the family skeletons.

- ❧ You do not want their treasured photographs or heirlooms.

- ❧ You are interested in their stories.

- ❧ You are creating a family tree on your computer and will be glad to print them some nice charts when you finish.

Interview your relatives separately if at all possible. Otherwise, you may discover, as I did, that Uncle John might challenge Aunt Thelma's version of an incident, a date, or a place, both insisting they are correct, of course. I was shocked to learn that my sister does not remember childhood events as I do. Obviously, her memory is faulty. However, don't argue when one relative's information disagrees with another's. You might mention that the information you have (without saying who provided it) is that a certain event took place on a different date or in another place. However, don't offend your relatives when they insist they are correct. Just smile and jot down the information. I once interviewed about a dozen family members at a family reunion, and learned that on many family stories none of them agreed; on a few stories only two or three agreed; and that in no instance did they all agree on anything—and some of them are still arguing.

> ❧ **TIP** ❧   *Your extended family can give you unique insights on your grandparents, parents, and yourself. Through their stories you will understand your family better. And by asking the right questions, you can obtain the genealogical data you need to pursue your family's history.*

Interviewing Friends and Neighbors

Definitely don't overlook the friends and neighbors of your parents and grandparents. Some of their lifelong friends or long-time neighbors will share information with you—or relate tales that your mother or grandfather told them. My mother's best friend told me more stories about my mother than anyone in her family ever did. Louise knew mother for 50 years—they reared their families together, vacationed together, went to church together, shared their prosperous and lean years, their grief and joy as mothers, wives, friends, and women. This dear family friend painted a picture of my mother that I, as a daughter, never knew. Even though your parents, grandparents, and closest relatives may all be gone, you can still find wonderful information about them from others who knew them. You never know what you can learn, unless you make the effort and ask.

Interviewing Techniques

Interviewing is a word that invokes images of the confrontational journalist badgering someone trying to hide something. That is not the technique to use if you want to gain information from your relatives. You want to talk to them to learn genealogical and biographical tidbits about family and friends. You want to stir their memories in order to help them recall specifics. The basic techniques apply whether the interview is conducted in person, or via phone, regular mail, or e-mail.

Oral Histories

Oral histories are simply information of historical or sociological importance. They are often obtained by tape-recorded interviews with persons whose experiences and memories are representative or whose lives have been of special significance. To the genealogist, the lives of all relatives are significant. While your mother's or grandfather's oral history may not be sought by historians, you, as the family historian, should obtain it. Wouldn't you love to find a story about your great-great-grandfather, as he told it, detailing the events of his life? Here are the secrets of obtaining oral histories and information from your relatives:

- Let your subjects talk about themselves.

- Gently interject questions that will stir their memories about particulars; memory must be led back gradually.

- Ask specific questions.

- Use some props (photographs, heirlooms, and Family Group Sheets).

- Meet several times, if possible.

- Be sensitive and diplomatic—some subjects might be too painful to approach casually. Respect your relatives' right to privacy.

- Take written notes (even if you are taping or video-recording).

- Ask for relationship clarification. Which "grandpa" is being referred to? Who was Cousin Rose from Joplin; whose cousin was she, and was McCready her maiden or married name?

- Listen—listen—listen.

Interviews by Phone and Mail

Some of your interviews will be in person, but probably many will be conducted by phone, e-mail, or old-fashioned paper mail. Years ago I corresponded with a distant cousin, who was in his late 80s at the time. His letters, albeit a bit disjointed and rambling at times, were sparkling gems of family lore and genealogy. His own children and grandchildren did not have much interest in family history—at the time—and he was delighted that I did. He sent photographs, old letters from other cousins, and details about my great-great-grandfather's Civil War service. He told about how his grandmother and her sister had a "falling out" over their children's squabble; and then how their husbands "got into a big fight" over the matter, with the result being that one sister and her family pulled up stakes and took off with the next wagon train to California. The sisters never heard from each other again, as far as my cousin knew. However, a descendant of the sister who went to California and I are now in touch, comparing family facts and lore.

> ❊ **TIP** ❊ *The easiest way to obtain copies of Family Group Sheets is to start on a family page and choose to print it. When the Print dialog box appears, check the Print Empty check box and then click on ok to print. You'll end up with a perfect data collection form. (See the section, "Organizing Information," later in this chapter for more information.)*

When you can't visit relatives in person and you are trying to obtain information, make the process easy for them. Again, remember you are the one asking for a

favor. Send copies of Family Group Sheets and ask your relatives to fill out what they know. Include some specific questions—and leave room for the answers. Send along a business-size (No. 10) SASE (self-addressed stamped envelope). If you have old photos that your correspondent might be able to identify, make photocopies of them—never send original pictures or documents—and send them along with your request for family information. Ask everyone about old family photos, papers, letters, and Bibles. You never know who has squirreled away such treasures. However, few people will be willing to part with their originals, so offer to pay costs for making copies of photographs, letters, and other records. Also, offer to share copies of your research with interested family members. Always ask if they know of other family members who might have information.

Most of us live busy lives, and taking the time to fill out a genealogy chart may not be high on the priority list of some of your relatives. Your request may arrive at an inopportune time. If you do not receive an answer within a reasonable period, send a polite follow-up note and another SASE or make a phone call to inquire if they received the material. Don't be pushy. Be patient—you do not want to alienate a possible source by demanding information. Some people hate to fill out charts, and remember many older people suffer from arthritis and, for them, writing can be a difficult chore. If you suspect either might be case, call that cousin and take the information by phone and fill in their Family Group Sheet yourself.

Jogging Memories

Memory is a selective thing. For example, your grandmother may not recall the exact dates her grandparents died, but by asking her if they died before she was married, or before or after World War II, you may jog her memory into a more precise time. For a genealogist, any time frame is helpful. Sometimes it is helpful to determine an approximate time frame by remembering the house in which you lived. Here are some questions you can use to stimulate remembrance when interviewing relatives:

> ❧ **Early childhood.** When and where were you born? In a hospital or at home? Were you the oldest, middle, or youngest child, or what number in the birth order?

❄ **School days.** What did you wear to school? Did you have a favorite teacher or subject? What games did you play? Were you involved in extracurricular activities? Sports, music, drama, or clubs? What about music and dances do you recall?

❄ **Teen years.** At what age were you allowed to date? What was your first date like—and with whom? Where did you go? Did you get an allowance? What were your responsibilities at home? What were some of the rules and restrictions in your family?

❄ **Religious traditions.** Describe your early religious training. How did your family observe religious holidays?

❄ **Vacations and special occasions.** How did you spend summers? Did the family go some place special every year? Did you have summer jobs? What about family reunions? Were you ever a flower girl, bridesmaid, ring bearer, or best man at a wedding? Are there any pictures?

❄ **Pets.** Were you allowed to have pets? What was the name of your first or favorite pet? Were you always bringing home strays? How did your parents handle that?

❄ **Wartime and news events.** Did you serve in the armed forces—drafted or enlisted? Which branch? Where were you stationed? What was basic training like? Did you serve overseas? When and where? Do you remember ration books? Where were you on Armistice Day, V-E or V-J Day, or when John F. Kennedy or Martin Luther King Jr. was assassinated?

❄ **Jobs.** First, favorite, or toughest. How much were you paid? What kind of hours did you work? How did you get back and forth to the job?

❄ **Courtship and marriage.** How and when did you meet your spouse? When and how did you decide to marry? Was there a formal proposal? An engagement ring? What was the family's reaction? When and where did you marry? Was it a big wedding? A religious or civil ceremony? Who attended? What was going on in

the world during the early days of your marriage? What did your first apartment or home look like? How much did it cost? Was it furnished? Did you inherit furniture from your families?

✿ **NOTE** ✿   *My mother recalled that the first apartment she and dad rented had only two rooms, it cost $6 a month, and was unfurnished. It is the little details like these that will enable you to turn a bare-bones genealogy into a family history.*

- ✿ **Parenthood.** When and where were your children born? How did you pick the names for the children?
- ✿ **Other subjects.** Divorce, adoption, and remarriage can all be sensitive subjects. Some family members will prefer not to discuss them. Don't insist.

Expressing Your Gratitude

Thanks and follow-ups are an important part of the process. It's a simple courtesy to let your relatives know you appreciate their help. It's often amazing how much more information they'll give you when you get back together because they're used to you and have had some time to think about what you're asking. After the interview:

- ✿ Thank people for their time and help.
- ✿ Compare (privately) notes of information from family members.
- ✿ Highlight any contradictory "facts" that you have obtained from different relatives and any other issues that might have come up during the conversation for follow-up interviews.

Going Beyond Information from the Family

Once you have talked to your relatives and friends and have compiled as much information as you can glean from them, you will want to begin the verification process of determining if the oral histories and basic data you have are correct. It is not that you don't trust Uncle Ron or your parents, but the genealogical research process involves verifying all the information you gather. Moreover, you will be eager to learn more about your family and find other cousins who may share information with you. Becoming a family historian is somewhat akin to becoming a detective. You want the facts. Stories are wonderful, and you will certainly want to weave those into your material, but first you need the facts.

Genealogical research is a classic example of a multi-tasking project. You probably will have several research activities going on at the same time most of the time. For example, you will write to various state vital records offices to obtain copies of death certificates, and write (the old-fashioned way) to county clerks requesting copies of marriage records. (No, not everything is online yet.) While you are waiting to hear back from those offices, you can explore other avenues such as:

- Searching for obituaries.
- Seeking cemetery and funeral home records.
- Exploring near and far libraries (covered later in this chapter).
- Learning more about the places where your ancestors lived.
- Combing the World Wide Web for genealogical and historical information.
- Tracking down family histories and genealogies—in print and online.
- Using the Family Archive CDs to search for additional information.

In genealogical research, each new clue leads to even more clues. You learn to explore many records and make use of various sources and finding aids. So what's a finding aid? What's a source? The two are often confused by newcomers to genealogy. They are similar, but serve different functions.

What's a Source?

You'll often hear genealogists talk about *sources*. When the cousins you find on the Internet ask, "What is your source for that information?" don't be offended. They are not questioning anyone's integrity or memory; they simply want to know whether the information came from oral tradition, a death certificate, census, will, newspaper article, family or county history, or what-have-you. "A blue book at the library" is not a proper citation of your source.

A *source*—in genealogical circles—is the means by which a particular bit of information came to the researcher. Genealogists borrowed this term from historians, who separate sources into two categories:

 ❊ **Primary sources.** The first or earliest documents in which a particular piece of information was recorded. Primary evidence is considered the most reliable, and in the case of a document, it is the original, the one actually written at or near the time of an event.

 ❊ **Secondary sources.** Published works, including those distributed electronically, either copied or compiled from primary sources, or reflecting the conclusions of a researcher.

EVALUATING EVIDENCE

Frequently you will encounter the term *evidence* relating to genealogy. If you watch *Court TV* or like to read stories and see movies dealing with court trials, you are familiar with this term. Evidence, in the legal sense, is simply the physical form in which information is presented. Evidence comes in three different types:

 ❊ **Oral.** A witness gives testimony.

 ❊ **Documentary.** A written document (sworn statement).

 ❊ **Physical.** A tangible object (a bloody knife).

The soundness of evidence can range widely from very reliable to highly suspect. In many ways a genealogist becomes both a judge and a jury when looking at evidence pertaining to family history. There is no inadmissible evidence in genealogy—you can consider everything you find. Most of the genealogical records you discover and deal with are documentary, but that interview with Aunt Rhonda is evidence, too—it's considered oral history.

For example, here is some evidence you might be using in your research. Say you interview Aunt Rhonda, and she provides this information about her mother (your maternal grandmother):

Sarah Elizabeth Case was born November 29, 1903 and married in 1925. She died March 1, 1985, in Boston, Massachusetts.

You send for your grandmother's birth, marriage, and death records from the Massachusetts Registry of Vital Records and Statistics (lucky you—Massachusetts is one of the few states with all these vital records in one place this early in the century). However, you discover the following discrepancies:

- Birth certificate says she was born November 29, 1902.

- Death certificate says her birth date was November 29, 1904.

- Tombstone says she was born November 29, 1903 and died March 1, 1986.

- Marriage record of June 20, 1925, lists her age as 23.

- In the 1910 federal (population schedule) census she is listed as age 7.

- In the 1920 federal census she is listed as age 17.

You might assume that if two or more sources or pieces of evidence agree, you should go with that information, but that would be incorrect. Here is where you learn to "weigh the evidence" and determine which record is more likely to be correct. Usually, this is the primary record—the original—created nearest to the time of the event, which in this instance would be the birth certificate. This doesn't mean it is completely correct or that primary sources are always right, but in this instance the birth certificate is more likely to be correct than Aunt Rhonda's memory, especially if she was not an eye-witness to the event, which, of course, she was not.

The death certificate information was provided by someone who may or may not have known for sure when your grandmother was born—or the clerk made an error in recording it. The tombstone information was created from information supplied by someone, and the stone carver might have misread the information, or simply made an error in the inscription. The marriage record, while considered a primary source for the wedding information, is a secondary source for the bride's age. Again, you don't know if your grandmother claimed to be 23 years old in June of 1925, if the clerk made an error, or perhaps the bridegroom gave the erroneous information. Perhaps he simply assumed that since she said she was born in 1902 she was 23 on the date of her marriage, not calculating correctly that she actually would not be 23 until her birthday in November of that year.

The census information is technically correct in this case, since the age information was supposed to be as of the official Census Day (not necessarily the day of the enumeration). In 1910, Census Day was April 15; in 1920, it was January 1. However, with census data, you don't know who gave the information or whether an error occurred in the recording or copying of these records.

DOCUMENTING SOURCES

If you neglect to record where you found information, you will have no way of judging the reliability of that pile of data, or deciding which of the pieces of evidence you have on anything is likeliest to be true. Worse, you will not remember where you obtained the so-called facts. Was great-grandma's name Jennie or Nancy Jane? Did your great-grandpa marry two different women or was Jennie a nickname for the woman named Nancy Jane? If you are the descendant of Jennie, not Nancy Jane, it is important that you identify your ancestor—otherwise you might be barking up the wrong tree, genealogically speaking. But how will you know which source is more likely to be correct if you neglect to record where you found them—and can find them again, easily, if need be.

Documentation—or the citation of sources by genealogists—was not considered so important in earlier times, even by scholars. Easier access to records and more careful methodology today reveal that many genealogies have been based on shoddy evidence, poor scholarship, and outright fraud. While we all wish to trace our ancestors back as far as possible, who wants the wrong characters hanging on the family tree? The argument that you are just doing it for your family is not a valid excuse for not documenting (recording) your sources. You will share your information with others—in print, in GEDCOM, or on your Web page—and someone will share that with someone else, and so on and so forth. Eventually it will wind up published in the Family History Library's Ancestral File or part of Family Tree Maker's World Family Tree.

> ❊ **TIP** ❊ *GEDCOM (Genealogical Data Communications) is a standard file format for exchanging information between genealogy programs.*

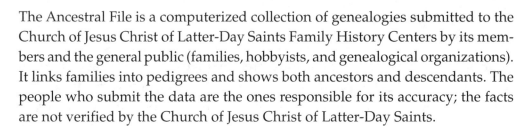
The Ancestral File is a computerized collection of genealogies submitted to the Church of Jesus Christ of Latter-Day Saints Family History Centers by its members and the general public (families, hobbyists, and genealogical organizations). It links families into pedigrees and shows both ancestors and descendants. The people who submit the data are the ones responsible for its accuracy; the facts are not verified by the Church of Jesus Christ of Latter-Day Saints.

The World Family Tree Project is sponsored by Brøderbund (Family Tree Maker's publisher) and is a massive, ever-growing, CD-ROM database consisting of thousands of family trees and millions of individuals. The information is submitted by family history enthusiasts who want to share their information.

> **TIP**   *As you collect information, note your sources completely. Leave a paper trail either you or anyone else—next week or years later—can follow. It does not matter whether the family Bible, a tombstone, or Uncle Jim's information is correct; what is important is exactly where you obtained the information. You will discover that many genealogical "facts" disagree with each other.*

Documenting is not difficult. Simply indicate where you obtained the information, along with enough additional information so that another researcher can determine what records you examined. When you jot down exactly where you

Value of Source Citations

You will really appreciate how worthwhile documentation can be some day when you discover an old family history about your ancestors, and the author claims that the information linking your line to, say, a Revolutionary War soldier, is found in the will of George Humphrey. But the author doesn't mention where—the repository or locality—this document was found. You'd love to see and obtain a copy of this old will, but you have no easy way to find it, because the author neglected to cite his source properly. Lack of citation forces you to reinvent the wheel on research—duplicating efforts and wasting money. It is a common problem, particularly with electronic genealogies, but as genealogists become more knowledgeable and careful in their work, they are citing their sources in more useful terms.

obtained your information, it makes it easier to judge which source is more likely to be correct. Frequently you will discover you need to reexamine sources for various reasons. If you have source citations you can quickly find them again.

> ❧ **NOTE** ❧   *Information you learned from an oral history interview can be cited simply as:*
>
> *John Henderson, personal interview with the author, Seattle Washington, 24 September 1997.*
>
> *If you found information in a book, list the author, name of the book, where it was published, name of the publisher, the date, and the page number:*
>
> *John Smith, Early Settlers of Texas (Dallas: Texas Publishing Co., 1983), p. 94.*

Seeking Documentation Tips

For some tips about documentation, read the following articles available from Family Tree Maker's Genealogy How-To Guide (**http://www.familytreemaker.com/issue19.html/**), as shown in Figure 3-1:

- 🏃 *Why Bother? The Value of Documentation in Family History Research* (**http://www.familytreemaker.com/19_kory.html**) by Kory Meyerink

- 🏃 *Carla's Tips for Sources* (**http://www.familytreemaker.com/19_carla.html**) by Carla Ridenour

- 🏃 *How To Cite Sources* (**http://www.familytreemaker.com/19_wylie.html**) by John Wylie

- 🏃 Tutorial: Using Family Tree Maker's New Source Documentation Features (**http://www.familytreemaker.com/19_ftwsrc.html**)

> ❧ **TIP** ❧   *You can find articles on documenting your sources at Family Maker Tree Online under the How-To Info section. Click on the How-To Articles from our Back Issues (www.familytreemaker.com/backissu.html) link.*

Because genealogists explore many and varied records and it's easy to forget how to cite them (properly), an excellent book for your personal library is *Evidence! Citation & Analysis for the Family Historian,* by Elizabeth Shown Mills

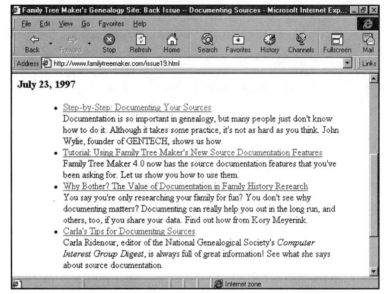

Figure 3-1

Read excellent articles
on documentation at
Family Tree Maker's
Web site.

(**http://www.genealogical.com/evidence.htm/**), which was published in 1997
and is the most up-to-date manual available on the subject. You learn by study-
ing genealogies published in scholarly periodicals such as the New England
Historical Genealogical Society's *Register*, the National Genealogical Society's
Quarterly, the New York Genealogical and Biographical Society's *Record,* and
The American Genealogist—TAG to its friends.

> ❧ **NOTE** ❧   *Among the most frequently used sources are vital records (cer-
> tificates), censuses, wills and probate records, Bible records, books, periodicals,
> CDs, and military and church records. Once you learn how to cite these and
> do it a few times, it will become second nature to you.*

What's a Finding Aid?

Anything that can help you find the information you seek about your ancestors
can be considered a *finding aid*. Some examples include:

❀ Census indexes

❀ Compiled marriage records

* ⚘ Name databases

* ⚘ Compiled but undocumented genealogies

* ⚘ Guides to various government records

* ⚘ Bibliographies

Use finding aids to locate the actual records and base your findings on those documents, not on the information in the finding aid. As you research your family, finding aids—especially those available on the Internet—will reduce the time it takes to learn about and find records that will enable you to compile information on your ancestors. Use any and all to help you in this quest.

> ⚘ **CAUTION** ⚘   *Just as you don't believe everything you find in print or read on the Internet, don't blindly accept information available in finding aids. Check the actual sources for yourself and verify the data.*

> ⚘ **TIP** ⚘   *Keep in mind that just because an index doesn't mention your great-grandfather, that doesn't mean you won't find him in the census or marriage record the index claims to cover—the people preparing it might well have misspelled or missed his name. It took me three tries to find my great-grandfather on the 1900 Indian Territory census, and I thought I was reading carefully.*

Finding cousins and other living relatives is much easier than it used to be. This is especially true if the surname of your family is not a common one. Many CDs are available that contain residential telephone numbers for different countries. Also, access to many of these databases is available on the Web.

FINDING A PHONE NUMBER

At Family Tree Maker Online, you'll find a Phone Number Search for U.S. and international phone directories. Look for the Phone/Address search link on the main page and click on it to go the search page (**http://www.familytreemaker.com/ww/wwphone.html**) shown in Figure 3-2. Scroll down and then type in the information you know for a U.S. name or address: name, city, and state if you've got them.

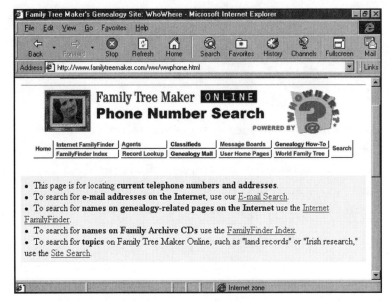

Figure 3-2

Family Tree Maker's
Web site offers several
search options for
phone numbers and
addresses.

Notice that at least the Last Name is required for this search (see Figure 3-3). However, entering each piece of information about which you are certain will help narrow the search and produce a shorter list.

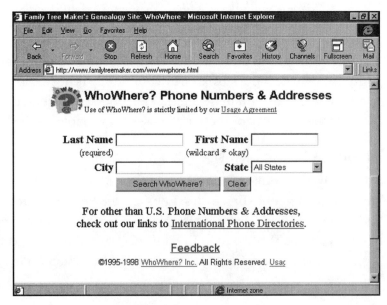

Figure 3-3

Enter search criteria to
locate a phone
number and address.

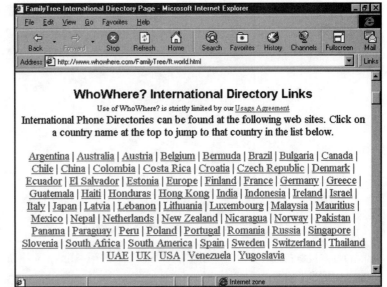

Figure 3-4

Search for international phone directories at Family Tree Maker's Web site.

To search for international phone numbers, click on the International Phone Directories (**http://www.whowhere.com/FamilyTree/ft.world.html**) link on the Phone Number Search page. It will take you to a list of directories around the world (see Figure 3-4).

OTHER ONLINE SEARCH AIDS

Another valuable finding aid is the SSDI (Social Security Death Index) available online and on CD (see Figure 3-5). Use the SSDI to learn more about relatives who have died and to find living relatives, too. The government computerized its records in 1962, and the file contains relatively little on people who died before this date—but it is extremely useful for information about those it does include. Information obtainable from the SSDI is often detailed enough so you can write for a copy of a death certificate or locate an obituary. This information can then lead you to living relatives.

The Internet is ablaze with potential genealogical connections, from forums and bulletin boards on commercial services to mailing lists, newsgroups, surname newsletters, and personal Web pages. Let others know of your interest in families with particular surnames.

Figure 3-5

The Social Security
Death Index is a
helpful finding aid for
genealogists.

You will also find form letters you can use to request information from family
members and repositories, plus other aids, in Family Tree Maker's online Genealogy "How-To" Guide (**http://www.familytreemaker.com/mainmenu.html**), as
shown in Figures 3-6 and 3-7.

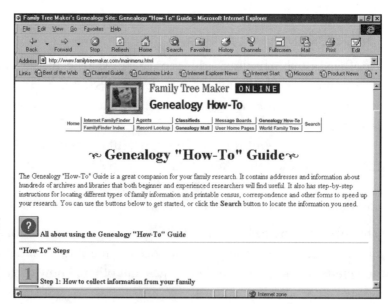

Figure 3-6

The Genealogy "How-
To" Guide is easy to
access from Family
Tree Maker.

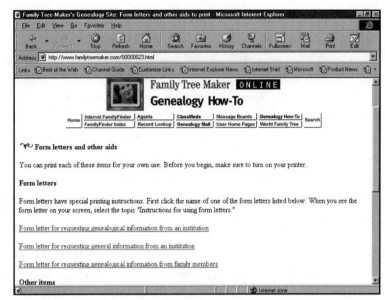

Figure 3-7

The Genealogy "How-To" Guide includes form letters for requesting information.

※ **NOTE** ※   *In Chapter Five, you will learn how to use Family Tree Maker's Family Archives and World Family Tree CDs; and Chapter Six will teach you tips on using the Genealogy Resource Finder, Internet FamilyFinder, and other Family Tree Maker online resources.*

Researching Libraries and Collections

While your first inclination may be to jump on a plane or drive back to the locality where your family once lived, an exploration in libraries near you may turn up valuable information about your ancestors. It is not always necessary to actually go to an area to find historical and genealogical data. Don't waste your valuable time and money seeking data that may be easily accessible locally.

All states have major repositories, such as a state library and archives. There may also be a fine collection in a historical society library, a regional branch of the National Archives university libraries, or in the public library, a few blocks from your home. Explore these first. Moreover, because so many records of genealogical value, such as censuses, have been microfilmed, you may be able to find copies nearby.

Family histories abound as do local histories. You may be surprised and delighted to discover that some distant cousin compiled and published a book about one of your family lines. Information of interest to you may be stashed away in obscure genealogical and historical societies' publications. Local libraries probably will have references that will be helpful to you. These include nationwide directories of funeral directories, cemeteries, newspapers, gazetteers, city directories, and biographies. There are also thousands of Family History Centers (FHCs)—branches of the famous LDS (Mormon) Family History Library in Salt Lake City—and through these repositories you will have access to microfilmed records of civil, religious, and private collections that have been gathered from around the world.

> ❋ **TIP** ❋ *Check out the material available at the Family Tree Maker Online site (**www.familytreemaker.com/links/c/c-libraries-and-archives**) and venture into the virtual world of what's out there pertaining to libraries and archives.*

It may be that you do not yet have enough information to fully utilize libraries near you, at least not until you have verified some of the information you have collected from family sources. I recommend that you obtain copies of death, marriage, and birth records first and then start with the 1920 census to find your American families. Once you have pinpointed where your families lived and can place them in those localities prior to 1920 you will be able to find many records.

Due to privacy laws, it can be difficult to find genealogical data, such as birth and marriages. For example, there is a 50-year restriction on death records in New York state; and a 75-year restriction on birth and marriage records. But, keep in mind that records that provide the information you seek are not necessarily limited to an official state or federal record. There may be other records in existence that will provide you with the information you need. Civil vital records (birth, marriage, and death records kept by states and municipalities) in America are fairly modern records and few exist, outside of New England prior to 1900. On the other hand, English researchers have access to such civil records dating back to 1837, and prior to that the information can be found in parish records.

Keeping a Research Journal

Develop good work habits when you begin your research: Keep a research journal (also known as a calendar or log)—either in a printed form or on a PIM (Personal Information Manager). It is simply a document that you use to keep track of where (repositories, as well as specific books, films, CDs, etc) you have looked for information and what you found or didn't find. A printed form usually works better than a PIM for genealogists since you can't always take your computer with you to the archive, library, or courthouse when you are researching. A research journal helps you avoid duplicating your research efforts. Genealogical research is not particularly difficult, but it can be time-consuming, and the volume of material available can be overwhelming. You need something to keep you focused. A research journal helps.

Family Tree Maker has a valuable tool called the Research Journal that is part To Do list and part research assistant (see Chapter 10 for instructions on how to use this feature). It helps you track research leads generated by the FamilyFinder Report, create your own To Do items, and track your research progress by marking To Do items as "Done!" The Research Journal also provides helpful features that let you sort the FamilyFinder Report as well as your customized To Do list. It's the only place you'll need to go to keep track of all your research activities.

Organizing Information

Rummage through old scrapbooks, photo albums, diaries, and newspaper clippings. Collect copies of birth, christening, marriage, and death certificates, plus all the naturalization papers, old passports, diplomas, letters, school yearbooks, military ribbons, wills, and deeds you can find—whatever family papers you or your parents might have saved or that you collected during the process of interviewing relatives. What you are doing is collecting foundational material—from every possible source. From these family papers and interviews, record what you have discovered about your family. No doubt you are eager to get started compiling your family tree. However, it will go more smoothly if you organize your material first. Most people work from paper rather than memory to input data into Family Tree Maker. That's because names and dates can be easily confused.

Creating Your First Family File

Family File is the name given to the database you create which holds the information you input about your family. You can think of it as an electronic folder into which you are placing details about each of your family members. If you have not yet done so, create your first Family File.

1. From the File menu, choose New Family File to open the New Family File dialog box.

2. In the File Name text box, enter a name for your new Family File—most people start with their surname.

3. Click on Save. Family Tree Maker creates the new Family File and displays the Family Page (see Figure 3-8).

Follow the easy on-screen form there by typing in the basic information you have collected about yourself and your parents. Then you can print blank (empty) charts from Family Tree Maker and use those, if you need to, for compiling and organizing your material or to send to aunts, uncles, and cousins for them to complete.

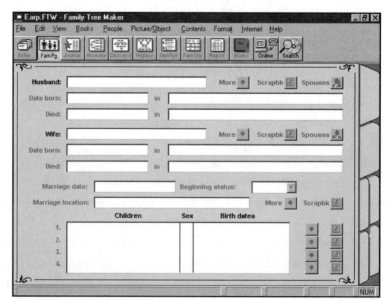

Figure 3-8

On the Family Page you can begin entering the information you have collected.

Using Family Group Sheets

The Family Group Sheet is the backbone of genealogy data, and I find it helps to complete these charts on paper first, and then input the data into the computer. It helps to familiarize yourself with the genealogy format and to learn what works for you regarding organization. Some people are clearly gifted with a talent for taking a pile of papers, notes, and memorabilia and converting it into neat groupings. Others, are, shall I say, organizationally impaired? I fall into the latter group, and as a result I need all the help I can get in finding the notes and making sense out of them before I start inputting data. Do whatever works best for you.

To print blank Family Group Sheets, follow these steps:

1.   Open your Family File, and then click on the Family Group button.

2.   From the <u>C</u>ontents menu, choose <u>I</u>tems to Include in Family Group Sheet. The <u>I</u>tems to Include in Family Group Sheet dialog box appears (see Figure 3-9).

3.   In the <u>A</u>vailable Items list box, select Standard Page with Pictures/Objects and then click on the > button.

4.   In the dialog box that appears, click on OK. The Standard Page with Pictures/Objects item appears in the Your Family Group Sheet <u>C</u>ontains box, on the right.

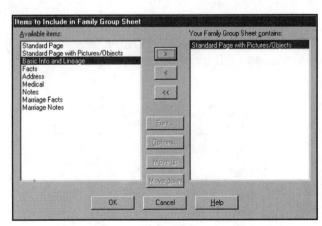

Figure 3-9

Select either Standard Page or Standard Page with Pictures/Objects.

5. Click on OK to close the dialog box.

6. Open the Eile menu and then choose Print Family Group Sheet (or press Ctrl+P) to open the Print Family Group Sheet dialog box (see Figure 3-10).

7. Select the Print Empty check box. In the Copies text box, type the number of blank (empty) copies you wish. Click on OK.

Now you have a supply of blank (empty) Family Group Sheets to send to your computer-less relatives. Ask them to fill in as best they can and return it to you. You can then enter the data in your Family File.

> ❧ **NOTE** ❧ *Depending on your printer, the fonts and styles you have selected, and how you have set up your configurations under Print Setup, you might want to change the margins—to fit your research notebook, for example. While computers are wonderful, it is not always possible to take them to libraries, repositories, or relatives' homes—as a result, you'll want to create research notes with information about your family that you can carry with you wherever you go.*

A Family Group Sheet helps you get organized. It enables you to focus on what data you have and what's missing. Every genealogy how-to manual I have ever read and every lecturer I have ever heard cautions family researchers to work with one family at a time. I will admonish you to do the same, knowing full well that you will ignore this advice and plunge headlong into trying to find all eight of your great-grandparents and all 16 of your great-greats. However, somewhere along the way, and usually soon, you'll discover

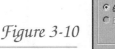

Figure 3-10

Select the Print Empty option and as many copies as you need.

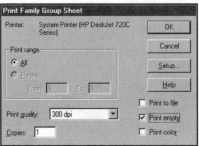

your mind is numb and you are buried in names, dates, and places, just spinning your wheels. When this happens, take a deep breath and select one family to research. And, remember, I told you so.

Multimedia Options

Genealogy is no longer musty old records and text. If you have a scanner, you can use it to make an electronic reproduction of almost any paper item—a photograph, newspaper clipping, or marriage certificate, for example. Scanning documents offers today's genealogist another way to preserve family memorabilia. Depending on your computer's capabilities, you may also be able to record or reproduce video or sounds. Currently, graphics and sounds occupy a great deal of storage on computers; while the technology offers great promise, you may wish to focus on your genealogy first and add the bells and whistles later. On the other hand, if you do have a scanner, you may want to go through family photos and papers and organize those that you want to include first. Additionally, since sound files can be added to Family Tree Maker Scrapbooks (discussed in Chapter Eleven), you should take a little time to become familiar with how to create and add .WAV files.

The History of George Howard Lafferty

George Howard Lafferty was born September 2, 1894 in Lenox township, Ashtabula County, Ohio, to Amber Amelia Wescott Lafferty and George Edwin Lafferty. A sister, Maud Irene, was born May 23, 1892.

A family of farmers, the Laffertys harvested the land where they lived. On May 9, 1919, they moved to Warren, Ohio, to a house on Forest Street NE. They lived next door to their daughter Maud, her husband Jay Rood Webster, and their three beautiful daughters, Reta, Shirley, and Marion.

As a youth, Lafferty went by "Howard" rather than "George" and signed his name as G. Howard Lafferty. After graduating from Lenox Township schools in 1911, he received a Teachers Certificate and became an educator and later a high school Principal. He then switched careers and ventured into banking just before World War I.

As a student at Ohio State University during the war, Howard Lafferty hoped to join the army but was classified 5G due to his glasses and other restrictions. In 1923 he received an L.L.B. degree and passed

Ancestors of George Howard Lafferty

Samuel Lafferty
1801 - 1873

Edwin F. Lafferty
1834 - 1907

Margaret McDowell
1803 - 1861

George F. Lafferty
1887 - 1936

Erastus Fowler
1793 - 1875

...elia Fowler
...1914

Temperence Merrill
1796 - 1871

Nathan Wescott
1818 - 1900

...iram Wescott

Sarah Ann McMichael
1820 - 1901

Samuel C. Amsden
1822 - 1899

Theresa Jerusa Amsden
1843 - 1934

Clarissa Hubbard
1820 - 1870

CHAPTER FOUR

Entering Basic Information

his chapter teaches you how to enter basic genealogical information, including sources, and how to use that information in various tree formats. In the process, you'll learn many of Family Tree Maker's commands and options, as well as how to handle some genealogical problems that you're likely to encounter with your own material.

For the examples in this chapter, you'll work with biographical and genealogical material for the family of Wyatt Earp—probably best known as a law enforcement officer in Dodge City, Kansas, in the late 1870s and as a participant in the famous gunfight at the OK Corral in Tombstone, Arizona, in 1881.

Getting Familiar with the Program

If you started a Family File for yourself in Chapter Three, set that aside for now. This chapter takes you through the steps of entering information about the Earp family, and you won't want to mix this up with information for your own people. Since I already have a collection of the names, dates, and places you will enter, you'll be able to practice all the Family Tree Maker features that you can later apply to your own Family File. To create the Earp Family File, follow these steps:

1. Start the Family Tree Maker program.

2. From the File menu, choose New Family File. The New Family File dialog box appears.

3. In the File Name text box, type **Earp**. This is the name you'll use for this family example.

4. Click on Save.

Family Tree Maker will create a new Family File called Earp and display an empty Family Page. The Family Page shows all members of a *nuclear family*—that is, two parents and their children. This page is where you enter basic information about a family. Family Tree Maker shows only one Family Page on the screen at a time, but it's easy to move about from page to page (more about that later). When you start a new Family File, you get a blank Family Page like the one in Figure 4-1.

Learning Screen Features

Take some time to get acquainted with the various screen elements and program features so you can use Family Tree Maker comfortably. The *menu bar* is that row of words (menu options) at the top of the screen. When you click on one of the menu options, a list of commands appears below it—this is called a

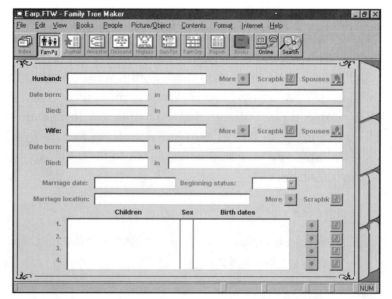

Figure 4-1

An empty Family Page shows fields and labels.

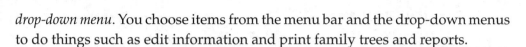

drop-down menu. You choose items from the menu bar and the drop-down menus to do things such as edit information and print family trees and reports.

Along the right-hand side of the Family Page are *tabs* (and they really do look like paper filing folder tabs). At this point they are blank; once you enter some names, you'll see how they work and how easy it is to use them to move back and forth among individuals. The Family Page also has several *buttons* that take you to other parts of the Family Tree Maker program. You'll learn these as you go.

You will notice that this Family Page resembles a paper form and consists of labeled boxes that you fill with information. These text boxes are called *fields*, and the descriptive labels that describe the text boxes are known as *field labels*. The fields have conventional labels, such as Husband, Wife, and Children.

NAVIGATING THE FIELDS

Some fields allow only certain information, and if you try to enter something else, Family Tree Maker will let you know that's a "no-no." Additionally, Family Tree Maker will catch conflicts with certain dates (like trying to enter a child's birth date that is earlier than the mother's birth date, for example). Some of the fields are what Family Tree Maker calls *Fastfields*. These fields keep track of the words you enter most often and fills them in for you when you begin to enter common data. This enables you to enter information more quickly. You will type information into the fields (text boxes), moving from field to field. You can move to another field in several ways:

- Press the Tab key
- Press the Enter key
- Press the up arrow and down arrow keys
- Click on the fields with your mouse pointer

Use whichever navigation option is easiest for you.

MOVING INFORMATION AROUND

You can save some typing time and effort by copying and pasting information from one field to another.

⚛ CAUTION ⚛   Do not cut and paste an individual's name. Cutting an individual's name does not delete or move that individual to another location. To delete someone, use the Delete Individual command; to move an individual and all the information associated with him or her, use the Detach and Attach commands. I'll explain these functions more fully in Chapter Nine.

⚛ TIP ⚛   If you make a mistake while typing an individual's name, just type over it. This corrects the spelling. If you make a mistake when entering a single piece of information, such as a date or location, simply type over the incorrect information. Do not use the Delete Individual option for these kinds of minor errors.

To cut and paste or copy and paste text in Family Tree Maker:

1. Highlight the text you wish to cut or copy by placing the mouse pointer in front of the first character you want to select. Press and hold the primary mouse button while dragging the mouse until the last character is highlighted, and then release the mouse button.

2. From the <u>E</u>dit menu, select either Cu<u>t</u> Text or <u>C</u>opy Text (this puts the text or a copy of it on the Windows Clipboard). If you prefer to use the keyboard, pressing Ctrl+X will cut and Ctrl+C will copy text to the Clipboard. You can also right-click on the selection and choose the appropriate command on the shortcut menu that appears.

    ⚛ NOTE ⚛   The Windows Clipboard is a temporary storage area in your computer's memory for items that you cut or copy. The text, picture, or other object on the Clipboard remains there, available for you to paste once or repeatedly, until you choose to cut or copy something else—or until you restart your computer.

3. Place the cursor where you want to paste the information. If you wish to replace a section of existing text with the information that you have just copied or cut, simply highlight that text.

4.   From the Edit menu, select Paste. (Pressing Ctrl+V will produce the same effect.) You can paste the same text as many times as you wish until you use the Copy or Cut command again.

❀ **TIP** ❀   *If you make a mistake, click on Edit and select the appropriate Undo command (Undo Paste or Undo Copy), or press Ctrl+Z. If you accidentally delete text using the Cut command, you can put your cursor where you wish to replace the text and paste it back in by going to the Edit menu and selecting Paste, or by pressing Ctrl+V.*

Entering Names, Dates, and Places

Names are *entered* (typed in) on the Family Page where you see the Husband, Wife, and Children fields. In the Children field, Family Tree Maker automatically inserts the husband's *surname* (last name) after the children's first and middle names. However, you can type over the name that Family Tree Maker inserts if the children have different surnames.

Use an individual's full given name, including the middle name if known, and enter the first name first. It is better not to use initials for the middle name, although sometimes that is all you have. Also use the *maiden name* of a woman— her birth surname; her name before she was married. Nicknames, name changes, missing surnames, and titles are handled differently; I'll get to them later in this chapter.

Entering genealogical data is much more convenient if you gather the information and have it ready in a format or arrangement that is easy to follow, which is why so many genealogists work from Family Group Sheets. Often your information will come from bits and pieces and various sources, and you'll have to shuffle through your notes at the keyboard if you haven't organized them first.

Starting a Family

On the Family Page you just created, you will enter information about Wyatt Earp and his family. Wyatt Berry Stapp Earp was born March 29, 1848, in

Monmouth, Warren County, Illinois. He died January 13, 1929, in Los Angeles, California. He was the son of Nicholas Porter Earp and Virginia Ann Cooksey. (Yes, they were married—but Family Tree Maker and genealogists alike track only a woman's maiden name, since those do not change. Determining the maiden name of a woman also enables you to identify her parents.) Follow these steps to enter the information for the father of Wyatt Earp on the Family Page:

1. In the Husband field, type **Nicholas Porter Earp**.

2. In the Date Born field, type **September 6, 1813**.

3. Tab to the In field and type **Lincoln County, North Carolina**.

4. In the Died field, type **November 12, 1907**.

5. Tab to the In field and type **Los Angeles County, California.**

Family Tree Maker saves the information you enter automatically as you leave each field to go to the next. You don't have to worry about saving the file as you work on it. Now enter information for the mother of Wyatt Earp in the Wife field:

1. In the Wife field, type **Virginia Ann Cooksey.** Remember to use the maiden names of your female ancestors, not their married names.

2. In the Date Born field, type **February 2, 1821**.

3. Tab to the In field and type **Kentucky**.

4. In the Died field, type **January 14, 1893**.

5. Tab to the In field and type **San Bernardino County, California.**

6. In the Marriage Date field, type **July 27, 1840**. In the Beginning Status field, "Married" (the default) already appears, which is OK.

7. In the Marriage Location field, type **Hartford, Ohio County, Kentucky**.

So far, the data you have entered should look like the data in Figure 4-2, except for the children's names and birth dates.

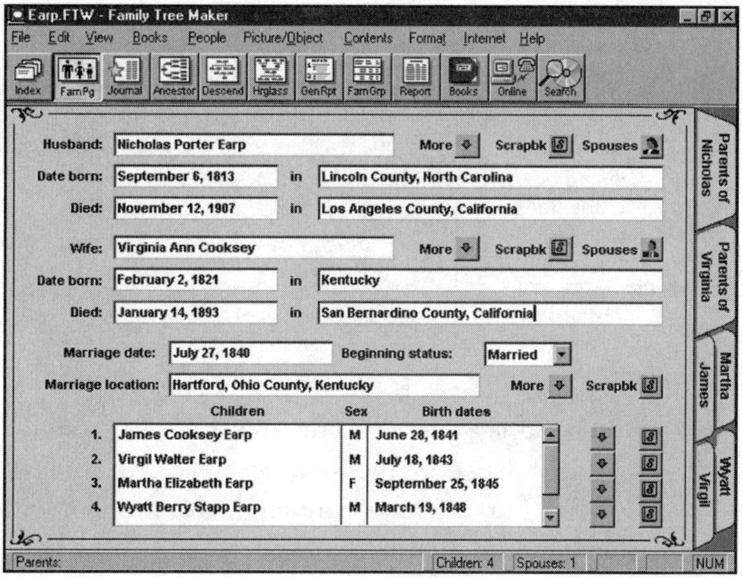

Figure 4-2

Start by entering
parents on the
Family Page.

CHANGING THE DATE FORMAT

Most genealogists around the world use the MDY order of a date. *MDY* is an acronym for month, day, year. However, the default order in Family Tree Maker is DMY (day, month, year). You can choose how you want dates to appear in your Family File by doing the following:

> ❧ **TIP** ❧ *You can type in a date in a short format and let Family Tree Maker convert it to the format you have set. For example, you could have typed **September 6, 1813**, for Nicholas Porter Earp's birth date and it would automatically show up as **6 Sep 1813**, if that is your default format.*

1. From the File menu, choose Preferences.

2. In the Preferences submenu, choose Dates & Measures. The Dates & Measures dialog box will appear, as shown in Figure 4-3.

3. If you want to change the date order from its current setting, select MDY for Month-Day-Year order or DMY for Day-Month-Year order.

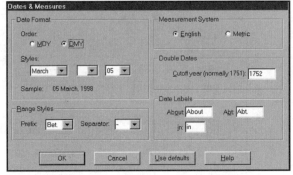

Figure 4-3

In the Dates & Measures dialog box, select the Date Format, Range Styles, Measurement System, Double Dates, and Date Labels you prefer.

4. In the first <u>S</u>tyles drop-down list, choose a style for the month: choose the entire month in text (March), abbreviated month in text (Mar), number for the month (3), or number with a leading zero for single-digit months (03).

   The default date punctuation places a comma and space before the year, as in March 5, 1998, or 5 March, 1998. Or if the month is a number instead of text, there are only spaces for punctuation, such as 3 5 1998 or 03 05 1998.

5. In the second <u>S</u>tyles drop-down list, choose the punctuation for the date format:

Punctuation	Examples
(blank)	March 5, 1998 or 03 05 1998
/	Mar/5/1998 or 3/5/1998
-	March-5-1998 or 3-5-1998
.	March.5.1998 or 3.5.1998

6. In the third <u>S</u>tyles drop-down list, choose the format for the day of the month, either with or without a leading zero for single-digit days as in 5 or 05.

7. If you wish to enter ranges of dates (when you have an idea of when someone was born, for example, but wish to approximate the date), use the two Range Style list boxes to adjust your settings.

8. If you want to change the Double Dates cutoff year, type a new year in the Cutoff year (normally 1751) text box. Until you have traced British or American lines back to the 18th century, you won't have to worry about this little problem, so don't be concerned about it at this point.

9. If you want to change to the Measurement System, select either English or Metric option buttons.

10. The Date Labels text boxes contain the words you wish to appear when making approximations about dates. The defaults of "about" and "abt" are sufficient for now.

   If the date format is changed, it is automatically applied throughout the program, and not just to data entered starting after the time the format was changed. Any change to preferences affects both previously entered information as well as any new information.

   ❧ **NOTE** ❧ *What happens if you enter a two-digit year? Try it! No, Family Tree Maker doesn't assume you want to enter a date in the current century. You will be presented with a tiny dialog box called Date Error. Choose the correct four-digit year in the drop-down list and then choose OK. And don't type two-digit years any more!*

ENTERING LOCATIONS

In providing information for the Earp family example, I have spelled out the names of states and used *County* instead of abbreviating the word to avoid confusion. However, you may choose any style you wish; just be consistent. Either abbreviate the states or spell them out. It is not necessary to include the word county or Co., but if you use it, be consistent. Put commas between city, county, state, and country names. It is not necessary to include the name of the country, especially if most of your family was born in one country. You might include the country for those who were born elsewhere, of course.

The location fields can contain up to 256 characters, which should cover names of most localities involved. The two-letter state abbreviations used by the Post Office in the United States are fine and conserve space, if that is what you want to do. Just remember to be consistent and use the same form all the time—don't mix your abbreviations so you wind up with three forms like PA, Pa., and Penn. for the same state.

Branching to Children

Now you are ready to enter the basic genealogical material about the children of Nicholas Porter Earp and Virginia Ann Cooksey. There are eight of them, which may seem excessive—but the practice will enable you to become familiar with the fields and the entry process. Then you will work with the peculiarities of nicknames, missing surnames, multiple marriages, children by other wives, nontraditional marriages, and missing or conflicting data. You will also learn how to cite the sources of your genealogical material and create reports, Ancestor trees, and Scrapbooks using this Earp family data.

Nicholas Porter Earp and Virginia Ann Cooksey had the following children:

 James Cooksey Earp, born June 18, 1841, in Hartford, Ohio County, Kentucky. He married Nellie "Bessie" Bartlett Ketchum on April 18, 1873, in Illinois. He died January 25, 1926, in Los Angeles, Los Angeles County, California. James Cooksey Earp (his middle name was his mother's maiden name—a popular naming practice, particularly among Southern families in this time period) fought during the Civil War and was unable to use his left arm due to a wound in the left shoulder. He drew a disability pension as a result of this.

 Virgil Walter Earp, born July 18, 1843, in Hartford, Ohio County, Kentucky. He died October 20, 1905, in Goldfield, Esmeralda County, Nevada. He first married Magdelana C. "Ellen" Rysdam on September 21, 1861, in Knoxville, Marion County, Iowa. He married second wife Rosella Dragoo in 1870 in Lamar, Barton County, Missouri. He married (or took as his common-law wife) Alvira "Allie" Packingham Sullivan, about 1874. Virgil was shot through the spinal column, biceps, and knee at Tombstone, Arizona, in 1881. He suffered from neuralgia of the stomach in 1888 and 1889, caused by wounds in the back. Virgil had one child—a daughter named Nellie Jane, by his first wife.

- **Martha Elizabeth Earp,** born September 25, 1845, in Kentucky. She died May 26, 1856, in Monmouth, Warren County, Illinois.

- **Wyatt Berry Stapp Earp** (named for his father's Mexican War company commander, Captain Wyatt Berry Stapp), born March 29, 1849, in Monmouth, Warren County, Illinois; died January 13, 1929, in Los Angeles, Los Angeles County, California. He married first Urilla Sutherland on January 10, 1870, in Lamar, Barton County, Missouri. Celia Ann Blaylock was evidently his common-law wife, as was probably his third wife, Josephine Sarah Marcus.

- **Morgan S. Earp,** born April 24, 1851, in Pella, Marion County, Iowa, and died March 18, 1882, in Tombstone, Cochise County, Arizona. He married Louise (called "Lou"), whose maiden name is unknown.

- **Warren Baxter Earp** was born March 9, 1855, and died July 8, 1900, in Willcox, Cochise County, Arizona.

- **Virginia A. Earp** was born February 28, 1858, in Monmouth, Warren County, Illinois, and died October 26, 1861, in Pella, Marion County, Iowa.

- **Adelia Douglas Earp** was born June 16, 1861, in Pella, Marion County, Iowa, and died January 16, 1941, in San Bernardino, San Bernardino County, California. She married William Thomas Edwards and had two children: Nicholas Edwards and Estelle Josphine Edwards.

Using this genealogical and biographical information, enter the basic data (there will be places to use the extra information later) about the eight children of Nicholas Porter Earp and Virginia Ann Cooksey. Start by typing in their oldest child:

1. Click on the first row of the Children text box. Type **James Cooksey**. Press Enter.

   Notice how Family Tree Maker automatically fills in the surname "Earp" for you (this is how the Fastfields feature works). As soon as the cursor moves to the Sex field, an "F" (for female, the default) appears.

2. Type **M** over the "F" in the Sex field to change the selection to male. (Lowercase typing is fine; Family Tree Maker will convert it to uppercase.) Press Enter.

3. In the Birth Dates field, type in the birth date, **June 18, 1841**. Press Enter.

   Family Tree Maker displays four children's names at a time, but you can enter up to 99 children (heaven forbid) for each marriage. Just use the scroll bar on the right side of the Birth Dates text box to enter or display the other children. Large families were not uncommon, with 7 to 10 children about average during the nineteenth century. However, be suspicious of one mother having more than 15 children unless there are multiple births involved.

4. Type in the next three children's information, referring to the earlier list.

   After you have entered the fourth child (Wyatt Berry Stapp Earp) of Nicholas Porter Earp and Virginia Ann Cooksey, press Enter. The list will scroll up, revealing space to add the rest of the children.

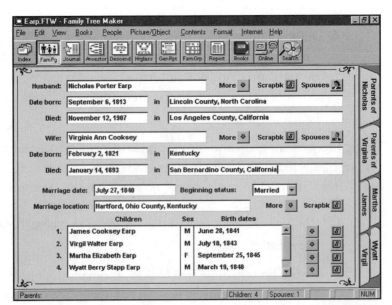

Figure 4-4

The four oldest children of Nicholas Porter Earp and Virginia Ann Cooksey

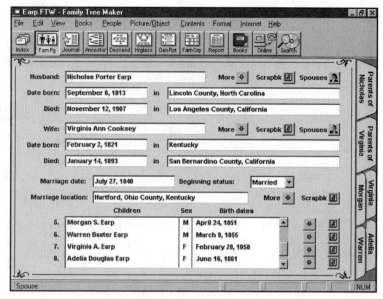

Figure 4-5

The four youngest children of Nicholas Porter Earp and Virginia Ann Cooksey

5. Type in the remaining four children's information. Notice after you type in each child's name that the first name appears on a tab at the right edge of the Family File. When you finish adding the rest of Wyatt's siblings, your screens should look like Figures 4-4 and 4-5.

Adding Additional Spouses

Wyatt Earp's father was married previously and had children by his first wife. Additionally, after the death of Wyatt's mother, Nicholas Porter Earp remarried late in life, but had no children by his third wife. Multiple marriages are common in family histories, and Family Tree Maker makes it easy to add additional spouses and children. When an individual has more than one marriage, you should create a separate Family Page for each additional spouse whether there were children by that spouse or not—otherwise the charts you produce will be incomplete. To add a Family Page for another spouse, follow these steps:

1. From the Family Page you just created showing Nicholas Porter Earp and his wife, Virginia Ann Cooksey, click on the Spouses button on the right of Nicholas' name (there are three options on that

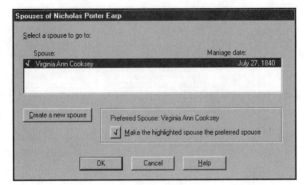

Figure 4-6

The spouse dialog
box of Nicholas
Porter Earp

line: More, Scrapbk, and Spouses). The Spouses dialog box appears,
as shown in Figure 4-6.

2. Click on the Create A New Spouse button in the Spouses dialog box.
Family Tree Maker asks if you want to "attach" the children you
listed under Nicholas Porter Earp and Virginia Ann Cooksey to the
new spouse (to appear on the new spouse's Family Page), as shown
in Figure 4-7.

※ **TIP** ※   *Family Tree Maker can create a step-relationship between the
children of one marriage and another spouse, but most genealogists prefer to
keep each family group separate to avoid confusion.*

3. Click on No. A new Family Page is created, containing information
about Nicholas Porter Earp.

FIRST SPOUSE'S FAMILY

On the new Family Page for Nicholas Porter Earp, enter the following information about his first wife, Abigail Storm, and the children they had:

Figure 4-7

Family Tree Maker
queries you when
there are children and
other spouses
involved.

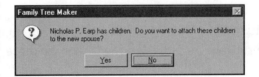

Abigail Storm was born September 21, 1813, probably in Kentucky, but we don't know for sure; place a question mark after her birth place. She died October 8, 1839, probably in Ohio County, Kentucky, but again we do not know for sure, so you can place a question mark after her death place too.

> ❧ **NOTE** ❧   *When you have information pertaining to your ancestors but do not have a specific source citation for it, it is best to place a question mark next to that field. The question marks remind you that citations are lacking and that you should check for additional verification. In this instance, there is a source indicating that Nicholas Porter Earp and Abigail Storm were married in Ohio County, Kentucky, in 1836, that their son, Newton Jasper Earp, was born in that county in 1837, and that Nicholas Porter Earp married his second wife, Virginia Ann Cooksey, in that same locality in 1840. While no source (found to date) reveals where Abigail Storm or her daughter, Marian Ann Earp, died, it appears likely that they both died in Ohio County, Kentucky. However, since you have no evidence to support this contention, it is best to mark it with a question mark until you have the opportunity to check for additional sources.*

Nicholas Porter Earp and Abigail Storm were married December 22, 1836, in Ohio County, Kentucky. They had two children:

1. **Newton Jasper Earp,** born October 7, 1837, in Ohio County, Kentucky; died December 18, 1928, probably in California. He married Nancy Jane Adams September 12, 1865, in Marion County, Missouri. They had the following children:

    A. Effie May Earp, born May 6, 1870, in Missouri.

    B. Wyatt Clyde Earp, born August 25, 1872, in Kansas.

    C. Mary Elizabeth Earp, born August 25, 1875, in Kansas; died before 1880, probably in Kansas.

    D. Alice Abigail Earp, born December 18, 1878, in Kansas, and married John E. Wells.

    E. Virgil Edwin Earp, born April 19, 1880, in Kansas; died after 1958. He married Grace J. Scott.

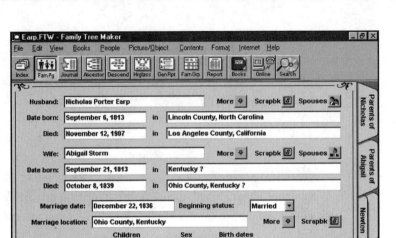

Figure 4-8

The Family Page for Nicholas Porter Earp's first spouse

2. **Mariah Ann Earp,** born February 12, 1838; died January 5, 1839, probably in Ohio County, Kentucky.

   Now you have completed the Family Page for Nicholas Porter Earp and Abigail Storm, which should look like Figure 4-8.

Now that you have entered information for the first spouse, Abigail Storm, you can repeat the process for another spouse. This time there are no children to enter.

THIRD SPOUSE'S INFORMATION

From the Family Page you just created showing Nicholas Porter Earp and his first wife, Abigail Storm, create another new spouse for Nicolas Porter Earp by clicking on the Spouses button on the same line as his name. Click on the Create a New Spouse button in the Spouses dialog box. Family Tree Maker asks if you want the children listed to appear on the new Family Page with the new spouse. Click on No. A new Family Page is created for Nicholas Porter Earp. Now enter this information:

Nicholas Porter Earp married his third wife, Annie Alexander, on October 14, 1893, in San Bernardino County, California. They did not have any children.

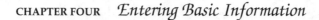

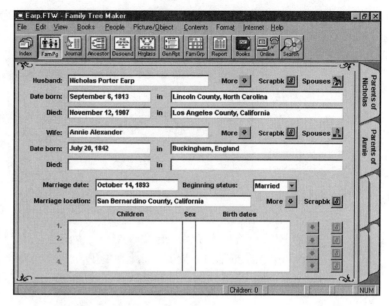

Figure 4-9

The Family Page for
Nicholas Porter Earp's
third spouse

Your completed Family Page for Nicholas Porter Earp and Annie Alexander should look like Figure 4-9.

DESIGNATING THE PREFERRED SPOUSE

Another option Family Tree Maker offers is the *preferred spouse*. This is the spouse whose information you would prefer to see on the Family Page. It doesn't refer to the favorite wives of the men in the tree. If you designate one of the spouses as preferred, the Family Page will display whichever wife you selected as the preferred spouse. Now that you have finished entering information about all three wives of Nicholas Porter Earp, you can select which Family Page should display first. To select the preferred spouse, follow these steps:

1. From the Family Page (showing any of the spouses), click on the Spouses button next to Nicholas Porter Earp. The Spouses dialog box appears, as shown in Figure 4-10. The first spouse you entered for Nicholas Porter Earp, Virginia Cooksey Earp, is checked already as the preferred spouse.

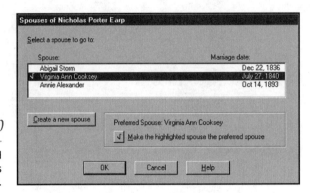

Figure 4-10

Select the preferred
spouse of Nicholas
Porter Earp.

✳ **TIP** ✳   *The buttons next to More, Scrapbk, and Spouses change when
something is added to them. You can tell if a person has more than one spouse
because the Spouse button includes two heads instead of one.*

2. In the Select a Spouse To Go To list box, select the name of the
    spouse you wish to be the preferred spouse.

    ✳ **TIP** ✳   *Of course, you can always display the Family Pages that con-
    tain the other spouses, no matter which one is the preferred spouse. You can
    go to the Family Page for any spouse by double-clicking on the spouse's name
    in the Spouses dialog box, or by selecting the name and clicking on OK.*

3. Click on the button next to Make The Highlighted Spouse The Pre-
    ferred Spouse. The check mark appears next to the preferred
    spouse's name.

4. Click on OK. Family Tree Maker displays the Family Page contain-
    ing the individual and the preferred spouse.

You can change the preferred spouse at any time simply by repeating these steps
and choosing another spouse.

Adding Parents and Siblings

Now that you have entered the basic information about Nicholas Porter Earp, his
three wives, and all of his children, you can add information about his parents.

Every individual will appear on at least two Family Pages in Family Tree Maker—as a child on his or her parents' Family Page and also as a husband, wife, or unmarried adult on another Family Page. When you enter an individual on one page, Family Tree Maker automatically copies that individual onto the other page to make it easy to add new information.

From any Family Page showing Nicholas Porter Earp, click on the tab on the right that says Parents of Nicholas. This takes you to a new page where you can enter the following information about his parents (in the Husband and Wife fields) and siblings (in the Children field):

Walter Earp was born in 1787 in Montgomery County, Maryland. He married Martha Ann Early in 1808 in Pittsylvania County, Virginia. He died January 30, 1853, in Monmouth, Warren County, Illinois. Martha Ann Early was born August 28, 1790, in North Carolina and died September 24, 1880, in Monmouth, Warren County, Illinois. They had the following children:

1. **Lorenzo Dow Earp,** born 1809 in North Carolina; died 1893 in Iowa.

2. **Elizabeth Earp,** born 1811 in North Carolina; died 1899 in Illinois.

3. **Nicholas Porter Earp,** born September 6, 1813, in Lincoln County, North Carolina; died November 12, 1907, in Los Angeles County, California.

4. **Josiah Jackson Earp,** born 1816.

5. **James O'Kelly Earp,** born about 1818.

6. **Francis Asbury Earp,** born 1821.

7. **Walter Cooksey Earp,** born 1824.

8. **Jonathan Douglas Earp,** born 1824.

9. **Sarah Ann Earp,** born 1827.

Whew. They sure had big families back then. Now you have created a small database about the Earp family, and with it you will learn how to handle some of the problems and genealogical peculiarities you may run into with your own families.

⚜ **NOTE** ⚜   *In most instances, genealogists include children only on the Family Page of their birth parents. However, there are other instances, particularly when adoption, divorce, remarriage, or other types of relationships are involved, when you might wish to create additional parents for a child.*

Family Tree Maker allows you to create multiple sets of parents for each child and then note the special nature of the relationships between the parents and child. When you create multiple sets of parents for a child, the child appears in trees and kinship reports more than once and also will appear in multiple Family Group Sheets (see Chapter Nine).

Refining Name Details

When you enter names, it is important to enter them with a first name, middle name, and surname (family name) initially. Don't worry, you can print names differently later. Family Tree Maker has additional pages where you can enter more detailed information about names, such as nicknames, name changes, surnames with suffixes, missing surnames, and titles. You access these pages by clicking on the More button next to the name field.

⚜ **TIP** ⚜   *Suffixes to surnames like Jr., Sr., and III should be entered on the Family Page.*

From the Family Page of Nicholas Porter Earp, click on the More button (located just to the right of his name). The More About window appears. This is where you can record additional information about people in your Family File. Each More About window has a vertical toolbar with buttons that take you to five supplementary More About windows:

- 🏃 Facts
- 🏃 Address
- 🏃 Medical
- 🏃 Lineage
- 🏃 Notes

For now, you will use the Lineage features to add information about names.

NICKNAMES

Nicknames are entered in the Lineage window. Here's how to enter nicknames:

1. In the More About window, click on the Lineage button. The Lineage window appears. It contains fields for recording special information about relationships, such as adoption or a step-relationship. However, it is also where you enter nicknames (that's what the *aka*—for "also known as"—box is for) and special titles that people use (Dr., Rev., Col., Mrs., etc.). On the Family page, the father of Wyatt Earp is recorded by his full name, Nicholas Porter Earp, but if his nickname was "Nick" then you would record it here.

2. In the field labeled This Person Is Also Known As (aka), type **Nick**, as shown in Figure 4-11.

NAME CHANGES AND HYPHENATED NAMES

When dealing with hyphenated married names, use the aka field in the Lineage window to record them. For example, if the parents of Wyatt Earp, Nicholas Porter Earp, and Virginia Ann Cooksey had used the compound (hyphenated

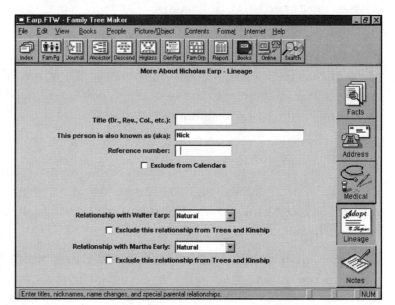

Figure 4-11

Nicknames are entered from the Lineage window.

surname) of Cooksey-Earp, then you would enter their birth names on their Family Pages, and put their hyphenated (compound) married names in the Lineage window.

If you have an ancestor who anglicized his name, or officially changed the name or its spelling, you can also enter that information in the aka field—the same field where you enter nicknames. For example, if Johann Zimmerman changed his name to John Carpenter, and his descendants go by the Carpenter surname, you could enter that he was known as Johann Zimmerman in the Lineage window.

Surnames with Suffixes

If there is a suffix attached to a surname (for example, Jr. or Sr.) you should separate it from the surname with a comma. Enter such names as John Smith, Jr. or John Smith, Sr. The comma after the surname tells Family Tree Maker that the suffix is not the surname, and will enable it to put the family name under the correct letter of the alphabet in the Index of Individuals and other lists. It is not necessary to use commas with Roman numerals (John Franklin Smith, III or William Lee Smith, IV, for example) after a surname, unless the number is greater than eight.

Missing and Unusual Surnames

Surnames or last names are not used in all cultures. The way to handle this is to place two backslash characters together, with no space between them at the end of the name. (The backslashes do not appear in the printed documents.) Native American names are one example of when you might need to use this option. The name Rattling Gourd should be entered like this:

Rattling Gourd\\

Family Tree Maker can usually distinguish surnames from other parts of an individual's name. However, there can be instances when unusual last names may not be recognized as such. Some cultures or nationalities don't use the last name as the surname.

For example, Family Tree Maker would assume that someone named Maria Campos Valenzuela uses the surname Valenzuela. However, it may be that Campos is the true surname under which this name should be indexed. To rectify this problem, type backslash characters around the surname. On the Family Page, this name should be entered as Maria \Campos\ Valenzuela.

Another style many genealogists use to indicate that a woman's surname is unknown is by recording her as Sarah Jane [--?--]. Many genealogical periodicals use this style with the brackets, em dashes, and a question mark. However, two hyphens instead of an em dash on either side of the question mark will work also—even though Family Tree Maker will question you about this style. You can treat this style as an unusual surname and put the backslashes around it so that Family Tree Maker will accept it as a surname:

Sarah Jane \[--?--]\

If you use this style, your female ancestors whose surnames are unknown will show up at the top of the alphabetical surname lists. It can be confusing when you have many Marys, Nancys, Elizabeths, and Sarah Janes whose surnames are unknown—but without this format, they appear in alphabetical order according to their given names, which is confusing too. You can use either style you wish when dealing with missing surnames—just be consistent.

TITLE PREFERENCES

Although courtesy titles (such as Mr. and Mrs.) are relatively rare in genealogical reports these days, Family Tree Maker provides an option for tracking them and putting them on trees, reports, and other views. You enter titles such as "Reverend," "Capt.," or "Dr." in the Lineage window—in the Title field, just above the aka field where you enter nicknames. You can select default titles for most of the people in your Family File by selecting File, Preferences, Titles. The Titles dialog box appears, as shown in Figure 4-12. You can enter titles for the following groupings of people:

- ✻ Married males
- ✻ Not Married males
- ✻ Children males
- ✻ Married females

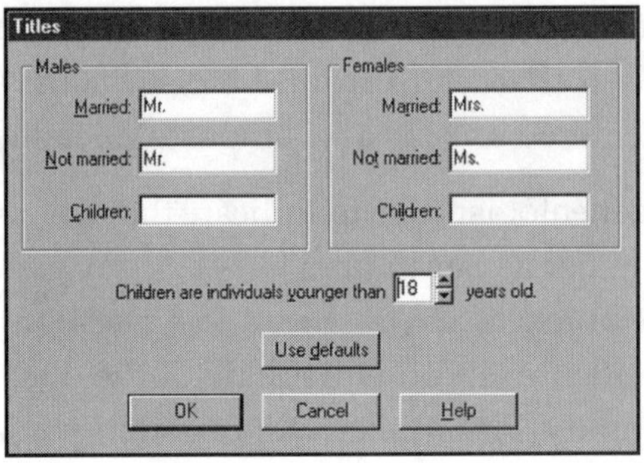

Figure 4-12

Courtesy titles can be
selected from the File
menu under
Preferences, Titles.

* Not Married females

* Children females

To define the age of children to whom you should apply the children's titles
(which are usually blank), assign a cutoff age in the spin box called Children Are
Individuals Younger Than X Years Old (the default age is 13). Click on the Use
Defaults button if you want to reset the titles and the children's cutoff age to
their default values. After you make your selections, click on OK.

Entering Sources as You Go

One of the most important things to do with your genealogy is to document
your sources of the information. Learning to cite your sources properly is not
difficult, but it takes some effort until you get the hang of it. Genealogists use
many sources to compile information about their ancestors. These include vital
records (copies and originals), family Bibles, books, deeds, wills and probate
files, newspapers, censuses, compiled data found on CDs, letters, e-mail messages, and Web pages. There are a number of fields in Family Tree Maker where
you can record your source information:

* Name

* Birth date and location

* Death date and location

* Marriage date and location

* Marriage ending date and location

* Marriage date and fact

* Each of the Fact fields

* Cause of death

* Medical information

To record source information for a field, follow these steps:

1. On the Family Page, click in the field for which you want to enter source information. For this example, click on the Husband field (where the name Nicholas Porter Earp appears).

2. From the View menu, choose Source. The Source-Citation dialog box appears.

3. In the Title of Source field (under Master Source Information) type **Earp Family Genealogy**. This is the name of a book in which you found this particular information.

4. Click on the Edit Master Source button, and type in the following information about this source in the Master Source dialog box.

   * Author/Originator: **Jean Whitten Edwards**

   * Publication Facts: **Breckenridge, Texas: Breck Printing, 1991**

   * Source Media: **Book**

   * Call Number: (leave blank in this instance)

   * Source Location: **Compiler's personal library, Seattle, Washington.** (You could include your complete address, or just the city and state.)

   * Comments: **Earp Family Genealogy: Mainly the Ancestors and Descendants of Brothers: Josiah and Philip Earp, Revolutionary War Patriots, was compiled by Jean Whitten Edwards.**

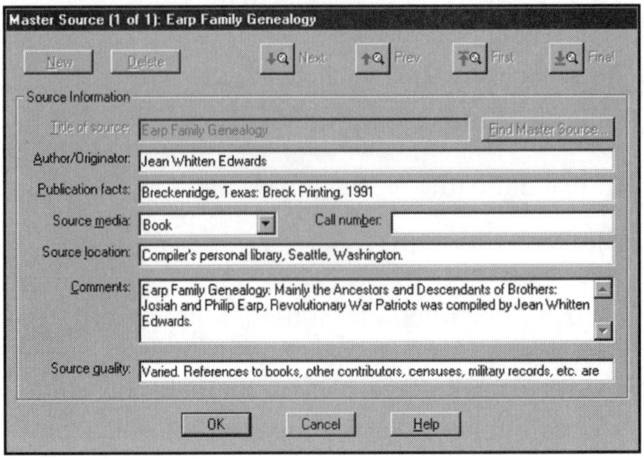

Figure 4-13

Create a Master
Source for your
references to make
citations easier
and faster.

⚸ Source Quality: **Varied.** (You might use a numerical scale of 1
to 4, or a scale of excellent, good, fair, or poor; and you may
indicate here whether the source is a primary or secondary
one, and an original or a copy of a record.)

The completed Master Source dialog box should look like the one in
Figure 4-13.

5. Click on OK to complete the Master Source entry. The Master
Source dialog box closes and you are returned to the Source-Citation
dialog box.

6. Click in the Citation Page field and type **p. 139**. You can spell out the
word *page* instead of using "p." if you wish—again, consistency is
the primary factor.

The Citation Text field contains what you found, or the major item
you found on the page cited in the Citation Page field. The Footnote
(Printed format) field shows you how this Source-Citation will appear when you print it.

❧ **NOTE** ❧   *The Footnote field text is automatically generated from the
information you typed in the Master Source dialog box. However, you can
create a custom footnote simply by typing over the default footnote text. Family*

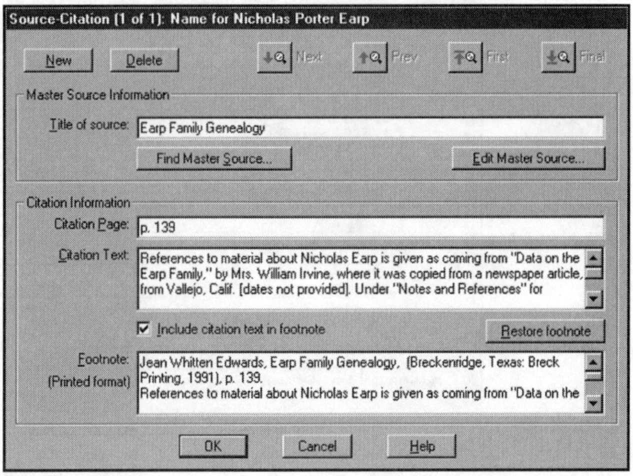

Figure 4-14

Use the Source-
Citation dialog box to
record information
about sources.

*Tree Maker gives you the option—should you change your mind about using
the original footnote text—to click on Restore Footnote, which will undo your
footnote changes.*

7. Click on the Include Citation Text in Footnote check box.

8. Check your entries (watch those typos—everyone makes them).

    Your completed Source-Citation dialog box should look like the one
    in Figure 4-14.

9. Click on OK.

Family Tree Maker will return to Nicholas Earp's name field and place an "s"
just to the right of it, indicating that you have recorded source information (see
Figure 4-15).

Once you have entered source information, it can be included as part of your
trees and custom reports. You'll learn more about these options in Chapters Ten
and Twelve.

After you create a Master Source, you can use it over and over. This is particularly useful when you have a lot of information that came from the same source,
such as a book or a census. To locate a source you have already entered in the
Master Sources dialog box, choose View, Source (the cursor can be in any field in

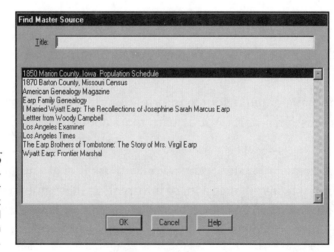

Figure 4-15

The "s" next to certain fields indicates that source information has been recorded.

the Family Page) or press Ctrl+S to open the Source-Citation dialog box. Click on the Find Master Source button to open the Find Master Source dialog box (see Figure 4-16). Select a Master Source from the list, and then click on OK. In the Source-Citation dialog box, you can click on the Edit Master Source button to add the page number where you found that particular reference.

Figure 4-16

The Find Master Source dialog box makes it easy to find and use sources again without retyping.

Displaying a Family Tree

In Family Tree Maker, you can create several types of trees. To understand how they differ and what will work best for you, experiment with the options. These are the three most commonly used types of trees:

- Ancestor
- Descendant
- Outline Descendant

Ancestor Tree

An Ancestor tree shows an individual's direct line—parents, grandparents, great-grandparents, and so on. It does not show aunts, uncles, nieces, nephews, or cousins. To display the Ancestor tree of Wyatt Earp, follow these steps:

1. Select Wyatt Earp as the primary individual by putting the cursor anywhere in one of his fields (name, birth date/location, or death date/location).

2. Click on the Ancestor button on the toolbar (or choose View, Ancestor Tree) and then choose Standard from the drop-down menu. The Standard Ancestor tree appears.

3. From the Format menu, select Tree Format. The Tree Format for Ancestor Tree dialog box appears (see Figure 4-17).

4. Select one of the Type options (Fit To Page, Book Layout, or Custom). For this example, the default Type option, Fit To Page, is selected.

5. In the Connections section, select the Detached button and then click on OK. The Ancestor tree appears (see Figure 4-18).

Play with the various options to see the differences in how an Ancestor tree can be displayed. You can return to the Family Page by clicking on the Family Page toolbar button.

Descendant Tree

The Descendant tree is also called a *drop chart* and is a popular format in England and Europe. It shows an individual's children, grandchildren,

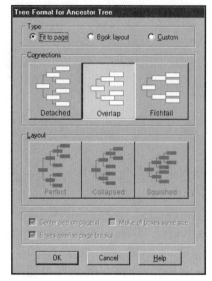

Figure 4-17

Choose a format for
displaying the
Ancestor tree.

great-grandchildren, and so on, with the primary individual appearing at the
top of the tree and the descendants in *branches* (boxes) below. To display the
descendant tree of Nicholas Earp, follow these steps:

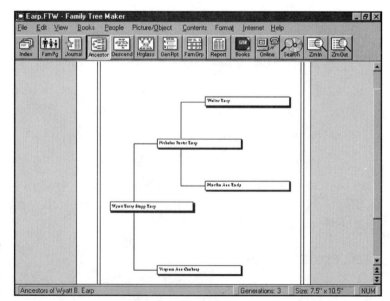

Figure 4-18

The Ancestor tree of
Wyatt Earp

1. Select Nicholas Porter Earp as the primary individual by putting the cursor anywhere in his field (name, birth date/location, or death date/location) on his Family Page.

2. Click on the Descend button on the toolbar (or choose View, Descendant Tree) and then choose Standard from the drop-down menu. The Standard Descendant Tree appears.

3. From the Format menu, select Tree Format. The Tree Format for Descendant Tree dialog box appears (see Figure 4-19).

4. Select one of the Type options.

5. If you chose Custom layout, click on a button in the Layout section.

   You also can center trees on the page and choose whether to have all the boxes the same size or not. Experiment with all the options.

6. Click on OK. The Descendent tree appears.

Outline Descendant Tree

To display an Outline Descendant tree of Nicholas Porter Earp, follow these steps:

1. Select Nicholas Porter Earp (primary individual) by placing the cursor on his name on his Family Page.

2. Click on View, and select Outline Descendant Tree. The Outline Descendant Tree dialog box appears.

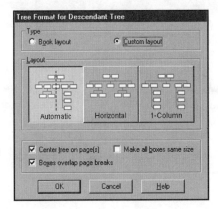

Figure 4-19

Tree Format for a
Descendant Tree

3. From the Format menu, select Tree Format. The Tree Format for Outline Descendant Tree dialog box appears (see Figure 4-20).

4. Select the Indentation options. One of most popular options is to use leader dots (. . . .) extending from the left margin of the page to each individual's name. To try this, enter a period (.) in the Indent With Which Character field.

   The Indent Each Generation By (in inches) box defaults to 0.30. That's fine. Leave it that way for this project.

5. Select the Generations Numbers options. Use the Starting with Generation No. 1 for this project.

6. Select the Size & Spacing options you prefer.

   All of the default options are fine for this project. You can fiddle with them later, if you wish.

7. Click on OK. The descendants of Nicholas Porter Earp (at least those you have entered so far) show up in the chart (see Figure 4-21).

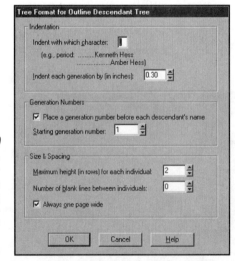

Figure 4-20

The Tree Format for Outline Descendant Tree dialog box provides choices for Indentation, Generation Numbers, and Size & Spacing.

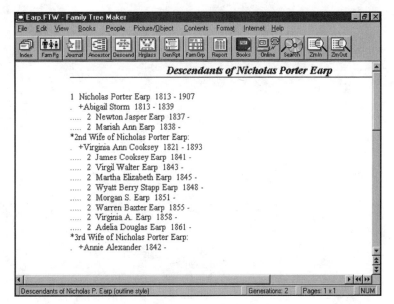

Figure 4-21

The Outline
Descendant Tree
format showing
Nicholas Porter Earp's
descendants

There are various options you can choose for these family trees. Brøderbund's Family Tree Maker user's manual provides detailed explanations about them and what they do. However, nothing beats just experimenting and trying various options until you become familiar with the styles and formats. Playing with the data and seeing the resulting information in different formats is a good way to relax after spending time inputting data and learning the features of the program. I like to see exactly how something will work; if you are the same, then just click and experiment with each and every option. It's fun.

PART II

Exploring Your Family Tree

Ancestors of George Howard Lafferty
Samuel Lafferty
1801 - 1873
Edwin E. Lafferty
1834 - 1907
Margaret McDowell
1803 - 1861
George E. Lafferty
1867 - 1936
Erastus Fowler
1793 - 1875
Temperence Merrill
1796 - 1871
Nathan Wescott
1818 - 1900
Sarah Ann McMichael
1820 - 1901
Samuel C. Amsden
1822 - 1899
Theresa Jerusa Amsden
1845 - 1934
Clarissa Hubbard
1820 - 1870
The History of George Howard Lafferty
George Howard Lafferty was born September 2, 1894 in Lenox township, Ashtabula County, Ohio, to Amber Amelia Wescott Lafferty and George Edwin Lafferty. A sister, Maud Irene, was born May 23, 1892.
A family of farmers, the Laffertys harvested the land where they lived. On May 9, 1919, they moved to Warren, Ohio, to a house on Forest Street NE. They lived next door to their daughter Maud, her husband Jay Rood Webster, and their three beautiful daughters, Reta, Shirley, and Marion.
As a youth, Lafferty went by "Howard" rather than "George" and signed his name as G. Howard Lafferty. After graduating from Lenox Township schools in 1911, he received a Teachers Certificate and became an educator and later a high school
Principal. He then switched careers and ventured into banking just before World War I.
As a student at Ohio State University during the war, Howard Lafferty hoped to join the army but was classified 5G due to his glasses and other restrictions. In 1923 he received an L.L.B. degree and passed

CHAPTER FIVE

Using the Family Archive CDs

amily Tree Maker's Family Archives is a large and growing CD-ROM collection that includes U.S. census information, a Social Security Death Index, selected U.S. and international marriage records, the World Family Tree military records, and ships passenger lists. The FamilyFinder Index, which is on two of the CDs that come with the Family Tree Maker program, is a unique list of approximately 170 million names that reveals which Family Archive CD includes information about a particular person and what type of information you will find there. Some versions of Family Tree Maker also contain selected Family Archive CDs. Additionally, you can purchase Family Archive CDs by choosing the Search button on the toolbar.

You learned in Chapter Three about sources and finding aids. Remember, you use finding aids to locate records that will lead you to other documents. The FamilyFinder Index on the Family Archive CDs is a finding aid that will lead you to sources of family information.

The FamilyFinder Index

Each of the Family Archive CDs includes references to thousands and thousands of historical records, ranging from military and church records to compiled family trees. Some of the CDs provide actual information gathered from particular sources, but most often the finding aids referred to will lead you to the actual source in various census or marriage indexes or to the actual census records, such as the *Virginia 1850 Census Microfilm Records* or books that have been reproduced on CD.

Searching the Index

In the steps that follow, you will continue to research the Earp family by exploring the Family Archive CDs. After you look up the Earp family, you can use the same methods to locate your own family members in the CD collection. To search the FamilyFinder Index for information on Wyatt Earp, follow these steps:

1. Start Family Tree Maker.

2. Open your Earp Family File. Family Tree Maker will display it automatically when you start if it's the most recent family file you've used (see Figure 5-1). If the Earp Family File is not onscreen already, you can choose File, Open Family File to display the Open Family File dialog box. Select the EARP.FTW file and then choose Open. (This assumes you actually created this file as described in Chapter Four.)

3. Insert into your CD-ROM drive the CD entitled Installation Program and FamilyFinder Index Volume 1: A-K. You won't see any starting banner appear onscreen, but the CD is now available to Family Tree Maker.

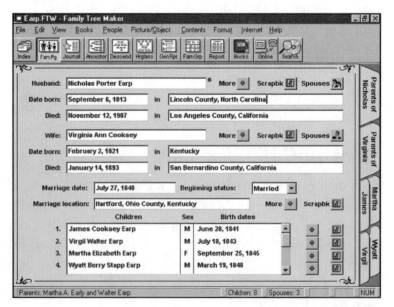

Figure 5-1

Display the Earp Family File before proceeding with the CD searches.

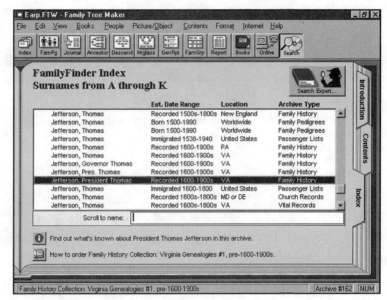

Figure 5-2

The first time you use the A-K FamilyFinder Index, the name President Thomas Jefferson appears.

4. Click on the Search button on the toolbar (it looks like a CD and a magnifying glass) or choose View, FamilyFinder (Search CD). (If the license agreement appears, read it and then choose OK.) The FamilyFinder Index for surnames from A through K appears with President Thomas Jefferson at the top of the list, as shown in Figure 5-2.

5. In the Scroll to Name field, type **Earp, Wyatt Berry Stapp.** Several listings of Wyatt Earp appear.

6. In the FamilyFinder window, click on the Search Expert button (the one that looks like Sherlock Holmes). The Search Expert window appears (see Figure 5-3).

7. Click on the Search for Someone From Your Family File button. When you select this option, Family Tree Maker uses the information in your Family File, such as birth dates, death dates, married names, maiden names, and nicknames to help find matches for the individual of interest. (The Search Expert will also search first name

Figure 5-3

The Search Expert asks
if you want to search
for someone from
your Family File—or
for someone else.

equivalents, such as Marge, Peggy, and even the initial M for the
name Margaret.)

❊ **TIP** ❊   *There are times when you will want to do a search for persons
not in your Family File. To do that just click on Search For Someone NOT
from Your Family File. When you want to find information about a specific
individual, it is best to use the Search Expert because it can search multiple
fields at the same time and locate matches quickly.*

The Search Expert locates the Earp family. Earp, Nicholas Porter is
highlighted by default because he is the primary individual on the
current Family Page, so you will need to select Wyatt, as shown in
Figure 5-4.

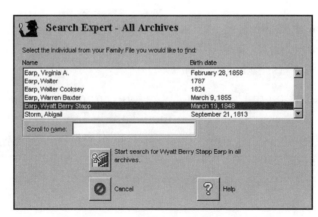

Figure 5-4

Search all archives
for Wyatt Berry
Stapp Earp.

8. In the list box (under Name) scroll to the entry for Earp, Wyatt Berry Stapp and select it. Alternatively, you can start typing **Earp, W** in the Scroll To <u>N</u>ame text box to find the name quickly.

9. Click on the button next to Start Search for Wyatt Berry Stapp Earp in All Archives. Family Tree Maker displays a status box while it conducts the search. It then places a magnifying glass to left of the matches found, highlighting the best match (see Figure 5-5).

❧ **NOTE** ❧   *When a field contains too much information to fit in the allotted space, you will see an ellipsis (. . .) to the right of it. Click on the Find Out What's Known button to see the rest of the information. Sometimes there are so many matches for a name that you will need to navigate through them either by moving forward or backward or jumping to the first or last entries. You can do this by clicking on the buttons to the right of Scroll To a Matching Name near the bottom of the FamilyFinder window, using the Page Up or Page Down keys on your keyboard, or using the scroll bars in the FamilyFinder window.*

Magnifying glass ——

Find button

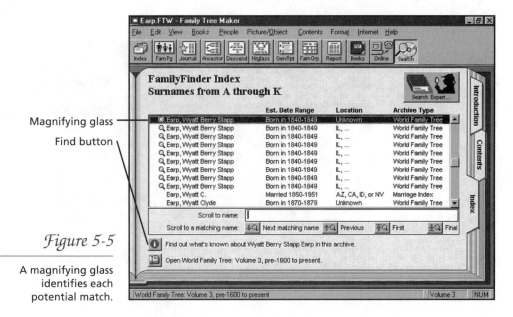

Figure 5-5

A magnifying glass
identifies each
potential match.

The search for information about Wyatt Earp reveals several variations on his name. (Remember, you need to investigate the evidence to be sure you have located the right person.) The man you're trying to trace may be listed as one of the following:

- Earp, Wyatt Berry Stapp

- Earp, Wyatt

- Earp, Wyatt S.

- Earp, W. S.

10. Highlight the *third* occurrence of the full name Earp, Wyatt Berry Stapp. (You'll see World Family Tree: Volume 3, Pre-1600 to Present displayed at the bottom of the screen.) Click on the Find Out What's Known About Wyatt Berry Stapp Earp button to display the More About information box (see Figure 5-6). There are details showing his name, his birth and death dates, the number of that tree submission, and its date. The information box also tells you that the source of this entry is the Family Archive CD World Family Tree: Volume 3. After seeing a few details of the archive, you can decide whether you want to view that source.

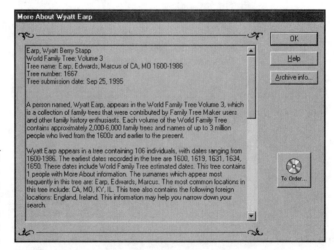

Figure 5-6

More information about Wyatt Earp is on Volume 3 of the World Family Tree in Tree No. 1667.

11. Click on OK to close the More About information box, and remove the FamilyFinder Index CD.

12. Insert the World Family Tree: Volume 3 CD in the drive. If this is the first time you have used this volume, you will see the license agreement (click on OK) and then the Volume 3 Introduction appears.

13. If the Index of People in this Archive window does not show Wyatt Berry Stapp Earp, click on the Search Expert button (as you did for the FamilyFinder Index), and then click on the appropriate buttons until The World Family Tree: Volume 3 Index of People in this Archive window appears. You can also click on the Index tab on the right side of the screen. If necessary, use the scroll bar or type **Earp, Wyatt Berry Stapp** in the Scroll to Name field to find Wyatt (see Figure 5-7).

14. From the Volume 3 Index page, click on the button Turn To Wyatt Stapp Earp in Pedigree Number 1667 in the lower left corner of the screen. Family Tree Maker displays this pedigree on a Family Page

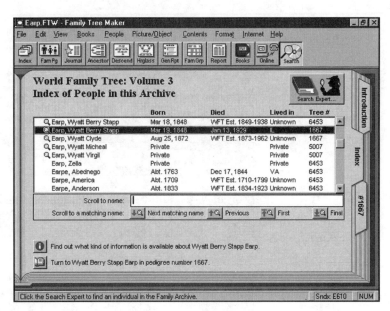

Figure 5-7

This index shows the contents of the World Family Tree: Volume 3 CD.

from the World Family Tree (see Figure 5-8). The World Family Tree resembles a regular Family Page. However, it has a different background color and a different toolbar.

You cannot add or change any of the information in the World Family Tree, but you can do the following:

* Move between Family Pages by clicking the tabs along the right edge of the screen.

* Display various reports and different types of trees using the toolbar or the View menu.

* Customize trees and reports and print them.

* Click on the More and Spouses buttons to find more information, if it has been provided in the CD.

15. Click on the Go Back button on the toolbar, or click on the View menu and select FamilyFinder (Search CD); you'll return to the Volume 3 Index view.

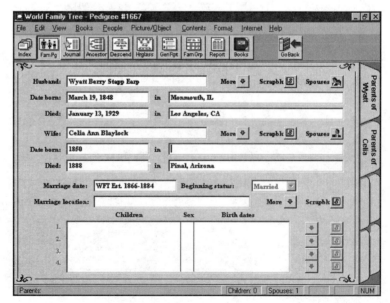

Figure 5-8

A World Family Tree pedigree page resembles a Family Page.

> ❋ **TIP** ❋   *You can look at some other entries on the same volume of the World Family Tree CD without going back to the FamilyFinder Index. Choose another item that has a magnifying glass icon or click on the Search Expert button to look up another name.*

When you finish searching the CDs, or even while you are still using an index on a CD, you can go back to viewing the primary individual's Family Page by clicking on the Family Page button on the toolbar. Clicking on the Search button will take you back to the index of whatever CD you have in the drive.

World Family Tree CDs

You can use the World Family Tree CDs to find more information about your ancestors and expand your own family tree. These CDs contain genealogical information that was contributed to the World Family Tree Project by other researchers. You can view and print information from these archives in Family Pages or in trees, reports, and Family Group Sheets. The information can be appended or merged into your own files, if you wish. You can also save the information you find as a separate file.

Merging a Pedigree

When you are using a World Family Tree CD, you will see a number to the far right of each name. This is the number of the tree in which you will find that name. Figure 5-8 shows how a Family Page looks in the World Family Tree. If you find there is a link to your family in a World Family Tree pedigree, you can append or merge the pedigree into your Family File. The search of the FamilyFinder Index done in the previous section indicated there is information about Wyatt Earp in the World Family Tree, Volume 3, Tree #1667.

To check out this lead, put World Family Tree Volume 3 CD in the CD-ROM drive to see if the information connects to the Wyatt Earp of interest to you. (Yes, there is even more than one Wyatt Earp.)

You can move more than one person's information if you find a pedigree that has one or more valid links to your family. Be sure you have the correct Family File (Earp.ftw) open before you begin this merge feature, and then follow these steps:

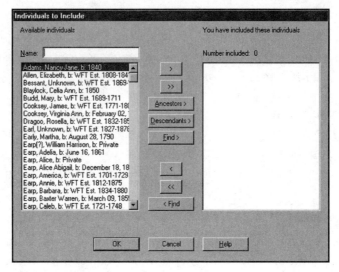

Figure 5-9

Individuals to Include
dialog box

1. Use the FamilyFinder Index to locate the name entry (and its corresponding World Family Tree CD and pedigree tree number) that you want to see and possibly merge.

2. Insert the correct World Family Tree CD (in this instance it is Volume 3) and find the reference to Wyatt Earp. Click on the Turn To button or double-click on the name to display the World Family Tree pedigree page.

3. From the People menu, select Merge Pedigrees. Family Tree Maker will remind you to back up your files if you have not already done so.

4. Click on OK if you have a current backup of your Family File. The Individuals to Include dialog box appears (see Figure 5-9).

5. Click on Earp, Wyatt Berry Stapp in the list of Available Individuals shown on the left. Click on the Ancestors button to include all of Wyatt's ancestors from this CD to merge with your family file. After you create a group of individuals to merge, click on OK. The Append File dialog box appears (see Figure 5-10).

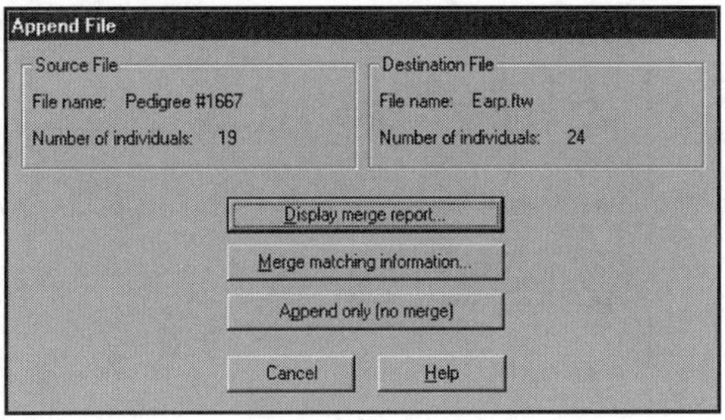

Figure 5-10

The Append File
dialog box

The Append File dialog box gives you information about both the source file and the destination file. In the Append File dialog box you can do three different things:

- **Display Merge Report.** Shows whether each of the individuals in the source file (the World Family Tree CD) is an exact match, possible match, or not a match for someone in the destination file.

- **Merge Matching Information.** Displays exact and possible matches one at a time so you can decide which information to keep and which to toss out.

- **Append Only (no merge).** Adds all the information in the source file to the destination file but does not merge anyone.

⊰ CAUTION ⊱   Before merging your Family File with another, be sure you understand the process and read the Merge Report so you will know in advance how Family Tree Maker will handle each individual if you proceed with a merge. After you merge files, print some reports and trees before you leave Family Tree Maker. Check to be sure there are no mistakes. If there are errors, then you can fix them by going to the Edit menu and selecting Undo before you quit Family Tree Maker.

6. Choose Display Merge Report, review the report for any problems (you can click on the Print button to print it), and then click on Done.

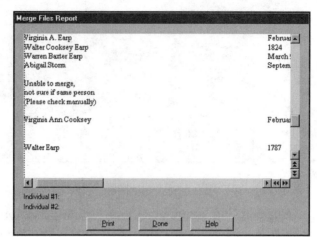

Figure 5-11

A Merge Files Report provides a guide to help determine if individuals match.

7. Click on <u>M</u>erge Matching Individuals. The merge will be completed and a Merge Files Report appears (see Figure 5-11).

8. Click on <u>D</u>one.

You also can use the Find command (from a World Family Tree pedigree page) to see the results of a merge. From the <u>E</u>dit menu, select <u>F</u>ind Individual to display the Find Individual dialog box (see Figure 5-12). Click on the arrow in the Search drop-down list box and choose Merged or Appended Individuals. In the For list box you have several choices from which to narrow your search, including Unchanged Individuals and New Individuals. After you make your choices, click on Search to see your merge results or Restart Search to begin again. When you are finished, click on Cancel.

Figure 5-12

Use the Find Individual dialog box to check the status of a pedigree after merging information.

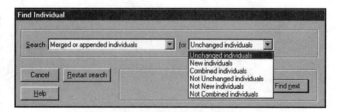

Trouble Finding a Name?

The World Family Tree CDs contain a great deal of information, but it is possible you will not find anything on a particular name you are seeking. Here are some additional hints for finding names:

- Watch out for those variant spellings—don't insist your name has always been spelled a particular way. Even if your family did always prefer one version, it probably has been spelled many ways by various clerks and enumerators.

- You can use Soundex codes and wildcards to help locate names spelled other than as you expect. (See the sidebar, "Understanding Soundex and Wildcards.")

- Take a look at entries in the FamilyFinder Index that are similar but not an exact match of a name. If you're still stumped, click on the Introduction tab in the Family Archive CD in which you are seeking a name. There you will find helpful tips and information about the material on that particular CD.

    ❀ **TIP** ❀ *Can't get the hang of Soundex? Use the Soundex Machine at the National Archives Genealogy Page (**http://www.nara.gov/genealogy/coding.html**).*

Social Security Death Index CDs

The U.S. Social Security Death Index (SSDI) is one of the most useful databases available to researchers. It is also one of the largest with information about more than 55 million people. You can use the SSDI to learn when and where an ancestor died, which in turn can lead you to additional information about a death certificate, an obituary, cemetery, or funeral home record, and perhaps a probate file, listing all the heirs.

    ❀ **NOTE** ❀ *The death certificate also can be helpful in finding living relatives as it will provide the place of death.*

The SSDI has some limitations. It does not include all those who died with a Social Security number—only those whose deaths were reported to the Social

Understanding Soundex and Wildcards

Soundex is a coded surname index based on the phonetic sound of the consonants in a surname rather than the way it is spelled. Soundex ignores all the vowels as well as W, Y, and H. A numeral code is assigned to the other letters. Every Soundex code consists of a letter and three numbers, like E610 (for Earp). The letter is always the first letter of the surname, and no matter how long or short a surname is, its Soundex code is always the first letter of the surname and three numbers.

Want to try your hand at Soundexing? Here's a Soundex Coding Guide:

The Number	Represents the letters
1	B P F V
2	C S K G J Q X Z
3	D T
4	L
5	M N
6	R

To determine the Soundex for your surname, write down your name and then, excluding the first letter, put a slash through all of the following letters:

A, E, I, O, U, W, Y, and H

If your surname has any double letters, like NN, put a slash in the second N. If your surname has a prefix—like Van, Von, De, Di, or Le—code it both with and without the prefix. Mc and Mac are not considered prefixes in this instance. One other little peculiarity is if a surname has different letters side by side that have the same number in the Soundex coding guide, they are treated as one letter. For example, Jackson is coded as J250 (J, 2 for the C, K is ignored, S is ignored, 5 for the N, and the 0 is added).

Long surname? Once you have coded the first three unslashed letters following the initial letter, disregard any additional ones. Short surname? Simply add zeroes to the end of the code.

For example, with the surname of Earp, the E is the initial letter. You put a slash through the A. The R number code is 6 and the P number code is 1. The code would then be E61—but you need at least three numbers and you've run out of surname, so just add a zero to come up with E610 for the Soundex code.

Another trick to successful searches, particularly with names, is to do some "wildcarding." For example, you can use an asterisk (a common wildcard character) in place of multiple letters. If you type Mary*, you will find all the names such as Maryann, Maryella, Mary-Louise, and so forth. The asterisk and question mark are the most commonly-used symbols to replace one or more characters in a name. The asterisk replaces a group of characters while the question mark only replaces one. Wildcarding can also be successfully used with many search engines.

Security Administration. This usually occurred when the spouse or a family member applied for a death benefit. While CD #110 indicates the SSDI covers the years 1937-1996, most of the deaths included in this database took place after 1962 when the Social Security Adminsitration started keeping this information on its computer.

Information found on the SSDI CDs usually includes:

- 衤 Social Security number
- 衤 Name (first and surname)
- 衤 Birth date
- 衤 Death date
- 衤 Issuing location of the original card (by a code)
- 衤 ZIP of last know residence
- 衤 ZIP of recipient if a lump sum payment was made

To search the SSDI CDs put either the Volume 1 CD (surnames A-L) or the Volume 2 CD (surnames M-Z) in your CD-ROM drive and click on Search on the main toolbar in Family Tree Maker. You can type in a name of interest and go right to that name. The Find Out Additional Information About option will provide you with data to help you determine whether or not you might want to copy information about that person to your Family File (see Figure 5-13).

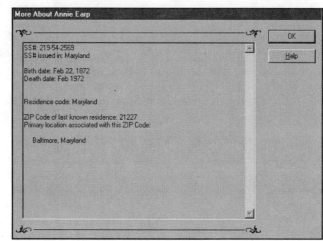

Figure 5-13

Find out more information in the Social Security Death Index

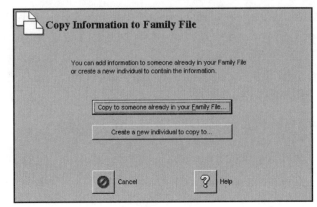

Figure 5-14

You can copy
information from
the SSDI.

If you would like to copy the information, click on Copy Information About to
Your Family File and the Copy Information to Family File dialog box appears
(see Figure 5-14).

After you choose whether to copy the information to someone already in your
Family File or to create a new individual to copy this information to, the Choose
Sex dialog box appears (see Figure 5-15). Choose Female, Male, or Unknown,
if you're not sure. Click on OK and the information will be copied to your
Family File.

Marriage Records CD

Another Family Tree Maker Family Archives CD you may find to be a helpful
finding aid is CD #403, Marriage Records: Selected U.S./International Marriage
Records, 1340-1980 from Yates Publishing (see Figure 5-16). It contains information for approximately 1.4 million individuals from all across the United States
and 32 other countries. The data was extracted from Family Group Sheets, from
unspecified electronic databases, biographies, wills, and other sources by Bill Yates.

Figure 5-15

The Choose Sex dialog
box is shown before
information is copied
to your Family File.

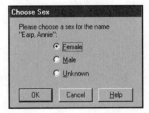

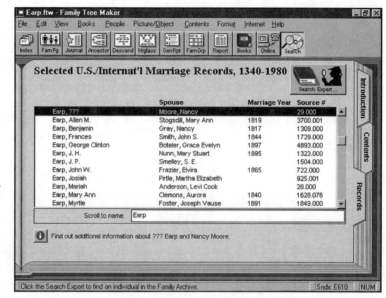

Figure 5-16

A search for Earp marriage records turns up a reference for Wyatt Earp's grandparents on CD #403.

If you find a possible ancestor listed, as shown in Figure 5-17, you can then write to Bill Yates and for a small charge of $1 per sheet, plus a mailing and handling fee, he will provide you with a copy of his source of the information.

The codes to the sources are given on the CD. They include F or X (Family Group Sheet), P (Pedigree Chart), C (Correspondence), and DB (Database).

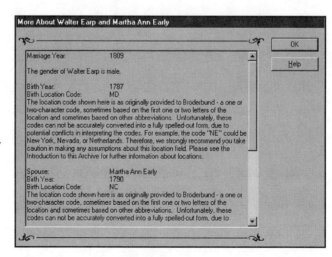

Figure 5-17

More about the marriage record pertaining to Walter Earp and Martha Ann Early is listed on CD #403.

The following text appears within the image (book pages shown in the photograph):

Ancestors of George Howard Lafferty

- Samuel Lafferty
  1801 - 1873
- Edwin E. Lafferty
  1834 - 1907
- Margaret McDowell
  1803 - 1861
- George E. Lafferty
  1867 - 1936
- Erastus Fowler
  1793 - 1875
- ...elia Fowler
  ... 1914
- Temperence Merrill
  1796 - 1871
- Nathan Wescott
  1818 - 1900
- ...ram Wescott
- Sarah Ann McMichael
  1820 - 1901
- ...George Wescott
- Samuel C. Amsden
  1822 - 1899
- Theresa Jerusa Amsden
  1845 - 1934
- Clarissa Hubbard
  1820 - 1870

The History of George Howard Lafferty

George Howard Lafferty was born September 2, 1894 in Lenox township, Ashtabula County, Ohio, to Amber Amelia Wescott Lafferty and George Edwin Lafferty. A sister, Maud Irene, was born May 25, 1892.

A family of farmers, the Laffertys harvested the land where they lived. On May 9, 1919, they moved to Warren, Ohio, to a house on Forest Street NE. They lived next door to their daughter Maud, her husband Jay Rood Webster, and their three beautiful daughters, Reta, Shirley, and Marion.

As a youth, Lafferty went by "Howard" rather than "George" and signed his name as G. Howard Lafferty. After graduating from Lenox Township schools in 1911, he received a Teachers Certificate and became an educator and later a high school Principal. He then switched careers and ventured into banking just before World War I.

As a student at Ohio State University during the war, Howard Lafferty hoped to join the army but was classified 5G due to his glasses and other restrictions. In 1923 he received an L.L.B. degree and passed

CHAPTER SIX

Family Tree Maker
Online

he recent explosion of genealogical data on the World Wide Web makes research faster, easier, and more exciting. Now you can join the cyberpioneers and learn to explore the Internet for information about your family. However, as many pioneers before you have discovered, there are some obstacles along the way, and you may have to make a few detours. The Web, as it is fondly called, is not perfect—not everything you find is accurate—and you will not be able to do all your research with a click of a mouse. Nevertheless, there is a whole new world online out there just waiting for you.

The Web is the graphical interface for certain parts of the Internet. You use what's called a *Web browser* (two of the most popular are Netscape Navigator and Microsoft Internet Explorer), and with a click-click here and a click-click there you move from one Web site to another. You can view information online, download files, or play tourist and gawk at all the sights you find at various Web pages.

> ❀ **NOTE** ❀ *The word* page *is somewhat of a misnomer since a Web page does not have the limitations of a printed page. Technically, the length of a Web page is unlimited.*

One of the main reasons the Web has become so popular, and is such a natural for genealogical material, is its ability to display both text and graphics in full color, plus sound and video. It is so easy to navigate—you jump from link to link, from page to page, across sites and servers, leaping over international boundaries with a click of your mouse. No passports or visas required. For genealogists, the Web is a giant library—open 24 hours a day, 7 days a week. You can browse to your heart's content.

Exploring Features of Family Tree Maker Online

You can access many genealogical resources and get your Web feet wet, virtually, at the Family Tree Maker Web site—called Family Tree Maker Online (**http://www.familytreemaker.com/**). First, make sure you have dialed your modem to connect to your Internet Service Provider (ISP) and that your Web browser is running.

> ❉ **TIP** ❉   *If you chose not to set up a Web browser during your installation of Family Tree Maker, you should re-run the setup to install and configure your browser.*

Follow these steps to go to Family Tree Maker Online:

1. Start your Family Tree Maker software.

   The Family Tree Maker screen appears, with the most recently used Family File open.

2. Click on the Online button on the toolbar, or from the Internet menu, choose Go Online.

   The home page screen for Family Tree Maker Online appears (see Figure 6-1).

   > ❉ **TIP** ❉   *Registration as a new user gives you access to special benefits. If you have not already registered, click the New User? link and follow the instructions onscreen to complete the Family Tree Maker Online Registration form. This will enable Family Tree Maker Online to identify you as a Family Tree Maker customer, entitling you to some special benefits, such as the ability to create your own user home page, access to the message boards, and free broadcasts of Family Archive CDs. (After completing the form, you'll return to the Family Tree Maker Home Page.)*

3. Use the scroll bar to move down and read the rest of the home page.

4. To move to other pages within the Web site, click on the *hyperlinks*—the colored, underlined text onscreen; or click on the menus at the top and bottom of the pages. To return to the home page, click on

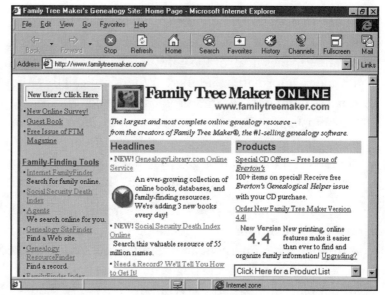

Figure 6-1

Welcome to Family
Tree Maker Online.

Home on the *navigation bar* (not your browser's Home button, which will take you to your own usual starting page), or use the Back and Forward buttons on your browser.

❧ **NOTE** ❧ *A* navigation bar *on a Web page is a menu of navigational links to other pages on the same site.*

The Family Tree Maker Online Home Page serves as a table of contents with links to each of the main sections of Family Tree Maker Online. Although (like most Web pages) its content changes frequently, in most instances you will find the navigational links on the left-hand side of the home page.

❧ **TIP** ❧ *If you want to keep sampling the Family Tree Maker Online features as I describe them in this chapter, stay online.*

You can spend a great deal of time at Family Tree Maker Online. Share your genealogy expertise and learn from others via the Genealogy Message Boards, or read the Success Stories to get inspired and see how others have solved research problems.

Internet FamilyFinder

Internet FamilyFinder was designed to be a single, comprehensive search tool for locating names in all of the genealogy data on the Web. There is a great deal of genealogy information out there. Where does all this information come from? Volunteers enter data for genealogical societies and for their localities of interest. Hobbyists post their home pages and include their family trees. While lists of links help, facing hundreds, even thousands, of possible links makes research too tedious and time-consuming. It is like going to a library that has no catalog. The information might be there in a book, but how do you find it?

Internet FamilyFinder is powerful. It searches the entire Internet and remembers all the names it finds on genealogically relevant pages. When you enter a name to search for, Internet FamilyFinder gives you a ranked list of all the mentions of that name on all the pages it knows about—which isn't quite the same as all the pages in existence. (While it constantly scours the Internet for new data, it does not search proprietary sites or fee databases.) However, it is designed to find all genealogy pages that are linked to information it already has. It already knows about millions of pages, and it is constantly growing. There are several other Internet search engines available—AltaVista, Infoseek, HotBot, WebCrawler, and Excite, to name a few—but Internet FamilyFinder is much better than these for genealogy research for the following reasons:

- It knows about names. If you search for John Smith with another search engine, you will get pages that have Johns and Smiths, but it might be John Jones and Mary Smith. Internet FamilyFinder also knows how to do Soundex searches and searches with initials.

- It knows about genealogy. Other search engines index all kinds of pages. If you search for Frank Case in another search engine, you may get the Frank Case who sells real estate in Kansas City. Internet FamilyFinder carefully selects only genealogically relevant pages for indexing, so the usefulness of the matches it returns is much higher.

- It gets all the information from a Web site so names buried on a list several pages deep will be found. Most other search engines only look at a few pages from each site.

> ❧ It shows the words around each match, which often contain dates, locations, or other family lines. This information lets you determine quickly which matches are relevant to your genealogy project.

> ❧ It looks at other kinds of information besides Web pages, including GEDCOM and text files that contain genealogical data.

Internet FamilyFinder scans the Internet and remembers all the names it has found, but the actual data does not reside in this search engine, nor generally on Family Tree Maker Online. The actual Web pages with the information remain on the Web site of the person or organization that created and entered them. (Remember, therefore, that the owners' usage rules and copyrights apply.)

Internet FamilyFinder is designed to make searching the Internet much easier and faster. Just type in a name and the program will search through hundreds of thousands of genealogy pages and give you links to likely matches in:

> ❧ Internet Web pages such as indexes, records, and family histories that others have posted; home pages containing trees, Ahnentafel (a German word meaning ancestor table), and files generated from GEDCOMS (GEnealogical Data COMmunication—a sort of ASCII for genealogy applications) into hypertext markup languages for the Web, and family association and name association pages, for example.

> ❧ Family Tree Maker Online Message Boards, Classified Ads, user home pages, reports on user home pages, and other content.

Using Internet FamilyFinder

Internet FamilyFinder does exactly what its name indicates—it searches the Internet for family names. Try it, you'll like it. To go to Internet FamilyFinder:

1. From the Family Tree Maker Home Page (refer back to Figure 6.1), locate the Internet FamilyFinder link, which is probably in the list of links on the left-hand side of the screen.

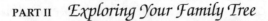
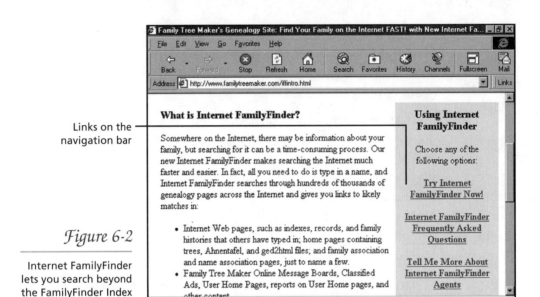

Links on the
navigation bar

Figure 6-2

Internet FamilyFinder
lets you search beyond
the FamilyFinder Index
on the CDs.

❋ **TIP** ❋   *You can recognize links not only by their alternate color and underlined text, but also by the mouse pointer changing to a hand when you are close to a link. Pictures can be links too; you'll see the mouse pointer change when it crosses a graphic that serves as a link.*

2. Click on Internet FamilyFinder. The Internet FamilyFinder page appears, with descriptions of its features (see Figure 6-2).

❋ **NOTE** ❋   *You get more than just a big list of links from Internet FamilyFinder. This feature sorts the list of links with the most likely matches at the top. Additionally, it displays some of the text from the matching pages to help you decide whether or not a particular page is worth your time and effort. You can also decide where it should search.*

3. Click on Try Internet FamilyFinder Now.

   You will be taken to a screen with a form like the one shown in Figure 6-3.

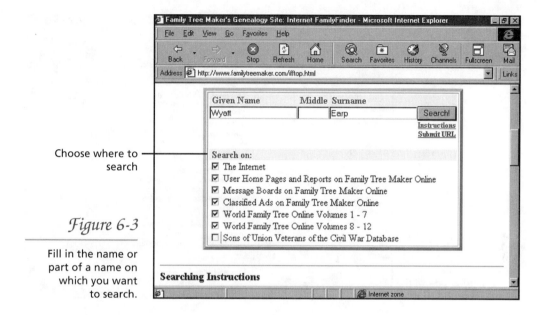

Choose where to search

Figure 6-3

Fill in the name or part of a name on which you want to search.

4. Type in the given name and surname, or just the surname if you wish, and then click on the appropriate boxes to direct Internet FamilyFinder to search any or all of the following options:

   ☀ The Internet

   ☀ User home pages and reports on Family Tree Maker Online

   ☀ Message Boards on Family Tree Maker Online

   ☀ Classified Ads on Family Tree Maker Online

   ☀ World Family Tree Online Volumes 1–7

   ☀ World Family Tree Online Volumes 8–12

   ☀ Civil War Databases--Union and Confederate Data

5. Click on the Search! button.

   A search for Wyatt Earp turned up several references (see Figure 6-4).

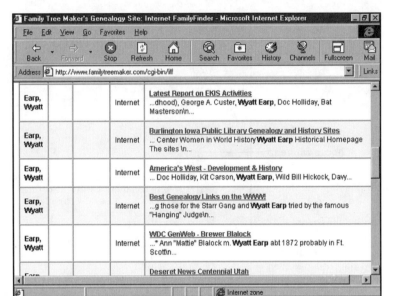

Figure 6-4

Results of a search for
Earp using Internet
FamilyFinder.

6. To try another search, click on the New Search link at the bottom of
the page, or click on your browser's Back button.

It is usually a good idea to leave the "Middle" name blank unless you really
only want an exact match. However, not all information may have included the
middle name, in which case you would not find those references if you limit
your search too much. Do not enter titles (like Dr. or Rev.) and leave off the
suffixes (Jr., Sr., and III).

To keep Internet FamilyFinder running fast, the number of results it will return
per search is limited to about 1,000. For more specific results, supply a first name
as well as a surname to search for. If that still results in too many matches, try
searching for a more uncommon name, such as the spouse's name or a close
relative, and perhaps the person you are searching for will be mentioned on the
same page. Also, to allow you to find names with the greatest chance of success,
Internet FamilyFinder takes the approach of remembering all names without
accent marks. When you're searching for a name with accented characters, do
not type the accents in your query—just use plain letters.

If you can't find the specific person, try just the surname. It may be necessary to experiment with variant spellings—you never know how a name might be listed in someone else's files or in other records. Some of the matches may not be what you hoped to find, while others may delight and surprise you with an enormous amount of detail on your ancestors.

Searching with FamilyFinder Index

The FamilyFinder Index is another valuable resource for searching. It contains more than 170 million names from census, marriage, and Social Security death records, and actual family trees.

1. Click on the FamilyFinder Index link on the navigation bar, or click on the link on the left side of the Family Tree Maker Online Home Page.

2. Click on the Search Expert button (see Figure 6-5). The Search Expert screen appears.

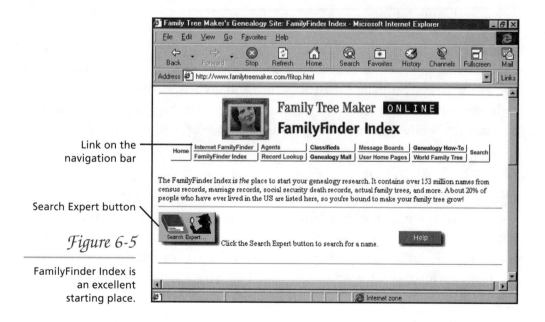

Link on the navigation bar

Search Expert button

Figure 6-5

FamilyFinder Index is an excellent starting place.

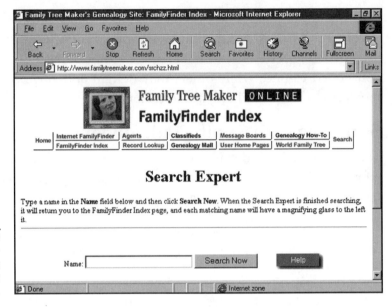

Figure 6-6

Simply type in a name
and let Search Expert
do the work.

3. Type the name you want to check in the appropriate box (see Figure 6-6).

A search for Earp, Wyatt reveals several links—under Earp, Wyatt Berry Stapp, as well as Earp, Wyatt, and other possible matches (see Figure 6-7). The search shows the name, estimated date, location, and archive type. The latter column indicates where the match was found. Some of these are from marriage and census CDs, while others are from Pedigree and World Family Tree CDs.

In the search results offered at Family Tree Maker Online several leads to information about Wyatt Earp were found. Following links to the various matches is always an adventure. You never know what may appear at the next click. In checking out one of the matches to Wyatt Earp, the trail from the Internet FamilyFinder led to a Web site that at first did not appear to have anything of interest (see Figure 6-8) or pertaining to Wyatt Earp. However, by using the Edit menu on the top menu bar and clicking on Find (see Figure 6-9), you can type in the name of interest and let the browser do the work for you.

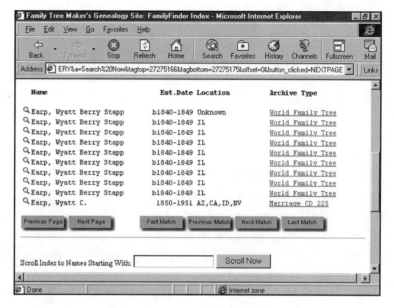

Figure 6-7

Several matches turn up for Wyatt Earp.

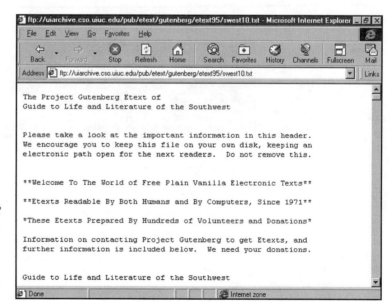

Figure 6-8

At first glance this page did not appear to have any connection to Wyatt Earp.

Figure 6-9

Using the Edit/Find option on the browser enables you to search for a specific name or word.

Another search to a Web site that did not appear at first glance to have any connections to Wyatt Earp turned up a reference to Ann "Mattie" Blalock and her family. Mattie was Wyatt's common-law wife about the time he went to Tombstone, Arizona, in 1880 (see Figure 6-10). Finding unexpected treasures of biographical and historical data is what makes following the links so much fun for genealogists. Don't be afraid to explore. You never know what you might find next.

Still another link led to the exploration of some historical sources pertaining to Kansas gunfighters and Dodge City, as shown in Figure 6-11. Wyatt Earp served in Dodge City as a policeman and assistant marshal in 1876, 1877, and 1878.

Figure 6-10

Genealogical information about Wyatt Earp's second wife was found here.

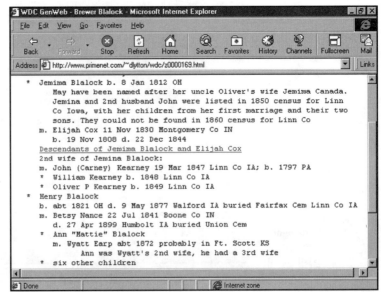

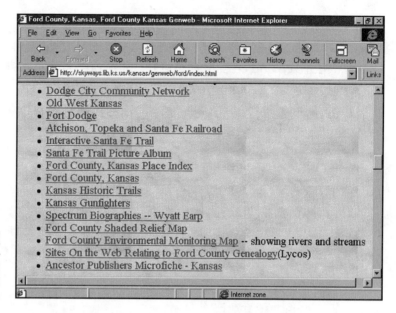

Figure 6-11

Genealogical material
is often found buried
at historical sites.

Using More Family Tree Maker Online Research Tools

Family Tree Maker's Home Page offers more tools to help you find information fast. Each of these options offers different help or services. They include:

- Genealogy SiteFinder

- Genealogy ResourceFinder

- GenealogyLibrary.com

- Research Services

- Reference Library

- WhoWhere? E-mail, Address, and Telephone Searches

- World Family Tree Vols. 1-7 Online

- FamilyFinder Report

- Internet FamilyFinder Agents

- Social Security Death Index (a searchable database)

Genealogy SiteFinder

The Genealogy SiteFinder provides tens of thousands of links to genealogy Web sites, categorized and cross-indexed to help you find what you need. The Genealogy Site Finder is compiled by Matt and April Helm. Choose Genealogy SiteFinder when you want to browse, look for ideas of other places to search for information, and learn more about genealogical research and records available. Figure 6-12 shows the Genealogy SiteFinder's search options—search by subject or by index of keywords.

The topics in the directory include:

- Abbreviations, Definitions, and Glossaries
- Adoption
- Calendars and Events
- Computers, Software, and the Internet
- Family History Centers

- Genealogical Education
- Groups and Societies
- History
- How-To and Help
- Libraries and Archives
- Magazines, Publications, and Television

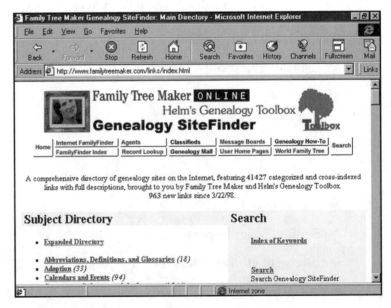

Figure 6-12

Genealogy SiteFinder features Helm's Genealogy Toolbox for searching by categories.

⚘ Maps

⚘ Microfilm, Microform, and Microfiche

⚘ Miscellaneous

⚘ National Archives and Records Administration

⚘ Numbering Systems

⚘ People

⚘ Photography and Video

⚘ Places

⚘ Records

⚘ Reunions

⚘ Search Engines

⚘ Supplies and Services

⚘ Technical Support

⚘ Time Periods

As you can see, there is much to discover and learn on the Internet. Finding the time to explore clues and various records becomes the major challenge. You can access the Genealogy SiteFinder link from the Family Tree Maker Online page. Figure 6-13 reveals more of the categories and search options available at Genealogy SiteFinder.

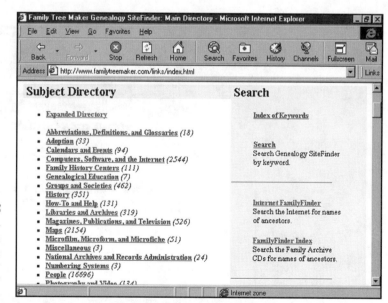

Figure 6-13

Searching by subjects or categories using Genealogy SiteFinder can lead to new discoveries.

Genealogy ResourceFinder

The Genealogy ResourceFinder (see Figure 6-14) helps locate some Family Tree Maker records. First, select a subject, such as Address or Age, to narrow your search and then just type in the time period, location, and type of information you wish to locate. ResourceFinder will make suggestions or refer you to a CD where you might find the answer. The ResourceFinder might direct you to Research Services, which is an online service available for obtaining various genealogical records such as marriage records, for fees ranging from about $7 to $10. It also might guide you to the Reference Library, which lists thousands of library, association, and county addresses and phone numbers. You'll find step-by-step research instructions here, plus a dictionary.

> ✳ **NOTE** ✳　*If you want to find phone numbers and e-mail and street addresses for living relatives (or friends), use the WhoWhere? E-mail, Address, and Telephone Searches option. This is an online national directory. (In Chapter Three, Figure 3-2 shows the WhoWhere? search screen.)*

> *World Family Tree Vols. 1-7 Online is a subscription offer that enables you to search and download information from this huge collection of family trees contributed by many genealogists, who are mostly amateurs.*

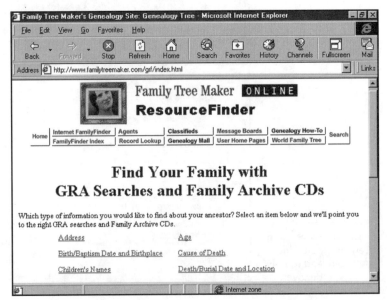

Figure 6-14

ResourceFinder directs you to Family Archive CDs and other references.

GenealogyLibrary.com

GenealogyLibrary.com is an ever-growing collection of online books, databases, and family-finding resources (see Figure 6-15). Three new books are added daily to the site. You can search a single book, an entire category, or all the books in the collection at once.

A search might turn up references in family histories, church histories, indexes to births and marriages in various counties and states, the gazetteer of the U.S., genealogies in the Library of Congress, and the "Land Fraud-Senate Doc 151."

After doing a search for you, GenealogyLibrary.com reveals the title of the matching book or document and offers you the option of seeing a description of it. It shows the "hits" (where the searched name appears in the reference) and offers related books.

The GenealogyLibrary.com also includes these features:

* **Social Security Death Index**

* **U.S. Geographical Names Information System.** Looking for a cemetery, creek, or town named for your family? Use this comprehensive list of landmarks throughout the U.S.

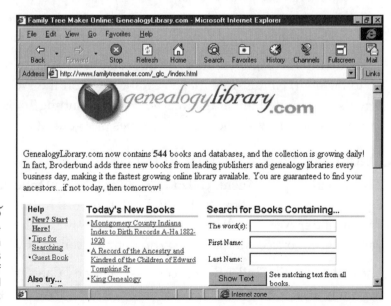

Figure 6-15

GenealogyLibrary.com offers subscribers access to hundreds of rare and hard-to-find books and documents.

- **Vital Records Assistant.** Learn how to order government-generated vital records and let the VRA do the writing for you.

- **Genealogy Discovery Articles.** Learn "how-to" with this comprehensive and growing collection of articles written by noted genealogists.

> ❧ **NOTE** ❧   *The GenealogyLibrary.com is a subscription library—$39.95 for an annual subscription or you can pay $5.99 per month (renewed automatically until you cancel). If you have the Family Tree Maker Deluxe 10 CD version, you will receive 6 months of free access to Genealogy Library.com.*

Using Agents

Tell the Agents which family names you want to find, and they will locate information about those names. There are two types of Agents: one is the Internet FamilyFinder Agent and the other is the Online FamilyFinder Report Agent.

INTERNET FAMILYFINDER AGENTS

Anyone with Web access can create reports with the Internet FamilyFinder Agents. The Agents can search for up to 10 different names at once, and the names don't have to be in your Family File. This type of Agent is ideal for locating all the information about a surname such as Coatney, or about an individual whose relationship to your family is unclear or not yet established.

To set up Internet FamilyFinder Agents, establish your Internet connection and go to the main Family Tree Maker Online page on the Web. Then click on the Agents link, located under the Internet Family-Finding Tools links. You'll jump to a page that tells you about the two types of Agents. (see Figure 6-16).

ONLINE FAMILYFINDER REPORT AGENTS

The second type of Agent, called the Online FamilyFinder Report Agent (see Figure 6-17), is created by the FamilyFinder Report. It differs from the Internet FamilyFinder Agents in that this Agent searches for all the individuals in your Family File at once—although you can define a subset of your choosing.

The Online FamilyFinder Report copies names and dates from your Family File to Family Tree Maker's secure Web server. Then its special search engines use

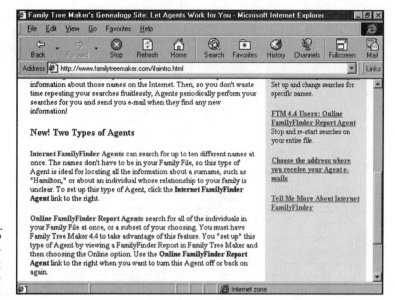

Figure 6-16

Put an Agent to work to save yourself some search effort.

that information to locate information about your family names. After searching the Internet for the individuals you select, it displays the matches in the FamilyFinder Report (see Figure 6-18).

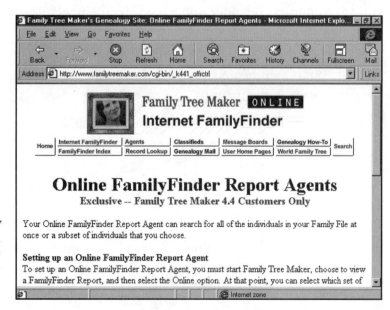

Figure 6-17

Obtain the aid of Online FamilyFinder Report Agents via a FamilyFinder Report.

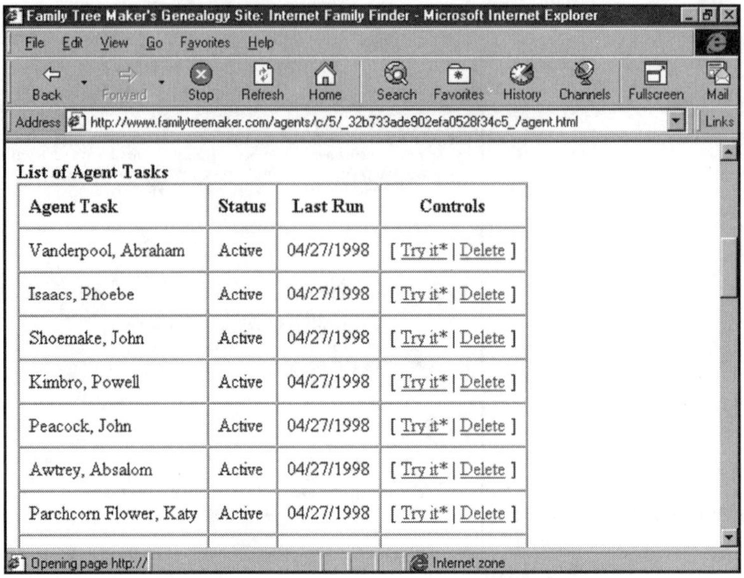

Family Tree Maker's Genealogy Site: Internet Family Finder - Microsoft Internet Explorer

File   Edit   View   Go   Favorites   Help

Back   Forward   Stop   Refresh   Home   Search   Favorites   History   Channels   Fullscreen   Mail

Address http://www.familytreemaker.com/agents/c/5/_32b733ade902efa0528f34c5_/agent.html   Links

List of Agent Tasks

Agent Task	Status	Last Run	Controls
Vanderpool, Abraham	Active	04/27/1998	[Try it* | Delete]
Isaacs, Phoebe	Active	04/27/1998	[Try it* | Delete]
Shoemake, John	Active	04/27/1998	[Try it* | Delete]
Kimbro, Powell	Active	04/27/1998	[Try it* | Delete]
Peacock, John	Active	04/27/1998	[Try it* | Delete]
Awtrey, Absalom	Active	04/27/1998	[Try it* | Delete]
Parchcorn Flower, Katy	Active	04/27/1998	[Try it* | Delete]

Opening page http://   Internet zone

Figure 6-18

Online FamilyFinder Report Agents search for information about your families and prepares reports.

The first time you run an online version of the FamilyFinder Report, Family Tree Maker automatically creates an Agent that continues to search for information about your family names even after you end your online session. When it finds new information, it will send you an e-mail message instructing you to run an online FamilyFinder Report to view the new information.

Here's how to run an online version of the FamilyFinder Report:

1. Start Family Tree Maker and open the Family File for which you want to run a report.

2. From the Research Journal menu, double-click on New FamilyFinder Report. The Create New FamilyFinder Report dialog box appears.

3. Select a search in either the Online or CD FamilyFinder Index options.

4. Select one of the following Include options:

   ❊ **All individuals.** Searches for information about everyone in your Family File.

❊ **Selected individuals.** Searches for information about specific individuals in your Family File. There is an Individuals To Include button that you click on to indicate which individuals you want in the search.

❊ **NOTE** ❊   *Rather than including several different family names, you might focus on one specific family and include all the spouses of the children and the in-laws of the mother and father. Searching expanded clusters of families is the key to successful genealogical research.*

5. Click on OK after you make your selections. Family Tree Maker will open your browser and connect you to Family Tree Maker Online and run the FamilyFinder Report. A progress meter indicates approximately how many minutes it will take to complete the process.

   While you are waiting for the FamilyFinder Report to finish downloading you can explore other options at Family Tree Maker Online.

6. Click on the Family Tree Maker button on the Taskbar to view the Family Tree Maker window where you can see the results of a search in the FamilyFinder Report. The first time you run the report, all the matches appear in the same section of the report. On subsequent reports, the matches you see now will appear in the "Based on your previous searches" section, and only the new matches will appear in the "New Matches" section. The best matches have five stars, the top rating, with the least likely matches having only one star.

7. Click on the folders next to a match to display additional information in the Online FamilyFinder Report, or click on the underlined information in the Possible Matches column to jump to that Internet site or to display information about the CD that contains the match.

8. After you review the information, close your browser and disconnect from your online service.

   ❊ **TIP** ❊   *See Chapter Ten for more information on FamilyFinder Reports.*

```
Family Tree Maker's Genealogy Site: Internet FamilyFinder - Microsoft Internet Explorer    _ 🗗 ✕
 File   Edit   View   Go   Favorites   Help                                                    e
  ⇦  ▾    ⇨  ▾      ⊗       ▣       🏠       ⊕        ⊡        ⊙         ⊙         ⊟          ⊠
 Back    Forward    Stop    Refresh   Home    Search   Favorites   History    Channels   Fullscreen   Mail
 Address 🗐 Thomas&last=Connally&fnoptions=fnex&lnoptions=lnse&submit=Create+Task+Now!&lo=li&lo=lu&lo=lm&lo=lc ▾   Links
```

Connally, **Thomas Dick**			Internet	... Carrington (b. ca. 1798), **Thomas Dick Connally** (ca. 1809-1846), Charles...
Connally, **Thomas**			User Home Page	**Family Tree Maker's Genealogy Site: User Home Page** **Genealogy Report: Ancestors of Charles Shields** **Mayfield** ... : Fact 1: 1713, married **Thomas Connally** per D. and W. 14, page 385,\n...
Connally, **Thomas**			User Home Page	**Family Tree Maker's Genealogy Site: User Home Page** **Book: OLDHAM : Register Report of William Oldham** ...; d. July 16, 1826. | |viii. | | **THOMAS CONNALLY**, b. September 12, 1738. | |ix. |...
Connally, **Thomas**			User Home Page	**Family Tree Maker's Genealogy Site: User Home Page** **Book: OLDHAM : Index** ... Report of William Oldham | **Connally, Thomas** | Register Report of William...
Connally, **Thomas Dick**			Internet	**Southern Plantations MS** ... Thomas Goode Boyd, **Thomas Dick Connally**, W. E. Davis, Robert...

```
🗐                                              🌐 Internet zone
```

Figure 6-19

Results of the Online
FamilyFinder Report
Agents for specific
individuals.

All of the search options of Family Tree Maker offer exciting ways to find information about your ancestors. A search for Thomas Connally (see Figure 6-19) and others from my Family File turned up several possibilities, including links to a report of a possible Connally cousin.

I found a great deal of genealogical data on several generations at a user's home page, including dates and localities that enabled me to determine that I probably have connections via my Connally, Oldham, Price, Lindsay, and Prescott families (see Figure 6-20). This is just one example of how valuable the search tools and Agents can be—and why the Internet excites genealogists.

> ⊛ **CAUTION** ⊛ *Never blindly accept information you find on the Internet (or anywhere else for that matter—there are many errors in published genealogies, too). Genealogy involves many details. It is easy to make mistakes when abstracting from records, to transpose numbers or mix generations (sorting out all the Williams in a family, for example, can be a major challenge). Use the Internet for what it is—a remarkable tool and finding aid. Verify the data you discover with primary sources, whenever possible.*

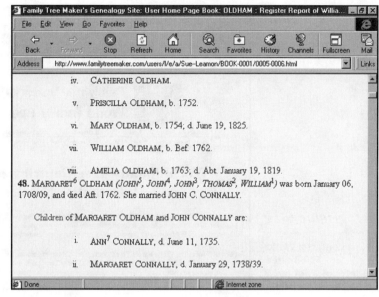

Figure 6-20

Several generations—
with genealogical
data—appear on a
cousin's home page.

Locating World Family Tree Contributors

Have you found a possible ancestor on one of the World Family Tree (WFT) CDs? You can contact the contributor. Hopefully she or he will have additional material to share with you (old family photos, the Family Bible, or letters) and can provide sources that might not have been included on the CD. Perhaps they have discovered more about your mutual family lines. Just click on Contact a WFT Contributor (it's a link on the left navigational bar at Family Tree Maker Online), and fill out the form, which asks for your name, address, and e-mail address, and optionally, your telephone number (see Figure 6-21).

You can ask for up to three names and addresses at a time. Be sure to include the following information:

- ❋ **World Family Tree Volume Number.**

- ❋ **Tree Number.** Each family tree in the World Family Tree has a unique identification number. This number shows up in the title bar at the top of the screen when you view the tree, and in the

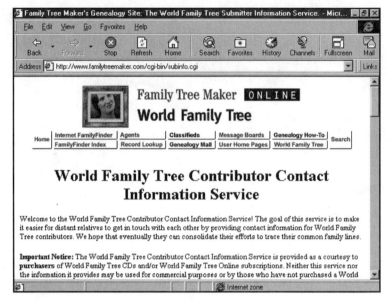

Figure 6-21

Contact a World
Family Tree
Contributor for more
family information.

Tree# column next to each individual in the index on the World
Family Tree CD. Use the tree number listed on the World Family
Tree CD rather than those in the FamilyFinder Index, as some of
the latter are incorrect.

✹ CD ID/World Family Tree Subscription Confirmation Number.
The CD ID is a seven-digit number that begins with "6" and is located in the lower right-hand corner of the back of the case that
holds your World Family Tree CD (or on the back of the CD folder, if
you have a multi-CD set). You may also use the seven-digit number
beginning with a "6" that is printed in the silver circle at the center
of your World Family Tree CD. For those with a World Family Tree
Subscription, just type in your order confirmation number in this
field instead of the CD ID. Your order confirmation number is seven
digits and begins with an "8."

After completing the form, click on the Continue button at the bottom of the
page. Then you will see a Web page that asks you a basic question, such as

"What color is the sky?" This is not a trick question—go ahead and type in the answer. These questions are asked to prevent commercial enterprises such as direct mail marketers from using a computer to automatically download all the contributor addresses at once. This technique works because computers can't answer simple questions the way real people can. After answering the question, click on the Submit Request button. You'll see a Web page confirming that the request has been received and explaining that you will receive the contributor information via e-mail.

Features Galore

Other features offered at Family Tree Maker's Home Page (**http://www.familytreemaker.com**) include:

- ⚘ **Social Security Death Index.** An incredible searchable database.

- ⚘ **Online University.** A place to sharpen your genealogy skills at your own pace.

- ⚘ **How-To Articles from Back Issues.** A growing and outstanding collection of informative genealogy articles written by the experts.

- ⚘ **Biography Writing Assistant.** Don't know what to ask your relatives to get the information you need? Need some help writing family stories? Here you will find more than 5,000 writing ideas that make it easy to record your family's memories. You can use the Biography Writing Assistant whether you use Family Tree Maker's Notes windows or a word processor. While using either of those programs, keep Biography Assistant's Writing Ideas handy by running your Web browser at the same time and pressing Alt+Tab to move back and forth between the two programs. Of course, you can also print out copies of the Writing Ideas. They make excellent scripts for interviewing your relatives on video or audio tape, or for doing oral histories.

- ⚘ **Classified Ads.** This is a virtual genealogy marketplace where you can advertise for information on a particular individual or let the world know about your family history book or compiled records

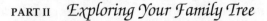

available for sale. Let others know of your interest in locating a particular book.

 Home Pages. You can create your own Web page and share your family history with cousins around the world. Need ideas? Chapter Fifteen covers how-to tips on creating a home page for yourself.

Just think—all these features at one Web site, Family Tree Maker Online. And, you have only just begun to explore the Web. Buckle up, it's time to hit the Information Superhighway.

CHAPTER SEVEN

Surfing for Genealogical Data

he Internet, and more particularly its best-known aspect, the Web, provides access to genealogical information like no other medium, and it is changing the way genealogists conduct their research. Like a giant spiderweb the Web ensnares and enthralls today's genealogists whose ancestors only a couple of generations back were mesmerized by moving pictures—the "WOW!" invention of their day.

What's Out There: History, Data, and More

The Internet is a network linking millions of computers. It was originally developed in 1969 for the U.S. military and gradually grew to include educational and research institutions. Today, *e-mail* (electronic mail) is probably the most popular use of the Internet. However, the World Wide Web is gaining ground fast. The Web—the graphical portion of the Internet—is a system of files called *Web pages* saved in a standard format known as Hypertext Markup Language (HTML). Web browsers are applications that view such files, finding them by means of addresses called *URLs* (Uniform Resource Locators) that work rather like your street and house number or post office box address. Web pages can contain text, graphics (pictures), and audio. They often include *hyperlinks* to other Web pages and files—pictures or words that users can click on to open other files or move around in the same file.

Locating Vital Records Online

The Web provides rapid access to information resources. Through the Internet you have easy, quick, and inexpensive communication via e-mail with cousins around the world; the traditional barriers of borders, distance, and time zones are gone. At your fingertips (or more likely, mouse-tip) is access to incredible online libraries containing catalogs as well as reference materials. You'll find how-to tutorials, maps, genealogical dictionaries, glossaries, foreign-language translations, and software you can download, try out, and purchase. You can also find genealogical and historical societies, libraries and archives, and genealogy publishers—around the world. The repositories on the Internet never close for lunch, evenings, weekends, or holidays.

EXPLORING VITAL RECORDS

Want to learn how to order a copy of your grandfather's death certificate and how much it will cost? If he died in the United States, it's easy. There's a Web site (see Figure 7-1) where you can get information about finding vital records from each state, territory, and county. Vital Records Information: United States is located at: **http://www.inlink.com/~nomi/vitalrec/**

> ❧ **NOTE** ❧   *The term* vital records *usually refers to official, government-created birth, marriage, divorce, and death documents, but can be any record pertaining to these events.*

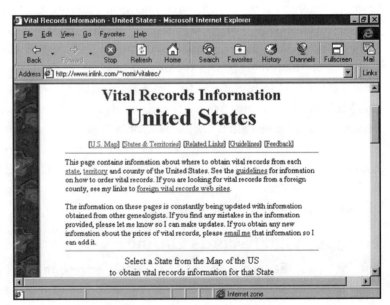

Figure 7-1

Vital Records
Information available
in the U.S.

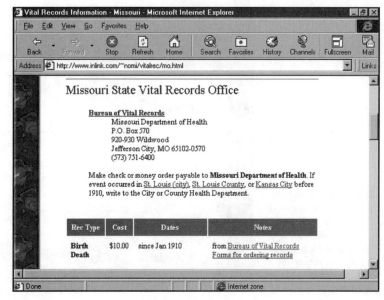

Figure 7-2

Information about
ordering a vital record
from the State of
Missouri with
complete address and
additional tips

From this Web site, you select the state you want to find out about (there's even a map to make it easier). If your grandfather died in Missouri, select that state and you will be whisked to the section about Missouri state vital records (see Figure 7-2).

Information there contains the complete address and phone number of the Missouri State Vital Records Office and instructions on making out a check or money order when ordering a copy of a vital record. You can drop down a level at the site for county records, and find tips as to who to ask for various kinds of information (see Figure 7-3).

If your grandfather died before Missouri began keeping these records on a statewide basis, the state won't be able to help you—but the Web site can. In this example, you see a note advising you to contact the county clerk for birth and death records prior to August 1909. Since costs of vital records constantly change, traditional published sources tend to be out of date before they get to your library or bookstore. The Web, with its ease of quick updating, is usually the most current source for costs and addresses. Some U.S. states now have searchable vital records indexes. Ohio, for example, has a searchable death certificate index

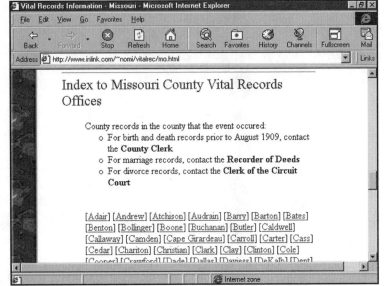

Figure 7-3

Additional tips on finding birth and death records prior to the time Missouri began keeping these records, and information about how to find marriage and divorce records in this state

(**http://www.inlink.com/~nomi/vitalrec/oh.html**) for the years 1913 through 1927 and 1933 through 1937 (see Figure 7-4).

Similar Web sites exist for many countries with details on what vital records exist and explicit instructions on how to order those you need. Here are a few examples:

- You will find indexes to births, deaths, and marriages reported in Calgary, Alberta newspapers between 1883 and 1899 at **http://www.freenet.calgary.ab.ca/afhs/news.html**.

- The Swedish Church Records Online (**http://slktfrsk.telia.se/slktfrsk/eindex.htm**) has an ambitious project underway to distribute original handwritten church records through a digital network. Its database will consist of images scanned from film, covering the 17th to the 20th century.

- You can find more than 1,700 marriage records that have been extracted from the Evangelical (Lutheran) church in Weil in Schoenbuch, Wurttemberg, Germany, from 1591 to 1705 in a

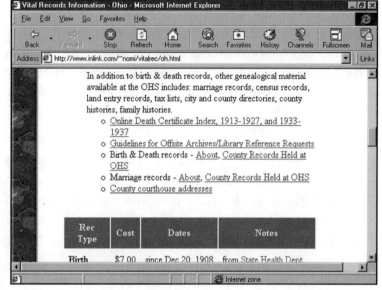

Figure 7-4

Web site showing
information about
vital records available
in Ohio, including a
hyperlink to a
searchable online
death certificate index
for certain years

searchable database at **http://www.kinquest.com/genealogy/marriages.html**.

🏃 The General Register Office for Scotland (**http://www.open.gov.uk/gros/index.htm**) is now online (click on the Services button at the home page) offering access to vital records in the Old Parish Registers from 1663 to 1854 and in Scotland's statutory registers from 1855. Details about obtaining the documents and paying for copies can be found here too.

Exploring vital records is only one example of how you can use the Web for genealogical research. It is not going to replace traditional methods in the near future—most of the records genealogists use are still either in manuscript or microform (film and fiche). However, a mind-boggling amount of hard data of interest and value to genealogists is being posted every day, and you can use the Internet as a giant finding aid to material that in the past took months and years to locate, let alone gain access to.

CHECKING CEMETERY RECORDS AND OBITUARIES

There are some cemetery records on the Web, but not many. However, as more and more genealogy volunteers join the online community and contribute time and talent to making information available, the long-time dream of finding an ancestor's final resting place via the computer may come true.

Canadian genealogists are doing an outstanding job of putting their cemetery records online. Pictou County of Nova Scotia is an example of what can be done by a dedicated volunteer with a computer. This locality has more than a dozen cemetery records posted at its site (**http://www.rootsweb.com/~pictou/**). Also, Edmonton Parks and Recreation of Alberta, Canada, has a database of names (nearly 60,000) of those interred 25 or more years ago in Edmonton municipal cemeteries (**http://www.gov.edmonton.ab.ca/parkrec/cemetery/search.htm**).

While search engines are useful (you'll read more about them later), you'll save yourself a great deal of time by going to Cyndi's List of Genealogy Sites on the Internet (**http://www.cyndislist.com/**) and check out the links there listed under the category called Cemeteries, Funeral Homes & Obituaries. It's arranged in strict alphabetical order by the name of the institution, not the state and county where it's located, so it may take you a while to find a particular site that might be useful in your research. Nevertheless, there are valuable links here.

> ❃ **TIP** ❃ *You can also go to Family Tree Maker's Genealogy SiteFinder (http://www.familytreemaker.com/links/c/c-records,cemetery.html) for cemetery listings.*

Eventually, online cemetery listings will probably be compiled geographically, or some technically-gifted person will figure out how to create a way to make these searches even easier. One of the largest compiled listings and links of cemeteries online currently can be found at the World Wide Index of Cemeteries on the Net Home Page (**http://www.inwd.com/death**).

> ❃ **TIP** ❃ *Another cemetery-related Web site is at the International Jewish Cemetery Project (http://www.jewishgen.org/cemetery/index.htm).*

For the most part, obituaries currently online are modern ones—from the past five years or so. However, a few older ones are popping up here and there. In a recent search, I found some at various USGenWeb state archives or county locations (**http://www.usgenweb.org/**). (See the section, "Linking to USGen Web," for more information.) Click on the state of interest and see what has been put in that state's archives as well as what is listed by county.

This provides you with a sampling of some of the hard data currently online. And the collection is growing daily. You will usually find it more easily by searching by the localities where your ancestors once lived than by surname searches.

Finding Genealogical Information

While some more cautious genealogists warn new online researchers about wasting time on the Internet, my advice is to explore it—if you have the time. At first you will be somewhat like a kid in a candy or toy store—darting hither and thither, clicking and scrolling, and on occasion following so many links that you lose your way and even forget the object of your initial search. I have observed the same behavior in researchers at the famous Family History Library in Salt Lake City, the DAR Library in Washington, D.C., and at the regional branches of the National Archives. It is OK to go crazy at first because exploring the Web is an educational process. Moreover, it is fun. Tracing your family tree should be fun, too. However, having fun does not mean you are not serious about your research and the genealogical material you are compiling to leave to your descendants.

One of the first questions a newcomer to genealogical online research asks is "What's online?"—usually followed by "How do you find it?" Almost anything you can imagine pertaining to genealogical and historical research is online—or will be tomorrow. However, that does not mean the marriage record of your great-grandparents is online or that you can type in your immigrant ancestor's name and learn the name of the ship he sailed on and date and port of entry. The information might be available, but like all genealogical and historical data, you will have to search for it. There is no giant computer database about everybody's ancestors that will spew forth any and all data at your request. Moreover, many records are protected by privacy laws and simply are not accessible.

Exploring Cyndi's List

A favorite Web site for finding genealogical information and for use as your launching pad to the wonders of the Web is Cyndi's List (**http://www.cyndislist.com/**). Some of the major categories of interest to genealogists are:

- Surname indexes and searchable databases

- Vital records

- Cemetery records

- Censuses

- Military records

- Ship passenger lists

- Newsgroups and Surname or One Name mailing lists and publications

- Historical records

From Cyndi's List you can easily find census indexes and records. Figure 7-5 shows a sampling of hyperlinks to various sources of international census information, including the 1871 Ontario (Canada) census index. Figure 7-6 reveals the variety of U.S. census records available—a growing source.

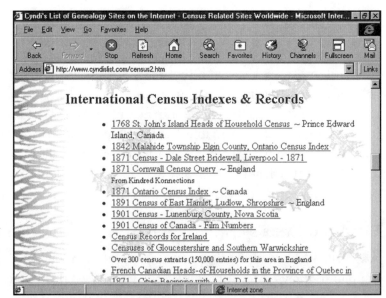

Figure 7-5

Cyndi's List is one of the busiest sites on the Web.

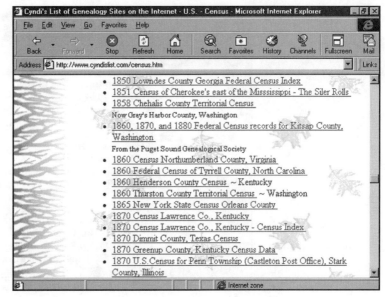

Figure 7-6

Here's some of the
U.S. census records,
arranged by date and
locality, that are
accessible from
Cyndi's List.

Interested in finding others who are researching the same family lines you are?
Want to learn if there is a family newsletter available? Look under Surnames,
Family Associations & Family Newsletters on Cyndi's List (see Figure 7-7).

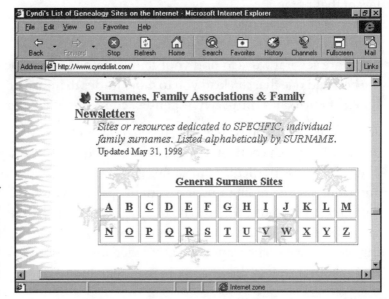

Figure 7-7

Surnames, Family
Associations & Family
Letters are accessible
from Cyndi's List,
arranged
alphabetically.

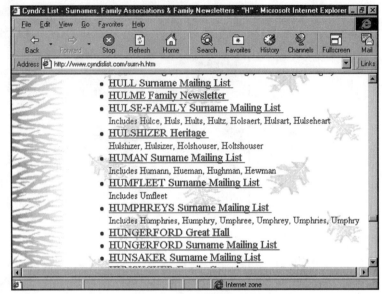

Figure 7-8

Surnames beginning with the letter H accessible from Cyndi's List

Click on "H," for example, and you are taken to the list showing the list of surnames beginning with that letter (see Figure 7-8). Click on the hyperlink to learn more about the associations, newsletters, or other individuals searching families of that name.

FINDING SURNAMES IN GENDEX

There are several ways to find your family names on the Web. However, one of the best and one that can lead you to more in-depth information is the GENDEX-Index of Surnames (**http://www.gendex.com**), shown in Figure 7-9.

At GENDEX, you can type in a surname or its prefix, or you can enter a surname and have a search conducted for its Soundex equivalents. If you're having difficulty finding a particular surname, try the Soundex option. Your American ancestors may be hiding under a variant spelling you have not yet discovered. Searching by Soundex will turn up the variant spellings of Stewart, such as Stuart, Steuart, Stuert, Steward, Steuard, and Stuard. There's even a Web site where you can have your surname automatically coded for Soundex searches (you'll find out more about it later in this chapter in the "Searching National Archives" section).

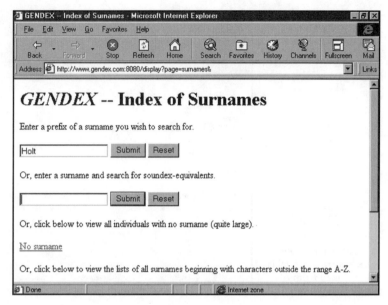

Figure 7-9

At the GENDEX Web page, you have two options for surname searches.

❧ **NOTE** ❧   *Soundex is an indexing system based on the phonetic sound of the consonants in a surname. Each name is assigned a letter and three numbers. The letter is always the first letter of the surname. (Refer to the sidebar, "Understanding Soundex and Wildcards," in Chapter Five for more information.)*

VIEWING TUPMAN'S LINKS

For the more experienced researcher who is looking for specific genealogical data online, particularly for British and Canadian links, a great site to visit often is the one compiled by Alan Tupman (**http://freespace.virgin.net/alan.tupman/ sites/**), shown in Figure 7-10.

At this site are links to vital records, marriages, deeds, and even executions. Want to check out some 18th-century ship passenger lists? You'll find some here (see Figure 7-11).

SEARCHING LAND RECORDS

The Web, as far as genealogical material goes, is in its toddler stage, but growing daily. Who would have dreamed a few years ago that you would be able to sit in

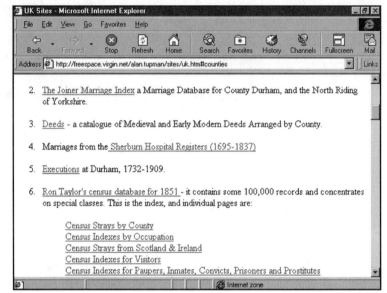

Figure 7-10

Some genealogical source material is linked from Alan Tupman's Web site.

the comfort of your home and search for your ancestors' Wisconsin or Florida land patents? The Bureau of Land Management's General Land Office, Eastern States, (**http://www.glorecords.blm.gov**) has been automating its millions of historic land records for several years now (see Figure 7-12).

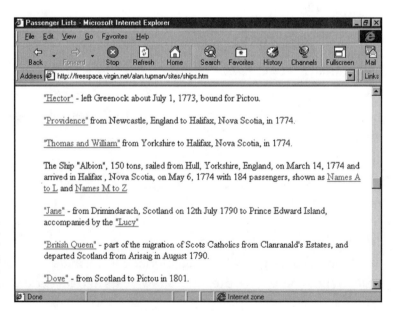

Figure 7-11

Ship passenger lists are available on the Web, linked from Alan Tupman's Web site.

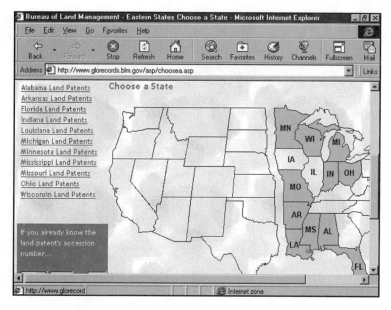

Figure 7-12

Various searchable American land patent records are available online at the General Land Office's Web site.

This repository has original land deeds issued to private owners by the U.S. government before 1908—and these documents include the landowner's name, legal land description, amount of acreage, document signature date, and in many instances, the actual signatures. A search by surname, particularly an uncommon one, can produce some surprising and delightful results (see Figure 7-13).

The search I conducted in Missouri land patents turned up 68 references to Vanderpools. Of those, four documents provided new localities (counties) and specific time periods in which to dig for more information on my family.

LINKING TO USGENWEB

One of the reasons for the phenomenal growth of genealogical material on the Web is the USGenWeb—short for United States Genealogical Web—project. The project began in April 1996 when a group of genealogists organized the Kentucky Comprehensive Genealogy Database Project. The idea was to provide a single entry point for all counties in Kentucky, where collected genealogical databases would be stored. Additionally, the databases would be indexed and cross-linked, so that a single search in the master index could locate all references to a particular surname across all pages and databases associated with the

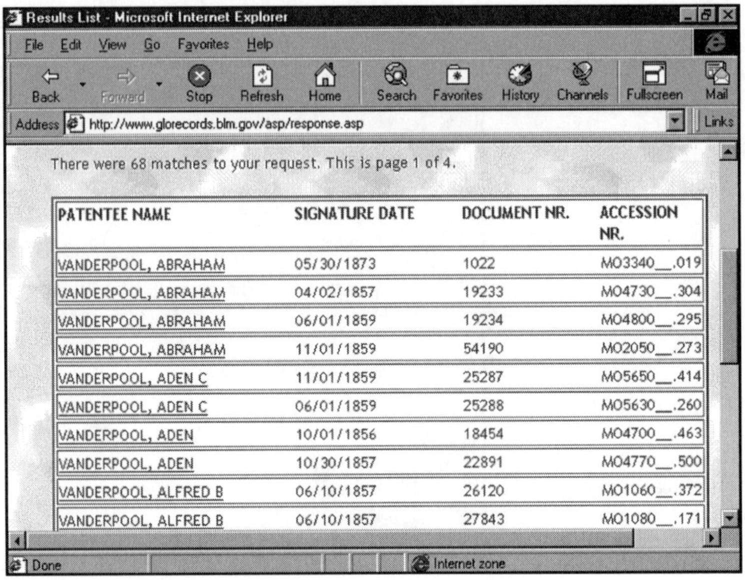

Figure 7-13

Search results for
ancestors in Missouri
land patents at the
General Land Office's
Web site

PATENTEE NAME	SIGNATURE DATE	DOCUMENT NR.	ACCESSION NR.
VANDERPOOL, ABRAHAM	05/30/1873	1022	MO3340___.019
VANDERPOOL, ABRAHAM	04/02/1857	19233	MO4730___.304
VANDERPOOL, ABRAHAM	06/01/1859	19234	MO4800___.295
VANDERPOOL, ABRAHAM	11/01/1859	54190	MO2050___.273
VANDERPOOL, ADEN C	11/01/1859	25287	MO5650___.414
VANDERPOOL, ADEN C	06/01/1859	25288	MO5630___.260
VANDERPOOL, ADEN	10/01/1856	18454	MO4700___.463
VANDERPOOL, ADEN	10/30/1857	22891	MO4770___.500
VANDERPOOL, ALFRED B	06/10/1857	26120	MO1060___.372
VANDERPOOL, ALFRED B	06/10/1857	27843	MO1080___.171

There were 68 matches to your request. This is page 1 of 4.

project. The framework for the project was laid out and the call went out for volunteers to coordinate the collection of databases and generally oversee the contents of the Web pages.

In June 1996, as the Kentucky project neared completion, it was decided to start a Web page for each of the other states, and to seek volunteers to create pages similar to Kentucky's. Thus the USGenWeb project was born. Volunteers were found to host the state projects and coordinate the county pages. The USGenWeb project introduced some new ideas for genealogical research on the Web.

- It organized data for research. Prior to this project, little real genealogical data was available for online research, and what was available was organized poorly.

- It created organization of data on a statewide, county-by-county basis.

- It created a nationwide umbrella group of grassroots volunteers whose efforts are coordinated and focused on specific goals.

Take a virtual tour of the USGenWeb by going to **http://www.usgenweb.org/ statelinks.html** and clicking on a state of interest (see Figure 7-14). Selecting

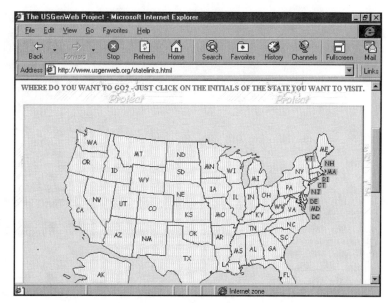

Figure 7-14

Home page of the
USGenWeb site

Kansas (**http://skyways.lib.ks.us/kansas/genweb/index.html**) takes you to the
Kansas home page with its links to Kansas counties and its statewide archives
and projects, as shown in Figure 7-15.

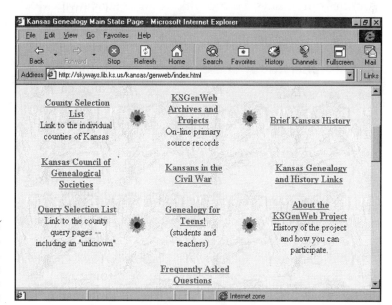

Figure 7-15

The home page of the
State of Kansas—part
of the USGenWeb
project

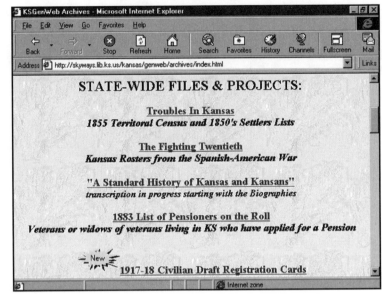

Figure 7-16

Statewide
genealogical projects
of Kansas, linked from
its home page, are all
part of the USGenWeb
project.

One of this state's projects is the transcription and indexing of biographies compiled from old Kansas histories (see Figure 7-16).

Counties online have a direct link from the state page. Most of these sites include:

- ⚡ Map of the county
- ⚡ Brief history of the county
- ⚡ Names of towns and cities in the county
- ⚡ Query pages and searchable indexes to them
- ⚡ Historical and genealogical files
- ⚡ Addresses and Internet links to historical and genealogical societies, county or municipal offices where genealogical data can be found, plus other links that might be of interest to those researching in that locality.

Some county pages greet you with, or allow you to click on an option that plays, music—called MIDI, an acronym that stands for Musical Instrument

Digital Interface. That's a program that acts as a go-between for an instrument and something that creates the sound. Many sites are ablaze in colors, textured backgrounds, animated icons, sounds, and images as well as text.

Some offer unique sources for genealogists and historians, such as the Rutland County, Vermont page (**http://homepages.together.net/~forguite//rut_vt.htm**). Here you will find a page for each town in the county with information about this locality's newspapers, cemeteries, church records, local histories, and early settlers.

SEARCHING NATIONAL ARCHIVES

National repositories are rapidly making data and finding aids to their treasures accessible online. The U.S. National Archives (**http://www.nara.gov/genealogy/genindex.html**) has an entire section devoted to genealogical research. Here you will find the Soundex Machine (see Figure 7-17) which can code your family name automatically into Soundex code—something you will need to know to search the 1880–1920 U.S. census available on microfilm.

The National Archives of Canada (**http://www.archives.ca/MenuPrincipal.html**) shown in Figure 7-18 is searchable in French and English. Go to the bottom of the main home page to change the language to English.

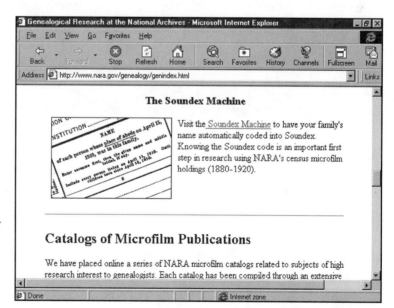

Figure 7-17

The Soundex Machine is available at the National Archives of the United States.

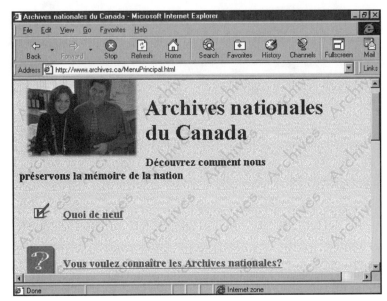

Figure 7-18

You can find many Canadian resources by clicking on the Genealogy Research link at this site.

USING SEARCH ENGINES

Search engines are Web sites that have robots (software) that search the Internet and prepare indexes of the visited sites. They catalog these sites by specific keywords, such as "genealogy," "census," or "Wyatt Earp." Type in a word or phrase and the search engine looks for this information in its index and gives you back the results of its search with the URLs of sites that may include the keywords you used.

Narrowing your searches in search engines is very important. For example, a friend who was new to genealogy went online and decided to use a search engine to find some information. He typed in "genealogy." The search engine twirled and spun and eventually delivered the news that there were several thousand references to the subject, and would he like to narrow the search? Yikes!

Each search engine works a bit differently and the only way to learn how to use them and find the ones that you like best is to try several. Some search engines will find mailing lists, newsgroups, and other Internet addresses as well as Web sites. Start your initial search using broad categories, and then narrow the search. AltaVista (**http://www.altavista.digital.com/**) shown in Figure 7-19, HotBot

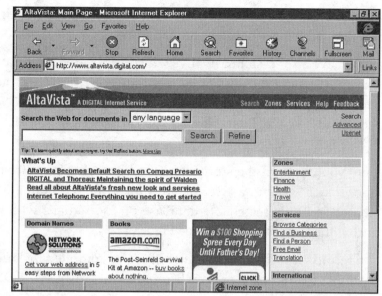

Figure 7-19

AltaVista is one of
several popular
search engines.

(**http://www.hotbot.com/**), and Yahoo! (**http://www.yahoo.com/**) are popular search engines. Try them.

More details about using search engines, exploring the Web and the Internet, and getting the most out of e-mail can be found in *Learn the Internet In a Weekend* by William Stanek (**http://www.primapublishing.com**).

Uncovering Historical Sources

A great deal of material of interest to genealogists is hidden at Web sites labeled *historical*. As your research advances and you become more comfortable searching online, explore historical topics—everything from general historical resources such as those found at The History Net: Where History Lives on the Web to specific ones covering eras or events such as the Irish Potato Famine or the Titanic sailing.

The best place to start for an introduction to historical sites on the Web is The History Net (**http://www.thehistorynet.com**), where you will find articles on an ever-changing array of subjects. Check out this site's archives: world history; American history; eyewitness accounts; personality profiles; great battles of the ages; arms, armies, and intrigue; interviews; historical travel; aviation and technology; and homes, heritage, and antiques.

If you have an ancestor or relative who disappeared in the latter part of the 19th century, consider the possibility that they were lured, like many others, to the Klondike gold rush. One of the most beautiful sites on the Web is the Ghosts of the Klondike Gold Rush Home Page (**http://www.Gold-Rush.org/**) shown in Figure 7-20.

Here you can read the stories of Klondike stampeders from North American cities under "Where Ya From, Gold Digger?" and try out the "Pan for Gold Databases" with its searchable database on individuals who were in the Yukon during the Gold Rush years (see Figure 7-21).

The records from which this database were compiled include sources you may never have considered or even heard about, such as:

- 🏃 Lists of victims of the killer avalanche on the Chilkoot in 1897

- 🏃 Notes kept by Clary Craig, a post office worker who listed people dying or leaving Klondike

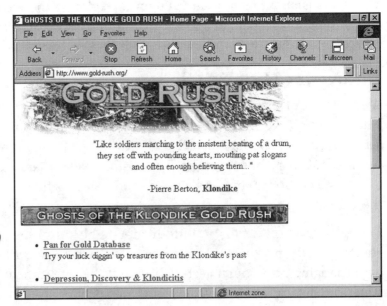

Figure 7-20

The home page of the Ghosts of the Klondike Gold Rush

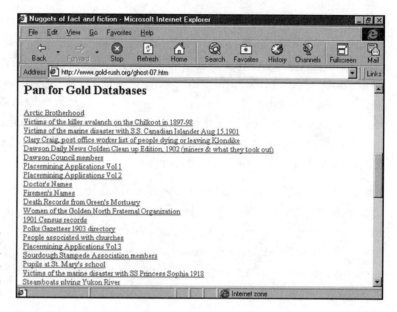

Figure 7-21

Did one of your ancestors succumb to gold rush fever?

🏃 The Dawson *Daily News* Golden Clean Up Edition, 1902 (miners and what they took out)

🏃 Death records from Green's Mortuary

🏃 1901 Census records

🏃 Placer mining applications

🏃 Northwest Mounted Police files listing their employees

History and genealogy are first cousins, and genealogists should be aware of this relationship. If you ignore one for the other, you may never solve some of your research puzzles. The Web sparkles like a golden nugget in the sunshine luring those who dare to explore the historical gems that lie buried therein. Like the prospectors of old (some of whom may perch upon your family tree) you'll have to dig for the riches. However, your hard work will be rewarded with a greater knowledge of the events and factors that influenced your families, and you may even find some missing links in your pedigree's chain.

Genealogists are often so eager to get to the old records that they neglect some valuable 20th-century sources. The value of *American Life Histories: Manuscripts from the Federal Writers' Project, 1936–1940* to your research may not be readily apparent, but it includes stories of people from 24 states and may include those of your ancestors or their neighbors. The entries describe the informant's family, education, income, occupation, political views, religion and mores, medical needs, diet, and miscellaneous observations. They are at the WPA Life Histories Home Page (**http://lcweb2.loc.gov/ammem/wpaintro/wpahome.html**) shown in Figure 7-22. This is part of the American Memory collection from the Manuscript Division of the Library of Congress.

The Library of Virginia and its LVA Digital Collections (**http://image.vtls.com/**), shown in Figure 7-23, is a jewel just waiting to be found by those researching in early Virginia. Click on the Virginia Colonial Records option and then the Electronic Card Indexes and discover one of the features that makes the Web so exciting. Additional sources in the card indexes include various newspaper and periodicals, such as:

    ⚘ *Confederate Veteran Magazine* 1893–1932 index

    ⚘ Magazine Index: Selected articles on Virginia circa 1900–1985

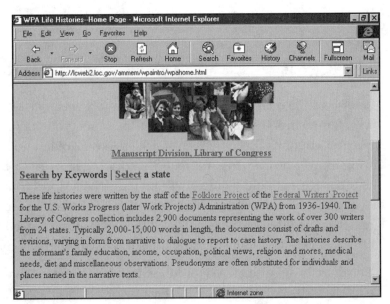

Figure 7-22

You can search by keywords or select a state in which you are interested.

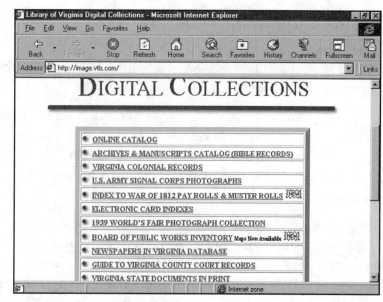

Figure 7-23

The Library of Virginia's Electronic Card Indexes

✱ Marriage Index: *Richmond Enquirer* 1804–1860, *Richmond Visitor* 1809–1810

✱ Newspaper Index: *Richmond Times Dispatch, Richmond News Leader* 1940s–1985

✱ Obituary Index: *Richmond Enquirer* 1804–1860, *Richmond Visitor* 1809–1810

Another place to start your exploration of historical sources is from Cyndi's List of Genealogy Sites on the Internet: Historical Events and People. Here you'll find links to history-related topics, as well as downloadable GEDCOMs and charts for some famous people such as American presidents, presidential wives, royalty, and nobility—and you'll even find Daniel Boone there. Looking for *Mayflower* lines, Oregon Trail pioneers, information about American railroads, Erie Canal, Salem Witch trials, or ancestors who fought at the Alamo? This is the site.

Even if you do not find genealogical material buried under historical topics, you will be enriched with a greater knowledge of the times and places in which your ancestors lived. And that knowledge may lead you to other sources that will enable you to find treasures untold.

Evaluating Electronic Sources

When you find information on the Internet, how do you know it is accurate? How do you determine its worth? The Information Superhighway is not without its bumps and potholes.

Evaluating evidence that enables you to compile an accurate family tree—and no one wants the wrong ancestors dangling from its branches—is a challenge with traditional sources. How to understand and handle the enormous amounts of data available via the Internet is a new problem that today's genealogists must face.

The downside of Internet research is you may find some exciting but possibly bogus information that cousin Joe Lee has published on his Web page. The genealogical data may connect your family with several noble or royal lines of Europe. Do you blindly accept it and tell everyone at the family reunion that they descend from royalty? When you ask cousin Joe for sources of his information and he tells you that it comes from a GEDCOM that cousin Kris sent him via e-mail, what do you do? Or say you locate the person who submitted this material and they tell you the royal lines came from a "blue book at the library." So much for real documentation and proper source citations. At this point you really don't know where the information came from, and as a result there is no way to evaluate it or determine its accuracy. All you can do is use it as clues and as a finding aid to track down the real evidence.

> ❀ **TIP** ❀ *Just as novice genealogists back in B.C. (Before Computers) used to believe anything in print or fall for fancy but false pedigrees that had been prepared by swindlers claiming to be genealogists, today's cyberpioneers must educate themselves about information that is largely unsourced. Moreover, you need to apply the same high research standards and methods of evaluating evidence to any piece of data you collect, no matter whether it is digital or in a "blue book at the library."*

A colleague confided to me that one of the biggest problems she has had with her family is dispelling a bogus claim that her grandmother fell for in the 1920s. It asserted that her family had a fortune tied up in England and all they had to do was prove they were connected to a particular family line. Of course, they

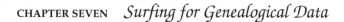

also had to contribute money to the "legal" fund in order to get their fortune. Scams like this were common in the late 19th and early 20th centuries in America, and the only ones who got rich were the swindlers. Yet one of my colleague's aunts still swears the family fortune story is true. Her argument is, "It was in all the newspapers."

Just because anything is in a newspaper or book—or on the Internet—does not make it so. Almost everything you are going to find on the Internet is secondary source data, which has been put there by some volunteer who has access to it and a computer. Most of it has been extracted, typed, and retyped or scanned in. Our technology, as wonderful as is, is not perfect. In scanning some text material for one of my county pages of the USGenWeb project, I discovered several errors. Even though I carefully proofread the final product, I was still working from a secondary source because someone else had done the extracting from the original records.

In doing a search for information about a problem ancestor (well, he is not a problem, but finding records about him is), I located three references to him posted on various home pages of other researchers. Now I have three more dates for his birth and three more death dates to go with my own estimations, and I haven't a clue as to where these researchers obtained their information. I contacted all of them, and sadly, none could provide a primary source—or even a secondary source—for their data.

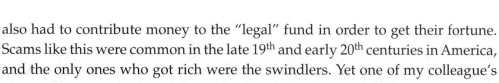

> **TIP** *The Internet is an incredible tool, but use it wisely—primarily as a finding tool. Don't be dazzled by the technology and neglect good methodology. Use original primary records whenever possible to verify all the information you collect—whether it comes from the Web, a GEDCOM, or your grandfather.*

Citing Electronic Sources

There is one hard-and-fast rule for general documentation and that is, *record enough information so you or another researcher can determine what you have searched.*

This applies to traditional sources as well as electronic sources. Cite your sources so you can remember where you found the information and avoid redundant research—and do it for the family researchers who will (hopefully) pick up your research where you leave off as well as for yourself. Without source citations, your grandson or niece will wonder how you knew your grandparents were married on a ship going to Australia. By compiling and leaving a record of the sources you consulted, you will save your descendants from having to reinvent the wheel, so to speak, or waste their time and money redoing your work.

Citing a source is more than saying you found the information in a census record or parish register. At the Family Tree Maker Online site is an excellent article by John Wylie titled *How to Cite Sources* (see Figure 7-24). Wylie's article includes the basic format for traditional citations, such as books, vital records, censuses, deeds, newspapers, personal letters, oral interviews, and photographs, plus online sources, such as e-mail, list server messages, articles found in a Newsgroup, extracts from a CD, and Web sites.

If genealogical source citation and documentation are new to you, you will also want to obtain copies of *Evidence, Citation, and Analysis for the Family Historian* by Elizabeth Shown Mills (Genealogical Publishing Co., Baltimore, 1998) and *Cite Your Sources—A Manual for Documenting Family Histories and Genealogical Records*, by Richard S. Lackey (New Orleans, Polyanthos, 1980). The authoritative source for citing anything is *The Chicago Manual of Style, 14th Edition*

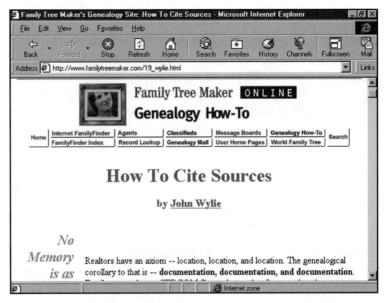

Figure 7-24

Print out a copy of this article and keep it next to your computer for easy reference.

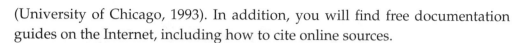

(University of Chicago, 1993). In addition, you will find free documentation guides on the Internet, including how to cite online sources.

Unless you work with many source citations on a regular basis, you will probably need to keep a copy of citation formats handy to consult. I do. Two of the major electronic sources you will probably cite often as you search for your ancestors—virtually—are Web pages and e-mail messages.

For Web pages, the URL and the date you viewed or downloaded data from it are critical. I recommend using angle brackets to set off the URL, as in the following example:

Klondike Gold Rush, Victims of the Killer Avalanche on the Chilkoot in 1897–98, <http://www.Gold-Rush.org/>, downloaded 7 February 1998.

> ❧ **NOTE** ❧   *The experts are still out on whether to put URLs in angle brackets or not; these brackets are not part of the URL, but for typesetting clarity, it is necessary to use something to show where a URL starts and stops. Angle brackets seem to work well for this purpose, especially when it's not convenient to use other forms of typographical highlighting.*

To cite an e-mail message, use this format:

Joanie Utley <jutley@greatnet.com> *(add postal mailing address, if known)*. Message to author, 15 September 1997. This message cites the 1893 death of Amanda Kelly, daughter of John Kelly and Sarah Anderson, in Newton County, Arkansas, as coming from a letter that Sarah (Anderson) Kelly wrote to her sister, Elizabeth (Anderson) Smith, who then resided in Clay County, Kentucky, in June 1893. Joanie Utley says she has in her possession a copy of this letter.

Electronic sources being used by today's genealogists are evolving, but it is important to record where and when you obtained any information. Citations provide you with logs of what you have researched and how to find the information again, should you need to (and you will refer to the same sources many times), and provide other researchers with the ability to evaluate the accuracy of your research. The most important things to identify are the author of a source, the type of source it is, the date of the source's publication, and any other additional information that will enable you and others to locate that source again—easily. "The Internet" is not enough and is not a proper citation.

Virtual Fishing for Ancestors

June was a favorite month when I was growing up in Oklahoma because that is when "Papa" (my maternal grandfather) and I went fishing. We would get the old cane poles out, dig up some worms, fill a fruit jar with cold water and pack a lunch (not necessarily in that order), and off we'd go down the hot, dusty road. At the old fishing hole on the creek we'd bait the hooks, drop our lines in the water, and then sit on the tree-shaded, cool bank and wait for the fish to bite.

Virtual fishing for ancestors is similar to the old-fashioned kind. First, you have to make some effort because the fish are not going to jump into your fish box, and second, you need to bait your hooks and throw out some lines. Fishing for ancestors online is one of the reasons the Internet has become so popular. Opening your e-mail and discovering a distant cousin in Ireland, Norway, Australia, or down the road who has information to share is like hitting the jackpot in a lottery.

One cousin found me by downloading my Ahnentafel from an online file library. It was a lucky bite for me. My family went to Arkansas while hers remained in Kentucky. I have information about the line that went West, but she recently found some old letters her grandmother had saved, filled with wonderful family gossip and tintypes that our families exchanged in the 1880s and 1890s.

Another online researcher contacted me because he discovered his Georgia ancestor listed on my Web page. He inquired about the evidence regarding the parents of his ancestor. I just happened to have a copy of the father's will, naming all 10 children. That made his day. Another fellow replied to my query regarding certain German families in 18th-century Orange County, North Carolina, with information about possible connections we might have. We both did some additional digging, and while we have not proved any cousinship yet, he gave me copies of some church records and I shared a few records I had that gave him some new material. In the process, I learned of another surname that possibly connects to my family. However, it was a visit to this county's Web site (part of the USGenWeb project) that yielded my biggest catch to date. Having this new surname to work with and knowing of a possible intermarriage between this man's family and mine, I looked at a record posted there that I probably would not have checked otherwise. It pertained to a 1787 inquest into the death of someone of this newly discovered surname. Guess whose ancestor is on that inquiry?

I also heard from a gentleman in Texas who has compiled two complete generations of descendants of the brother of my ancestor that had eluded me for years. I found this connection by using the search engine for the Roots surname list (**http://www. rootsweb.com/**). From a clue on an online bulletin board pertaining to Virginia sources, I learned there is a database online for the purported maiden name of the wife of one of my ancestors. I checked it out, and three more generations—including the gateway ancestor—leaped into my net. Of course I must verify the data, but that is the fun part of genealogy. A recent response to a query pertaining to the terribly common surname of Jackson suggests my line might be off a Quaker branch, one that left the faith. The researcher provided me with the name of the creek (in Orange County, North Carolina) near which this family resided in the time frame of interest. There is nothing like a new clue to excite a genealogist. My fish box overrunneth.

You too can go virtual fishing for your ancestors on the Internet. Bait your hooks. Get your lines in the water and catch some big ones. Just don't neglect to document those fishing holes and exactly where you caught those fish. You might need to go back to that same spot.

PART III

Shaping Your Family Tree

Ancestors of George Howard Lafferty

			Samuel Lafferty 1801 - 1873
	Edwin E. Lafferty 1834 - 1907		
			Margaret McDowell 1803 - 1861
George E. Lafferty 1867 - 1936			
			Erastus Fowler 1793 - 1875
	...elia Fowler ...1914		
			Temperence Merrill 1796 - 1871
		Nathan Wescott 1818 - 1900	
	...ram Wescott		
			Sarah Ann McMichael 1820 - 1901
	...a Wescott ...1963		
			Samuel C. Amsden 1822 - 1899
	Theresa Jerusa Amsden 1845 - 1934		
			Clarissa Hubbard 1820 - 1870

The History of George Howard Lafferty

George Howard Lafferty was born September 2, 1894 in Lenox township, Ashtabula County, Ohio, to Amber Amelia Wescott Lafferty and George Edwin Lafferty. A sister, Maud Irene, was born May 23, 1892.

A family of farmers, the Laffertys harvested the land where they lived. On May 9, 1919, they moved to Warren, Ohio, to a house on Forest Street NE. They lived next door to their daughter Maud, her husband Jay Rood Webster, and their three beautiful daughters, Reta, Shirley, and Marion.

As a youth, Lafferty went by "Howard" rather than "George" and signed his name as G. Howard Lafferty. After graduating from Lenox Township schools in 1911, he received a Teachers Certificate and became an educator and later a high school Principal. He then switched careers and ventured into banking just before World War I.

As a student at Ohio State University during the war, Howard Lafferty hoped to join the army but was classified 5G due to his glasses and other restrictions. In 1923 he received an L.L.B. degree and passed

CHAPTER EIGHT

Entering Additional Family Data

n genealogy, the rule is to start with yourself and then list your mother, father, and siblings. This is a nuclear family. Back in B.C.—Before Computers—information about each family was hand-written or typed on a Family Group Sheet. Many genealogists still create and keep paper copies of Family Group Sheets, but Family Tree Maker and other genealogy software programs offer greater legibility, easier updating, and quicker production all around.

This chapter focuses not only on Family Group Sheets but on those More About information boxes you met briefly in previous chapters. As you collect family data, you'll have many interesting details to record. Family Tree Maker simplifies things for you by organizing the facts into categories for individuals and marriages. Yet there is built-in flexibility, allowing you to enter any kind of data you choose, even stories.

Importance of the Family Unit

The family unit and its importance to genealogical research and compilation cannot be underestimated. Try to focus on each family group as you research, and take care to enter the data correctly. Once you have the information in the Family File, you'll be able to use it easily in Family Tree Maker's various trees, charts, and reports. It also shows up on printed Family Group Sheets, of course, giving you excellent research references to carry with you to libraries, archives, and courthouses.

Initially, you are probably interested in researching your so-called direct line—your father's father's family as far back as you can trace it—but you will discover that searching for a specific ancestor often can be like looking for the proverbial needle in a haystack. However, while you may not be able to find out much about your ancestor under his own name, the information you seek pertaining to him or his parents might turn up in his brother's file. Additionally, if his sister married someone of importance in the community, the brother-in-law's biography may appear in a county or local history, along with some information about his wife's family (sister to your ancestor)—perhaps revealing the family's previous residence or origins. The value of learning and recording information about the entire family group becomes obvious as you become more experienced in genealogical research.

> ❁ **TIP** ❁   *Be sure to record information about those siblings and in-laws. They might turn out to be the links that enable you to untangle those family roots and branches.*

Sorting Out the Family Group Sheet

There are several styles of Family Group Sheets, but in addition to basic data about the mother and father, they all contain places to record names of each child, dates and places of birth, marriage (or marriages), and death, plus names of the children's spouses. Figure 8-1 shows the Family Group Sheet of Nicholas Porter Earp and Virginia Ann Cooksey. Having the children in proper birth order enables you to determine approximately when the parents married—in the old days that was usually a year or less prior to the birth of the first child.

Up until the early part of the 20th century (before birth control became widely available and used by American families), children were usually born about two years apart. A gap of more than four years between children alerts you to the possibility that a child died young or that there was a miscarriage.

A Family Group Sheet enables you to see at a glance when and where the children in a family began marrying and setting up their own homes. (Figure 8-2 shows all the siblings of Wyatt Earp with information about who and when they married.) You will also discover that brothers and sisters of one family frequently intermarried with sisters and brothers of another family—they were often neighbors or belonged to the same church or ethnic group. Each clue and every record becomes important in genealogy, and the further back in time you research, the

Family Group
Sheet button

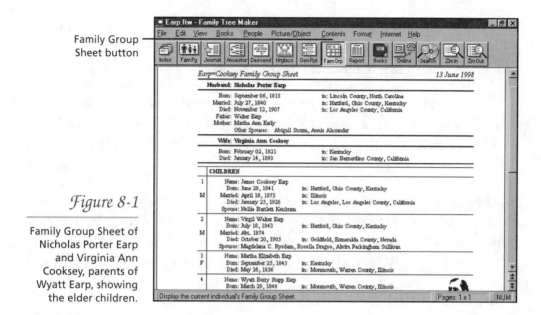

Figure 8-1

Family Group Sheet of
Nicholas Porter Earp
and Virginia Ann
Cooksey, parents of
Wyatt Earp, showing
the elder children.

more valuable they are. On occasion you will simply lose track of the parents in census records, for example. However, knowing the names of their sons-in-law allows you to search for them in the households of their married or widowed

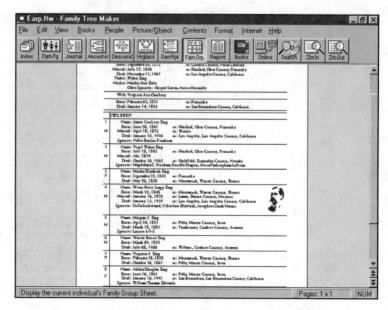

Figure 8-2

Family Group Sheet
showing Wyatt Earp
and his seven siblings.

daughters. If you neglect to determine who these sons-in-law are, you won't have the clues to work with. One often finds the widowed mother or father living with one of their children in their later years.

> ❊ **TIP** ❊ *If you have entered information in a Family File, that information is already available in a Family Group Sheet. To access the Family Group Sheet in Family Tree Maker, open a Family File, and then click on the toolbar button labeled* **Fam Grp.**

The family unit—shown in a capsule format on the Family Group Sheet—is your road map to researching your family. Without it, you could easily get lost, or find yourself wasting time and money climbing the wrong family tree. Figure 8-3 gives a closer look at Wyatt Earp's section of the Earp-Cooksey Family Group sheet.

Keeping Families Straight

The only way to keep families straight is to identify yours from the masses—and you will not be able to do it just by the spelling of the surname or names of the wives. You'll probably be surprised to discover how many people of the same name you will encounter in the records.

Figure 8-3

You can scan photos—like this one of Wyatt Earp—and include them with Family Group Sheets.

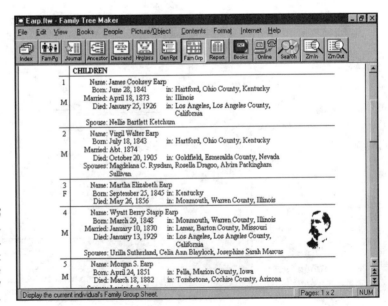

❧ **NOTE** ❧   *Years ago I requested copies from the National Archives of the Civil War military records for a John Vanderpool, born somewhere between 1830 and 1845. I thought that was more than sufficient information. How many John Vanderpools could there be who fit that description? After all, my maiden name is somewhat rare—or so I thought. It turned out there were records for eight men with the same name and born in the specified time frame. I narrowed my request to those who served from Missouri and still came up with five who fit the profile. Genealogical research can get expensive in a hurry, which is another reason to learn as much as possible about your ancestors so you can identify yours from others of the same name.*

As you work your way back in time, you might discover you have (to your horror) three Jones families—evidently unrelated. Perhaps two are on your father's side and one on your mother's. Or possibly you have a Jones line in Tennessee and discover your spouse's pedigree includes Jones families in Kentucky and Virginia. Do they connect? Perhaps. Perhaps not. It can be mass confusion in these instances, particularly to a brand-new researcher.

❧ **TIP** ❧   *You may want to do as many experienced genealogists do— keep some lines in different Family Files until you can sort them out and determine which, if any, really belong in your family tree. Later you can merge such files into the appropriate Family File.*

To make matters worse, you may discover that your great-grandfather, David Jones, married an Elizabeth Jones back in the late 1800s in Ohio. Are they related? Or do they just have the same common surname? You should include details about these families as you research them, to distinguish them from others. One hopes for an uncommon surname to work with, but the same situation often arises with uncommon surnames of ancestors who have the same given names. In my own families, I have three Abraham Vanderpools and three Samuel Isaacs to sort out. Some of these fellows had the temerity to marry women with the same given name—just to give me a challenge, I'm sure.

Keeping families of the same surname straight is a problem you probably will have to deal with at some point. So be prepared for it. Most of the time it's safe to use a surname alone as the name of your Family Tree Maker Family File—but you might want to create one or more that have the same surname, but may or may not connect to your lines. You could create a Family File named "Djones" and one named "Ajones" to help you remember that one file pertains to your David Jones family and one to the Andrew Jones family. Later, when you have determined that the data is correct and have figured out whether or not the lines of David Jones and Andrew Jones belong in your family tree, you can merge those files into your main Family File.

> ✧ **CAUTION** ✧   *Remember you can create a Family File in Family Tree Maker under any name you wish to use—but watch out when dealing with common surnames, and name the files carefully.*

Detailing Individuals

As you begin to sort out the family on a group level, you will also need to record information you've collected about each individual. You may be able to locate a great deal of biographical information about some of your ancestors but very little about others. Finding personal details about female ancestors is often a challenge, since fewer records pertaining to women exist in earlier times. Nevertheless, a careful and persistent family historian will learn bits and pieces about many ancestors—male and female. Suppose you discover that one of your ancestors, like one of my early female Dutch progenitors, was a midwife? Where would you record that information? There is no place to put it on the Family Page. In the More About windows you will discover several choices of listing data about an individual.

Using the More About Options

Family Tree Maker's More About windows are where you can record some of that additional information you collect—those little biographical details that enable you to paint portraits of your ancestors as real people, not just names on a chart. To record that personal information, just click on the More button that appears to the right of the Husband or Wife name field, the marriage fields, or each of the children's names on the Family Page. You can also access the More About options by placing the cursor in the appropriate field, and then choose <u>M</u>ore About from the <u>V</u>iew menu. For each individual there are five different More About options:

* Facts
* Address
* Medical
* Lineage
* Notes

> ❧ **NOTE** ❧   *Each marriage also has More About options for Facts and Notes in which you can record special information. I'll get to them later in this chapter.*

The More About windows give you a place to keep track of special events such as immigration and baptism, medical histories, and all the minutiae you uncover about your ancestors and help you get to know them as real people (see Figure 8-4).

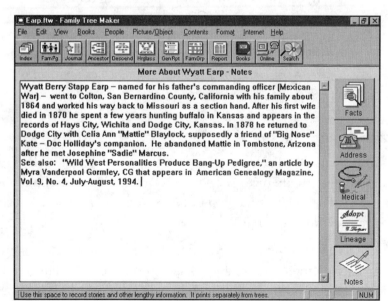

Figure 8-4

The Notes window can be used to record details about an individual, keep track of sources you'd like to locate, and to list conflicting information.

Each of the More About windows has two parts:

❉ The main window is the area where you can record information about the individual or the marriage. The name of the individual appears at the top of the window.

❉ The vertical toolbar has five buttons that let you move to other More About windows—Facts, Address, Medical, Lineage, and Notes.

❋ **TIP** ❋ *You can switch among all five More About windows by using the vertical toolbar.*

If you want to keep paper copies of the biographical details in a separate file, the information in the More About windows can be printed:

1. Go to any of the More About windows for the chosen individual.

2. From the File menu, choose Print More About Individual.

3. Click on OK in the message box about formatting text.

4. In the Print More About Individual dialog box, change settings as needed and then click on OK.

❋ **TIP** ❋ *In any More About window other than Notes, choosing to print will print out the first four windows of information. If you are in Notes, choosing to print will print out the Notes window.*

RECORDING FACTS

You can use the Facts window to create a personal timeline of specific events in an ancestor's life or to keep track of whatever miscellaneous information you collect. The information you put here does not have to be in chronological order, and dates are optional.

The Facts window lists information about an individual's life using predefined or user-defined fact types. These can be special events, activities, or personal characteristics. You might include such things as graduation from high school or college, christening, bar mitzvah, changes of residence, and burial date and place. Figure 8-5 shows dates and events in the early adult life of Wyatt Earp. To enter detailed Facts information for an individual, follow these steps:

1. Click on the Facts button on the vertical toolbar in the More About information window.

2. From the Fact drop-down list box, click on one of the many kinds of facts or events listed.

3. Fill in the Date and Comment/Location fields and press Enter. Each fact you enter for this individual will be added to the list boxes. When your collection of facts fills the available boxes, a scroll bar appears. You can list more facts than are visible on the screen at one time.

If you add facts that appear to be duplicated or conflicting, such as two "Died" dates, click on the Pref'd box next to the entry that is most likely correct. That makes it the preferred (first choice) entry.

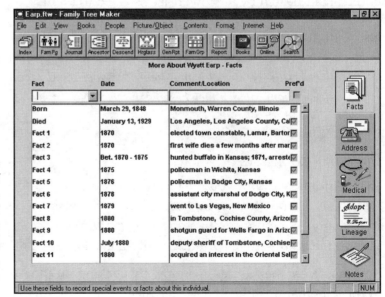

Figure 8-5

The More About Wyatt Earp - Facts window, showing an abbreviated chronology of his early adult life from about 1870 to 1901

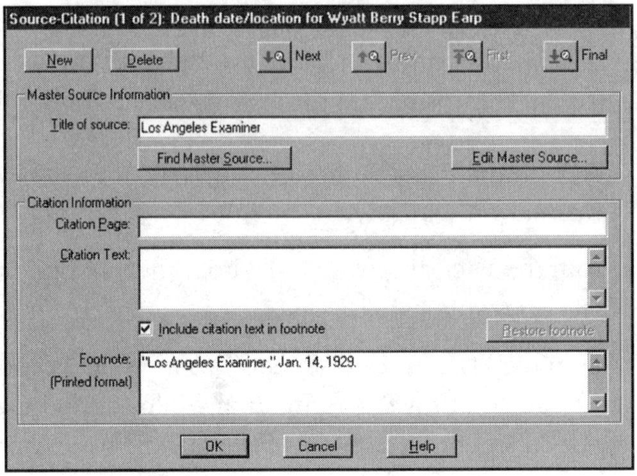

Figure 8-6

Entries with sources that have been referenced are shown with a lowercase "s" to the right of the item.

You can reference your Facts sources (see Figure 8-6) as you would an event by clicking on the item, and then pressing Ctrl+S. The facts that have been referenced are indicated by the lowercase "s" next to them.

> **TIP** *You can type in a Fact name that doesn't already appear in the drop-down list box. After you complete the Comment/Location field for your entry, the New Fact Name dialog box appears. Click on OK to accept the new Fact name, which then becomes a selectable name on the Fact drop-down list box for this Family File.*

Entering Addresses

In the Address window you can record an individual's address and phone number. This is a handy feature for keeping track of cousins who might be interested in a family reunion or exchanging information with you. Family Tree Maker obtains the addresses for printing mailing labels from the Address window.

You can access the Address window by clicking on the Address button on the vertical toolbar. Family Tree Maker fills in the individual's name for you; you can then type the address information in the appropriate fields.

LISTING MEDICAL INFORMATION

The Medical window has fields in which you can record such details as height (in feet and inches or meters), weight (in pounds and ounces or kilograms), cause of death, and additional health problems or medical information. You might also want to record injuries sustained, surgeries, allergies, diseases, or serious illnesses an ancestor experienced. The Medical window is especially useful to note disorders that might have genetic links.

You can access the Medical window by clicking on the Medical button on the vertical toolbar. Family Tree Maker will fill in the individual's name for you, and you can type in any appropriate medical information.

> ❋ **TIP** ❋   *If the amount of information you have for an individual exceeds what will fit in the Medical Information field, you can continue in the Notes window.*

RECORDING LINEAGE

The Lineage window contains fields where you can record special information about an individual, such as titles, other names by which an individual was known, and the relationship between an individual and his or her parents. These relationships might include an adoption or a step-relationship. You can access the Lineage window by clicking on the Lineage button on the vertical toolbar. Figure 8-7 shows the relationship options available in the Relationship drop-down list box.

> ❋ **NOTE** ❋   *If you want to display other sets of parents, first open the parents' Family Page and place the cursor in the child's name. From the People menu, select Other Parents. In the Parents Of dialog box you can create a new selection for parents and change the preferred parents.*

To record a special relationship between a child and either parent, click on the appropriate parent's drop-down list box and select from the following options:

❋ **Adopted**

❋ **Foster**

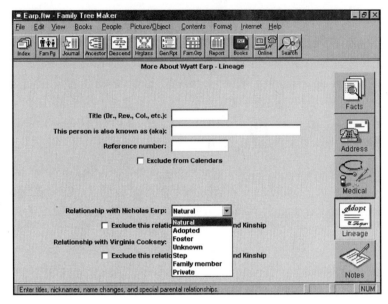

Figure 8-7

Special relationships
between parent and
child can be recorded
in the Lineage
window.

❀ **Unknown**

❀ **Step**

❀ **Family Member**

❀ **Private.** Imported information from a World Family Tree CD may
have this designation to protect the privacy of living individuals.

❀ **Natural (default).** A child can only have one natural father and one
natural mother.

❀ **NOTE** ❀ *If you do not want a particular individual to appear in Calendars that you create from your Family File, check the Exclude From
Calendars box in the Lineage window. This affects only a specific individual—
not his or her ancestors and descendants. To exclude several individuals from
Calendars use the Individuals To Include dialog box, click on the View menu
and select Calendar, and then open the Contents menu and choose Individuals To Include. There you can select the group of individuals you wish to
include in your Calendars.*

You may have occasion to exclude information about certain relationships from your trees or from the Kinship report (see Chapter Ten). There are two options in the Lineage window where you can elect to exclude this relationship between the child and either or both parents. If you select the Exclude This Relationship from Trees And Kinship check box, here's what will happen:

* In Kinship reports, the child will appear, but his or her maternal or paternal ancestors will not appear in the tree—depending on which parent's check box you selected. (You can select both.)

* In Ancestor trees, the child will appear, but his or her maternal or paternal ancestors will not—depending on which parent's check box you selected. (You can select both.)

* In Descendant trees, checking either box excludes the child and any of the child's descendants. However, the child's siblings and their descendants will appear.

Lining Up the Children

If you wish to record everyone who makes up a family, you can enter adopted, foster, and stepchildren along with the natural children at the bottom of the Family Page. (Although, technically, genealogy is the study of bloodline relationships, it's useful to keep track of everyone as you may well find information about blood relations in records about people who were brought into the family instead of born into it.) You can use the Lineage window to indicate the special nature of various relationships. When entering children on a Family Page, it is best to list them in the order in which they were born, starting with the oldest child. However, often you will not know the exact birth date. In those instances, provide an approximate birth date using such terms as before, after, about, circa, or estimate. This will help sort the children in the correct birth order. Often you will discover additional children who need to be inserted between those already listed, or you will find an error in a child's birth date that will force the rearrangement of the birth order. Do not attempt to rearrange children by typing over their names—that can get you into a lot of trouble. There are three commands to use for rearranging the children on a Family Page:

* Insert Child

* Move Child

* Sort Children

To insert a new child within the children's list, follow these steps:

1. In the Children list on the Family Page, place the cursor on the row where you want the new child's name.

2. From the People menu, choose Insert Child. The child's name at the cursor and children below the cursor are moved down one position, creating a blank line for you to enter a child.

To move a child within the Children list (this doesn't work for moving to a different Family Page), follow these steps:

1. In the Children list on the Family Page, place the cursor on the child you want to move.

2. From the People menu, choose Move Child From. A message box appears, informing you that you will be moving this child to a new position.

3. Click on OK.

4. In the Children list on the same Family Page, put the cursor on the row where you want the child to appear. If necessary, you can scroll the Children list to find the right position.

5. From the People menu, select Move Child To. The child's info will show up in the new position on the list.

    ❊ **TIP** ❊   *If you make an error in the move, you can undo it: From the Edit menu, choose Undo Move Child. This only works for a move you just made, so pay attention and make sure the new location is the one you wanted!*

If you want to transpose two children whose names are adjacent in a Children list, select the lower child as the one to move, and move that child upward.

You can enter children on the Family Page without regard to their birth order, and then sort them by date later. However, be sure not to leave the Birth Dates field blank for any children or they will be sorted to the top of the list. To sort children by birth order on a Family Page:

1. Select Sort Children from the People menu. A message box asks if you want to arrange the children in birth order (oldest first).

2. Click on OK. The children are sorted according to the contents of their Birth Dates fields.

Family Tree Maker sorts the children by putting the oldest child's information at the top of the list and the youngest child at the bottom. Twins or triplets stay in the order in which you entered them. If the Birth Dates field has a question mark (because you don't know the date of birth or are unsure of the information for whatever reason) that child will appear at the bottom of the list. If you know that Mary was younger than James, you can use the After date prefix so she will appear after him in birth order.

You can enter a date almost any way you wish, and Family Tree Maker will automatically put it into a standard format. If you leave a date field blank it means the event hasn't happened; entering a question mark means that you know the event happened, but are not sure when. You can also type "dead" or "deceased" in death date fields. If you do not know the exact date, you can use such traditional genealogical designations as: circa, est, about, before, after, and between (see Table 8-1).

Family Tree Maker can display double dates to account for the crossover between the Julian and Gregorian calendars. If you enter a date that falls between January 1 and March 25 for any year before 1752, a double date appears.

ENTERING NOTES AND STORIES

Using the Notes window is like typing in a word processor. Information in the Notes window will not appear on your family trees, but you can print these notes in Family Group Sheets or add them to a Book you create. The Notes window is an ideal place to include a short biography about an ancestor (see Figure 8-8) or any other information that doesn't fit elsewhere.

Table 8-1   Date Prefixes

Type This	You Get This
1776	1776
est 7/4/1776	Abt. July 4, 1776
abt 7/4/1776	Abt. July 4, 1776
about 7/4/1776	Abt. July 4, 1776
circa 7/4/1776	Abt. July 4, 1776
bef 7/4/1776	Bef. July 4, 1776
before 7/4/1776	Bef. July 4, 1776
aft 7/4/1776	Aft. July 4, 1776
after 7/4/1776	Aft. July 4, 1776
July 1-4, 1776	Bet. July 1-4, 1776
June 1776-July 1776	Bet. June 1776-July 1776
Bet. 7/4/1776 and 8/4/1777	Bet. July 4, 1776-Aug. 4, 1777
?	Unknown

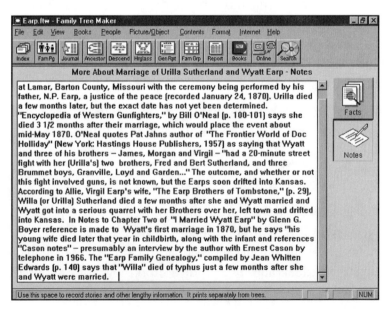

Figure 8-8

Additional information pertaining to an individual can be entered in the Notes window.

Copying and Moving Notes

You can edit your text in the Notes window just as in any word processor. In addition to the cut, copy, and paste functions, you can delete information, undo editing, and add extra lines and spaces. You can also move or copy sections of text from one individual's Notes window to another's. Access the Notes window by clicking on the Notes button on the vertical toolbar. To copy or move Notes window text, follow these steps:

1. Open the Notes window of the person whose text you want to copy or move.

2. Highlight the text you want to copy or move.

3. From the Edit menu, choose Cut (if you want to move the text) or Copy (if you want to copy the text to another Notes window).

    ❋ **TIP** ❋ *You can also right-click to choose the Cut and Copy commands on the shortcut menu. Alternatively, you can use keyboard shortcuts: Ctrl+X for Cut and Ctrl+C for Copy.*

4. From the View menu, select Index Of Individuals. The Index of Individuals dialog box appears.

5. Select the individual to whom you want to transfer the text; click on OK. The Notes window appears for the individual you selected. (Be sure the name at the top of the Notes window is the one you want.)

6. Position the cursor where you want to insert the text. If you want to use the new text to replace a section of old text, highlight the old text first.

7. From the Edit menu, select Paste Text. The text is pasted in the new location.

    ❋ **TIP** ❋ *You can also right-click to choose the Paste command on the shortcut menu. Alternatively, you can use the keyboard shortcut Ctrl+V.*

Finding Text in Notes

Sometimes you might have a Notes window with a large amount of text stored in it. A quick way to find text without reading the entire Note is to use the Find command. First make sure the Notes window you wish to search is onscreen. To find text, follow these steps:

1. From the Edit menu, choose Find. The Find dialog box appears (see Figure 8-9).

2. In the Find What text box, type in the text you want to find. (You can also select the Match Whole Word Only or Match Case check box or both).

3. Click on the Find Next button. If a match is found, it is indicated by highlighted text in the Notes window.

4. Click on Find Next to look for more occurrences of the text or on Cancel to end the search.

Formatting Notes for Printing

You can also format text in the Notes window. This option allows you to format all the notes for one individual.

> ❧ **NOTE** ❧ *The formatted text appears in printed copies, but not on the screen.*

1. From the Format menu, select Text Font, Style, & Size. A message box informs you that the formatting choices you make will appear only when you print.

2. Click on OK. The Text Font, Style, & Size for Notes dialog box appears (see Figure 8-10).

Figure 8-9

You can locate text in a Notes window without reading the entire contents.

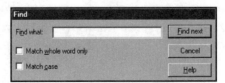

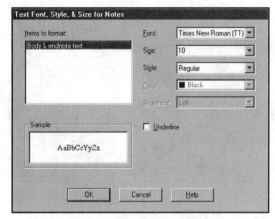

Figure 8-10

You can change the font used when you print information from the Notes windows.

3. Make formatting selections from the drop-down lists on the right side of the dialog box.

4. Click on OK. This returns you to the Notes window.

Copying or Importing Text to Notes

In addition to copying and pasting text into the Notes window, you can import ASCII text from another program such as a word processor. (The difference with importing is that you are transferring the contents of an entire file, not just copying and pasting a portion of text.) First, export the material from the other program to an ASCII file. To import the ASCII file, do the following:

1. Open the Notes window where you want to place the text.

2. Put the cursor where you want to insert the text.

3. From the File menu, select Import Text File. The Import Text File dialog box appears (see Figure 8-11).

4. In the Look In drop-down list box, select the drive where the file you want to import is located.

5. Double-click on the folder containing the file you want to import.

6. Select the proper file type (ASCII) from the File of Type drop-down list box. Use ASCII (ANSI) for Windows-created files.

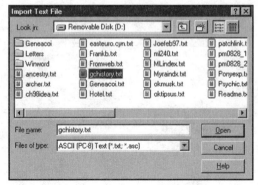

Figure 8-11

Importing a text file
into the Notes
window is an easy,
handy feature.

7. In the list box, click on the file you want to import.

8. Click on the Open button. The text from the file appears in the Notes window.

Exporting Notes

Text from a Notes window can also be exported to another word processor. To do this, you create an ASCII text file with Family Tree Maker and then import it into the other program.

1. Open the Notes window that has the text you want to export.

2. From the File menu, choose Export Notes. The Export Notes dialog box appears (see Figure 8-12).

Figure 8-12

Export information
from the Notes
window in plain text
(ASCII) to any file.

3. In the Save In drop-down list box, select the drive where you want to put the file you are creating.

4. Double-click on the folder in which you want to place the file you are creating.

5. Select the correct file type ASCII (ANSI) from the Save as Type drop-down list box.

   ❋ **TIP** ❋   *If you're exporting information from a Notes window to a DOS application, use the ASCII (PC-8). If you're exporting to Windows, choose ASCII (ANSI).*

6. Type a name for the file in the File Name text box.

7. Click on Save. The Notes window text is saved in the file you created.

Detailing Marriages and Other Relationships

Each marriage in Family Tree Maker has its own set of More About information—a Facts window and a Notes window. You can use these to record information about marriages, notations about special anniversaries, or perhaps information about activities a couple likes to share (see Figure 8-13). Additionally, if the relationship has ended, you can record the date and reason (divorce, death, or whatever).

To display the More About window for a marriage, go to the Family Page of the couple. Either click on the More button next to the marriage on the Family Page or follow these steps:

1. Place the cursor in one of the marriage fields (Marriage Date, Beginning Status, or Marriage Location).

2. From the View menu, select More About; from the submenu, select the name of the view you want to see, either Facts or Notes. The specified view appears.

   Whichever you choose, you'll see a vertical toolbar on the right, with two buttons that enable you to switch between the Facts window and the Notes window for the marriage.

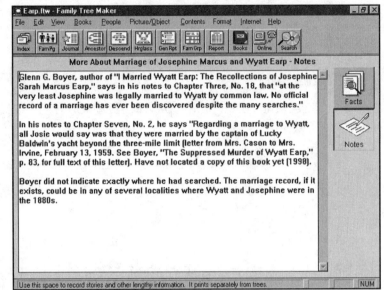

Figure 8-13

The More About
Marriage window,
showing information
about the marriage of
Josephine Marcus and
Wyatt Earp.

Marriage Facts

The rather murky marital history of Wyatt Earp and his three wives presents a
unique opportunity to include information not commonly found in genealogies. You may also encounter some ancestors with similar situations. Family
Tree Maker has five fields in the Facts window where you can record details
about a marriage:

- ❋ Ending Status
- ❋ Reference Number
- ❋ Marriage Fact
- ❋ Date
- ❋ Comment/Location
- ❋ Pref'd (Preferred) checkbox

Like the Facts window for individuals, the Marriage Fact window allows you to
enter as many facts as needed by choosing a marriage event from the drop-

down list box. In the Ending Status field, click on the drop-down list box and select the relevant option.

The Reference Number field is an optional one. It can contain any numbers or letters you choose. You can use this field to record a reference to your filing system, for example.

Wyatt Earp was legally married at least once. He later lived with two other women, but whether he legally married Mattie Blaylock or Josephine "Sadie" Marcus has never been determined by historians or genealogists. Common-law marriages were not rare in the West at the time—the latter part of the 19th century—but it is not always easy to know how to record such situations.

Family Tree Maker offers several choices in the Beginning Status field on the Family Page: Friends, Married, Other, Partners, Private, Single, and Unknown. If it is not certain that a couple ever married, choose "Unknown." When you choose Partners or Friends, Family Tree Maker automatically substitutes the words "Meeting Date" for the "Marriage Date" in the records pertaining to the two individuals listed. Additionally, when Partners or Friends is selected, then the Husband and Wife labels are changed to Partners.

Marriage Notes

You can use the Marriage Notes window to include additional information about a marriage or relationship. Click on the Notes button on the vertical toolbar to access the Notes window from the Facts window.

In the example of Wyatt Earp and Mattie Blaylock, the relationship actually ended about 1881 when he left Mattie for Sadie Marcus. In the Marriage Notes window, you would be able to record details about their relationship and cite the facts about Mattie's suicide in 1888 and the sources of the information.

Ancestors of George Howard Lafferty

Samuel Lafferty
1801 - 1873

Edwin E. Lafferty
1834 - 1907

Margaret McDowell
1803 - 1861

George E. Lafferty
1867 - 1936

Erastus Fowler
1793 - 1875

...ella Fowler
...1914

Temperance Merrill
1796 - 1871

Nathan Wescott
1818 - 1900

...iram Wescott

Sarah Ann McMichael
1820 - 1901

...n Wescott
...1903

Samuel C. Amsden
1822 - 1899

Theresa Jerusa Amsden
1845 - 1934

Clarissa Hubbard
1820 - 1870

The History of George Howard Lafferty

George Howard Lafferty was born September 2, 1894 in Lenox township, Ashtabula County, Ohio, to Amber Amelia Wescott Lafferty and George Edwin Lafferty. A sister, Maud Irene, was born May 23, 1892.

A family of farmers, the Laffertys harvested the land where they lived. On May 9, 1919, they moved to Warren, Ohio, to a house on Forest Street NE. They lived next door to their daughter Maud, her husband Jay Rood Webster, and their three beautiful daughters, Reta, Shirley, and Marion.

As a youth, Lafferty went by "Howard" rather than "George" and signed his name as G. Howard Lafferty. After graduating from Lenox Township schools in 1911, he received a Teachers Certificate and became an educator and later a high school Principal. He then switched careers and ventured into banking just before World War I.

As a student at Ohio State University during the war, Howard Lafferty hoped to join the army but was classified 5G due to his glasses and other restrictions. In 1923 he received an L.L.B. degree and passed

CHAPTER NINE

Pruning Your Family Tree

ou've added many family members to your family tree, but how do you find them all? If you've accumulated dozens of names from the World Family Tree CDs, GEDCOMs, or online resources, you may not remember all the names or how they are related to one another. You need a way to see a list of them and jump right to their branches of the tree. You may even want to focus on a particular date range or location instead of finding a name. Family Tree Maker makes all this possible with its Index of Individuals.

Family Tree Maker checks spelling and looks for other data entry and relationship errors for you, too. This chapter helps you navigate the Family File using the Index of Individuals, and also assists you with cleaning up different types of errors you may have inadvertently introduced.

Using Family Tree Maker's Index of Individuals

The Index of Individuals shows the name, birth date, and death date of every person in your Family File. It is an easy and quick way to see information you have on anyone.

From the View menu, choose Index of Individuals. This opens the Index of Individuals dialog box, displaying names listed alphabetically by surname with birth and death dates shown on the right (see Figure 9-1). Individuals that have nicknames (aka) appear twice in the index—under both of their names. You can use this feature to locate and sort out people of the same name that wind up in your Family Files and to check if you have entered information about a particular individual.

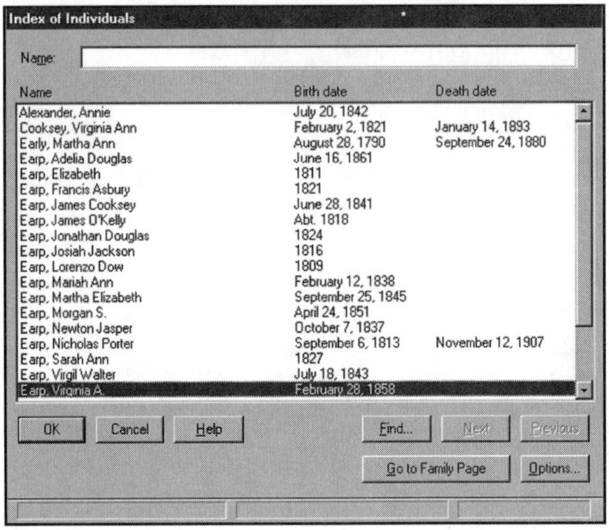

Figure 9-1

The Index of
Individuals is arranged
alphabetically by
surname.

You can move up and down through the names by using the scroll arrows or by using the Page Up and Page Down keys on your keyboard.

Quick Search by Name

You can locate a person in the Index of Individuals by using the Quick Search feature. This feature only works when the Index of Individuals is arranged alphabetically. To use the Quick Search feature:

1. Click on the Name text box at the top of the Index of Individuals.

2. Type the surname (last name) of the individual you wish to find, followed by a comma and space, and then the first (given) name, and finally the middle name. The first matching name is highlighted in the Index of Individuals.

   ❋ **TIP** ❋   *You probably won't have to finish typing the entire name. Quick Search takes you to the name that matches as you type each letter. The search is not case-sensitive—you can type in uppercase or lowercase letters and it won't affect the search.*

Whether you have the Index of Individuals sorted by name or date, you can also use the Find feature to locate a name. To use the Find feature in the Index of Individuals:

1. Click on the Find button (located at the bottom of the Index of Individuals dialog box). The Find Name dialog box appears.

2. In the Name text box, type an individual's name (you can type any part of the name), as shown in Figure 9-2.

3. Click on OK to begin searching.

    The Find dialog box closes, and the first matching name is highlighted in the Index of Individuals. If there is no match, an error message box advises you to try again. Click on OK and go back to step 2.

4. To continue searching through the list of names, click on the Next button to move to the next name that meets the criterion. (Click on the Previous button to return to the previous matches).

    ❦ **NOTE** ❦ *It may be surprising to find out that a few of your ancestors bear the same names. It is not unusual to have several persons of the same name born at about the same time, and in the same locality. Moreover, you may discover that your ancestor married two women named Elizabeth, but you do not yet know their maiden names. Problems, problems, problems. Never assume anything in genealogy. Check and double-check your data.*

Figure 9-2

Locate an Individual in the index using the Find Name dialog box.

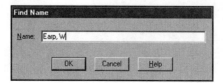

Rearranging the Index

You can sort the Index of Individuals list by clicking on the Options button to open the Sort Individuals dialog box (see Figure 9-3). This dialog box offers four options for sorting:

- **Last Name (A First).** This gives you surnames in alphabetical order.

- **Last Name (Z First).** This gives you surnames in reverse alphabetical order.

- **Birth Date (Oldest First).**

- **Birth Date (Youngest First).**

Choose one of these option buttons and then click on OK. The index is sorted in the order you selected. Notice that the Name text box is not available for a Quick Search unless you choose the first option.

> ❋ **TIP** ❋   *You may wish to find all the Zumwalt ancestors in your Family File. To get to them in a hurry, rather than scroll down to the end of the list, type a "Z" in the Name field. You also can choose Options/Sort Individuals, and then select the Last Name (Z First) option button in the Sort Individuals dialog box.*
>
> *You can find the oldest person in your Family File by selecting the Birth Date (Oldest First) option in the Sort Individuals dialog box, or you can find the youngest person by selecting Birth Date (Youngest First) in the Sort Individuals dialog box.*

Figure 9-3

Rearrange the Index
using the Sort
Individuals dialog box.

Jumping to the Individual's Family File

Once you find the name of an individual in the Index of Individuals, you can click on the <u>G</u>o To Family Page button, which takes you to the Family Page containing the individual (shown as either a husband or wife) whose name is highlighted. If the individual has been married more than once, Family Tree Maker selects the Family Page that contains the preferred spouse.

Instead of choosing the <u>G</u>o To Family Page button, you can click on OK to go to the current view of the individual whose name is highlighted. Family Tree Maker takes you to the view that you were in before you opened the Index of Individuals—a Tree, Family Group Sheet, Scrapbook, Report, Family Page, and so on. You can see the individual's name in that view, and also switch to other views for this individual.

> ❧ **NOTE** ❧   *By double-clicking on the individual's name, you go to the current view.*

Using the Find Individual Feature

Family Tree Maker doesn't limit you to locating individuals through the Index of Individuals. There is another feature, called Find Individual, which gives you more flexibility in defining your search. The Find Individual search option allows you to locate anyone in your Family File, plus you can search for individuals using almost any type of information: names, dates, comments, items in Scrapbooks, and even phrases in the Notes window.

The Find Individual feature is also useful for finding groups of individuals. For example, you can search for all the Earps or Smiths, or search for everyone that has the same birthplace. When Family Tree Maker finds the individual for you, you can edit that individual's information and then continue the search. You don't need to tell Family Tree Maker what to search for again.

Searching by Name

If you wish to locate a particular person in your Family File, one way is to search by name. Go to any Family Page, and then follow these steps:

Figure 9-4

The Find Individual dialog box allows you to search by name and other fields.

1. From the Edit menu, choose Find Individual. The Find Individual dialog box appears (see Figure 9-4).

2. In the Search drop-down list, select Name.

3. In the For text box, type the name you wish to find—or type any part of it.

4. Click on Find Next to start the search. If there are no matches, Family Tree Maker displays a message saying so. If this is the case, click on OK in the message box and then try another search.

5. Click on Find Next to continue the search. You can go through the same search again by clicking on the Restart Search button.

6. To quit searching, click on Cancel.

Searching for Other Information in Your Files

You can also use the Find Individual dialog box to find dates, locations, sources, and comments. Using this feature will enable you to find individuals who are parentless or childless (at least in your database) as well as individuals who have been merged or unmerged in your Family File. To find any information other than by name, go to any Family Page and then follow these steps:

1. From the Edit menu, choose Find Individual. The Find Individual dialog box appears.

2. In the Search drop-down list, select the item you want to search for, such as Birth date (see Figure 9-5).

3. In the For field, type in the information you wish to find. For example, if you choose Birth Date in the Search drop-down list and

Figure 9-5

The Find Individual dialog box allows you to search by various fields, such as birth dates.

want to find everyone born in February, just type **February.** If you want to find everyone who was born before the 1920 census was taken, type in **<January 1920** (Note the "<" sign—it's important).

4. Click on Find <u>N</u>ext to start the search. If you follow this example, you'll see the first birth date located before January 1920 highlighted in an individual's Date Born field.

5. Click on Find <u>N</u>ext to continue the search. You can go through the same search again by clicking on the <u>R</u>estart Search button.

6. To quit searching, click on Cancel.

❋ **TIP** ❋   *Take the time to explore the search feature early on while you still have a small database.*

Privacy Considerations

Each state has its own laws regarding privacy and access to records. Some records of the Immigration and Naturalization Service are restricted for 25 to 50 years, and most U.S. states have restrictions on their vital records, particularly birth records. Currently, the 1920 census is the most recent U.S. (federal) census available to researchers. If you have family members born after 1920 who are still living, you should obtain their written permission before sharing any genealogical or biographical information about them with others—even with other cousins. This is common courtesy, but sometimes genealogists get so caught up in their projects they forget that even though it is family information, data about living persons should not shared with the world without permission. You also run the risk of being sued for invasion of privacy if you aren't careful.

SEARCHING BY DATE

After names, dates are probably the most widely explored fields in a genealogical database. You can learn a great deal about your families by studying time frames. After all, most people's lives fit into time frames and cycles—birth, youth, marriage, middle age, old age, and death. Of course, there are exceptions in every family tree. Some of your ancestors may have married much later in life than most people, for example. However, in looking at many families over many time frames and localities, I've found that it is amazing how closely most ancestors from generation to generation adhere to basic time frames of life cycles. Dates or time frames can be useful in helping you sort out generations. If a couple married in 1850 and had the average number of children who survived to adulthood, those children were probably born between about 1850 and 1875, which means they, in turn, probably married in the time frame of about 1868 to 1900. When you use the date search options in Family Tree Maker, you can use any allowable date formats. Figure 9-6 shows how to search for all birth dates in your Family File that occur after January, 1880.

> ❀ **TIP** ❀   *You can type a date to search on in several different formats, and the date will still be found in the date field regardless of the current display format. To choose a date format preference for the way dates look in date fields, choose File, Preferences, Dates & Measures, and set your preferences in the dialog box that appears.*

The following are examples of allowable date formats you can enter for searches:

- ☆ Jan 1, 1920
- ☆ 1 Jan 1920
- ☆ 01.01.1920

Figure 9-6

You can use the Find Individual dialog box to search for all birth dates occurring after a certain date.

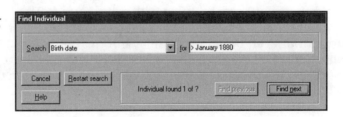

Find Individual

Search | Birth date | for | > January 1880

Cancel   Restart search

Help

Individual found 1 of ?   Find previous   Find next

Figure 9-7

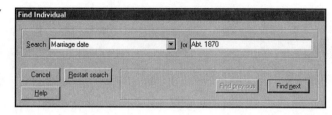

To find a marriage that took place in about 1870, select Marriage Date for the search and type in **Abt. 1870.**

 01-01-1920

 01/01/1920

In searching for dates (or numbers), you can use the mathematical operators— >, <, >=, and <=. You can also use X..Y (where X and Y are dates) to combine with the other operators to specify a date range. Consider the examples in Table 9-1 for the date search criteria you can use in the For text box of the Find Individual dialog box.

You can search for an approximate date of a particular event also. Figure 9-7 shows how to search for a marriage date of about 1870.

SEARCHING BY LOCATION

You also can search your Family File by location. Figure 9-8 shows how to conduct a search for all deaths that took place in California, for example.

Techniques for Searching in Family Files

There are a number of ways to do a search in the Family File:

     To find all the empty fields in a Family File, type = (equal sign) in the For text box.

     To search for a field that is not empty, type != (exclamation point and an equal sign) in the For text box.

     To search for a specific date, but not in any particular field, select Any and all date fields from the Search field.

     To search for a specific set of words, but not in any particular field, select Any and all text fields from the Search field.

Table 9-1   Entering Date Search Criteria

Enter This	To Find This
01/01/1920	All occurrences of January 1, 1920
<01/01/1920	Dates before January 1, 1920
<=1/1/1920	The date January 1, 1920 and all dates before it
BEFORE 01/01/1920	Dates before January 1, 1920
BEF 01/01/1920	Dates before January 1, 1920
>01/01/1920	Dates after January 1920
AFTER 01/01/1920	Dates after January 1920
AFT 01/01/1920	Dates after January 1920
ABOUT 01/01/1920	Dates entered as About January 1, 1920
CIRCA 01/01/1920	Dates entered as Circa January 1, 1920
EST 01/01/1920	Dates entered as Est January 1, 1920
01/01/1920..01/01/1921	Dates between January 1, 1920 and January 1, 1921, including those two days
>01/01/1920..<01/01/1921	Dates between January 1, 1920 and January 1, 1921, excluding those two days

Locality searches let you sort information according to where things happened—which may seem useless at first glance, but can come in handy. Locality information is helpful in preparing research strategies before visiting libraries, archives, and other repositories with genealogical collections. By arranging

Figure 9-8

A search through your Family File for all the deaths that occurred in the same state can help you better organize your research notes.

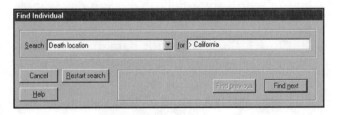

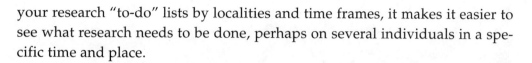

your research "to-do" lists by localities and time frames, it makes it easier to see what research needs to be done, perhaps on several individuals in a specific time and place.

> ❈ **TIP** ❈   *When searching for localities, remember to search for abbreviations you might have entered in the fields. No matter how carefully you try to keep things consistent as you enter data, you will probably discover some discrepancies. Check all the options you might have used.*

LOCATING SOURCES

An easy way to determine if you have entered the source of material is to use the != (exclamation point and equal sign) and search through the fields of the Find Individual dialog box. By asking for a search in the birth source information, you can learn if you have documented this information. It's easy to get so eager to enter material that you neglect to include the source, or you get interrupted and skip fields.

LOCATING COMMENTS

You can search for almost any information in your Family File, including items in comments. Want to know whether you put that medical information in about your great-grandfather? Do a search in the Find Individual dialog box for Medical info and use the != to show you all the places where that field contains information.

> ❈ **TIP** ❈   *The Find Individual feature is much more than just a name search option. You can use it to determine what information you have and have not entered in your Family File. It's a great checker for your data.*

Correcting Family File Errors

Everybody makes mistakes—and when you're entering seemingly endless piles of names, dates, and strangely-named places, mistakes are easy to make. Few genealogists have the luxury of a personal editor who can check their databases (Family Files), so you must rely upon yourself for the most part. However,

Family Tree Maker provides some ways for you to check for and correct certain kinds of mistakes commonly found in Family Files.

Using Family Tree Maker's Spell Check Feature

The Spell Check is an option that even the best of spellers and typists appreciate. It proofreads the text in your Notes and Books. You can spell check:

- ✗ All notes and text items in a Family File.

- ✗ All text items in a Book.

- ✗ A specific text item in a Book.

- ✗ Notes for a specific individual or marriage.

To spell check in a Family File, display the Family Page, Tree, or Report for the family you're interested in. From the Edit menu, select Spell Check All to begin checking the text (see Figure 9-9).

When Family Tree Maker finds a potential spelling error (see Figure 9-10), the Spell Check dialog box appears and makes alternate spelling suggestions or indicates that the word is not in the dictionary.

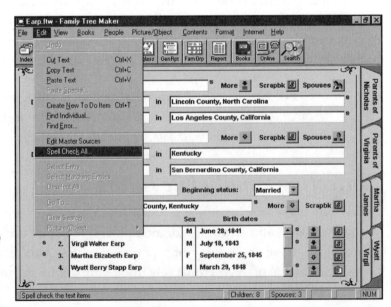

Figure 9-9

Check your pages for potential spelling errors.

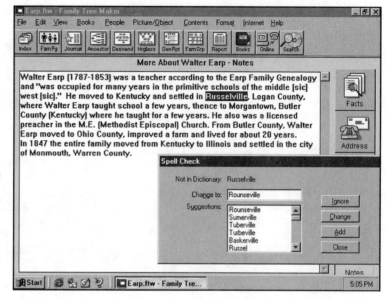

Figure 9-10

Spell Check detects a potential spelling error with "Russelville" and displays the Not in Dictionary error message.

Many of the personal names and locality names genealogists use are unique. Also, one may find towns and parishes that are spelled one way in one locale and another way elsewhere. For example, there are numerous Russellville localities in different states. There is also a Russelville in Illinois and one in West Virginia, and just to confuse genealogists, there is a Russellville and a Russeville in Kentucky.

In Figure 9-10, the reference is to the town in Logan County, Kentucky, which should be correctly spelled Russellville. Since this word is not in the dictionary, you can add it.

Click on the <u>A</u>dd button and type in the word you want to add to the dictionary—Russellville in this example. The word is added to the dictionary and the Spell Check continues.

In this example, Spell Check also stops (see Figure 9-11) at the spelling of Morgantown (Butler County, Kentucky). It asks whether this should be two words and shows other possible options. Again, you can type in words that are not in the Spell Check dictionary.

❧ **TIP** ❧ *It is a good idea to do the Spell Check routine when you have the time to double-check your references and won't be interrupted.*

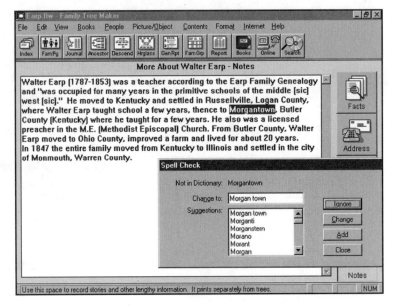

Figure 9-11

When Spell Check detects a potential spelling error, it gives you an opportunity to ignore or change it, or add the word to the dictionary.

❧ **NOTE** ❧   *Many towns in Europe have the same names. Foreign words and American locality names with their variant possibilities can make the Spell Check hop and stop like one of Mark Twain's Calaveras County frogs. Take your time and make sure of the spellings the first time you run the Spell Check feature, adding to the dictionary as you go. The results will be worth the effort.*

Click on the Ignore button whenever you know the word prompting the Not In Dictionary error is spelled correctly but you don't want to add it to the dictionary. By choosing Ignore, you skip adding the word to the dictionary, and Spell Check will prompt you when it encounters that word again.

You can also choose Ignore if you don't want to bother with confirming the spelling right away—you could jot it down to verify later, knowing that Spell Check will stop on it again next time you run Spell Check for the same Family File.

If you see a correct spelling for the word in the Suggestions list box, you can select it and then click on the Change button. The word is then replaced in the occurrence where Spell Check found it, and the Spell Check continues.

Continue clicking on Add, Change, or Ignore until the Spell Check is complete. Click on OK when you see the message telling you the Spell Check is complete.

❀ **TIP** ❀ *If you want to quit checking spelling while Spell Check is still running, you can click on the Close button in the Spell Check dialog box.*

The procedure for Spell Checking only Notes (in the Notes window) or Books (a feature I'll tell you more about in Chapter Thirteen) is similar to the steps you just saw. To check spelling in a Notes window, display the Notes window you want to check; from the <u>E</u>dit menu, choose Spell Chec<u>k</u> Note. To check spelling in a Book, display the Book you want to check; from the <u>E</u>dit menu, choose Spell Chec<u>k</u> Book. The Spell Check dialog box appears if there are any words not found in the Family Tree Maker dictionary. At that point, all you need to do is follow the steps in this section—Spell Check doesn't care how you get to it.

Untying the Knot

What happens if you "marry" John Smith to the wrong woman? It happens. In fact, it probably happens more often than anybody likes to admit (in Family Tree Maker and in real life, only with different people). Especially before the 20th century, siblings in one family often married siblings from another—and that frequently puts a lot of similar names close together. When working from Family Group Sheets, it is quite easy to pick up the wrong spouse for someone. Some of your ancestors probably married offspring of their parents' neighbors, while others found their mates among members of the same religious group— other sources of clusters of similar names.

❀ **NOTE** ❀ *One of my Tennessee families had four marriages between children of two families. This produced some unique relationships, such as double first cousins who were also parallel (or ortho) and cross cousins. And you thought figuring out relationships was easy now that you have a software program to help you!*

If two Smith brothers marry two Jones sisters, their offspring will be double first cousins. Double first cousins share all lineal and collateral relatives. Additionally, these offspring are also parallel (or ortho) first cousins. Parallel cousins are the children of two brothers or two sisters. If a brother of these Jones sisters married a sister of the Smith brothers, then their children would be cross (not cranky) cousins.

You have plenty to do to untangle family branches without marrying up the wrong people in your Family File. But should this happen, you can use the Detach Spouse command to unmarry them. If these individuals have children listed on their Family Page, the children will remain with the spouse who is *not* being detached.

1. Display the Family Page that has the couple you have incorrectly listed as husband and wife. You must use the page where the individual is shown as a husband or wife, not as a child.

2. Click to place the cursor on the spouse you want to detach.

3. From the People menu, choose Fix Relationship Mistakes and then choose Detach Spouse (see Figure 9-12). A warning box appears, asking you if you are sure you want to detach this individual and informing you if there are children who will lose a parent.

4. Click on the Yes button to confirm—or click on the No button if you aren't sure.

As I said, if the husband or wife you are detaching has children, the children will remain with the spouse who is not detached. Another option (Linking

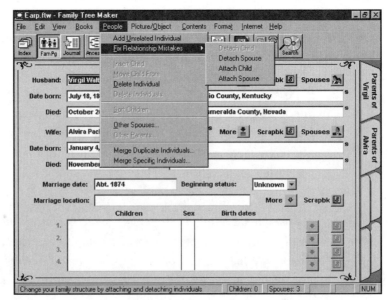

Figure 9-12

Selecting the Fix Relationship Mistakes option presents other choices in the submenu shown here.

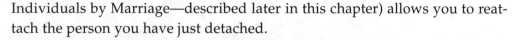

Individuals by Marriage—described later in this chapter) allows you to reattach the person you have just detached.

Do not use the Detach Spouse option to enter information about divorces. Divorces should be recorded in the More About Marriage window for that couple (click on the More button for the marriage and then open the Facts window and choose Divorce in the Fact drop-down list).

Removing People from Your Files

Occasionally you will discover that you have added someone to your Family File who does not belong there. To erase one person from the file, use the Delete Individual command. If you have a group of people to delete, use the Delete Individuals command, as explained later in this section.

DELETING ONE PERSON

The Delete Individual command eliminates all ties that a person has with all other individuals in your tree, so be careful before using this option. If the mistake you've made is an incorrect date or location, just type over the incorrect data. Don't use Delete Individual for these kinds of errors. However, the only time you should type over a person's name is to change its spelling. If you need to move an individual to a different Family Page, then you should use the Attach and Detach commands (see later sections in this chapter). To delete someone:

1. Display the Family Page that lists the person you want to delete.

2. Click to place the cursor on the name to delete.

3. From the People menu, select Delete Individual (see Figure 9-13). A message box appears, asking if you're sure you want to delete all information about the person.

4. Click on the Yes button. The person is deleted from the Family File.

DELETING A GROUP OF PEOPLE

To purge your Family File permanently of more than one individual, use the Delete Individuals command available from the People menu. To use this option, you need to display a Custom Report, Ancestor Tree, Descendant Tree, or

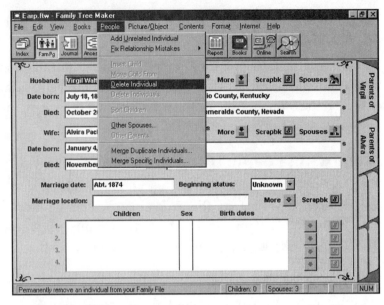

Figure 9-13

Use Delete Individual to remove the selected person completely from your Family File.

Outline Descendant Tree that contains the group of individuals you want to delete. Review the document carefully, making sure it contains only the group of individuals you wish to delete—once you select them, Family Tree Maker will delete all information associated with them in the Family File. To delete more than one individual:

> ❋ **TIP** ❋ *You may want to create a backup copy of your Family File before doing any irreversible deletions.*

1. In the Family File, display an Ancestor Tree, Descendant Tree, Outline Descendant Tree, or Custom Report that contains only the people you want to delete.

2. From the People menu, select Delete Individuals. The specific command depends on which tree or report you have displayed. If you have displayed a report, the People menu will show Delete Individuals In Report, and a variation on that if you have displayed a tree. A message box appears, asking if you're sure you want to delete these individuals from your Family File.

3. Click on the Yes button. The individuals are deleted from the Family File.

Checking the Family File for Errors

Family Tree Maker provides three types of error-checking options. One runs automatically as you are entering the data, another runs when you request its services, and a third prints out a report of possible data errors to check manually. Of course, the program does not know whether you have the correct Mary Smith married to your ancestor, or where she was born or how she spells her name. But it can identify certain kinds of conflicting data. The three techniques are as follows:

* **Data Entry Checking.** This helps you catch such errors as inconsistencies in birth and death dates while you are entering data, as well as name errors such as too many or too few capital letters.

* **Find Error Command.** This searches a Family File for possible errors and fixes them on the spot when it finds them. It is similar to a spell checker, but it also finds date errors such as someone's death date being before the birth date.

* **Data Errors Report.** This valuable option prints out a report of possible errors in your file. Use it to go through your Family File and manually fix the mistakes. It takes time to do this, but it is the most thorough method.

USING DATA ENTRY CHECKING

The Data Entry Checking feature is one you should keep turned on, because it detects certain errors as you enter the information. It prompts you to take a closer look at the things you type (probably where most mistakes are made), and gives you an opportunity to fix them, if necessary.

There are certain kinds of errors, such as entering titles in a name, that Family Tree Maker always prompts you to fix, regardless of whether the Data Entry Checking feature is turned on or off. To turn on the error checking options:

1. From the File menu, choose Preferences and then choose Error Checking. The Error Checking dialog box appears (see Figure 9-14).

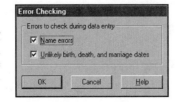

Figure 9-14

Select the type of errors you want Family Tree Maker to catch.

2. Select one or both options. Checking both Name Errors and Unlikely Birth, Death, and Marriage dates is a wise choice. Click on OK.

With the Data Entry Checking feature turned on, Family Tree maker will catch a typing error such as a 1960 birth date, instead of 1860, for Josephine Sarah Marcus, who died in 1944 (see Figure 9-15). Notice that the Data Entry Error dialog box contains an Ignore Error check box so you can keep the entry that is suggested to be in error. In this case, the AutoFix button is not available because Family Tree Maker doesn't know how to fix the error. You need to type in the correct dates, or choose Ignore Error for now and fix the error when you know the correct date.

USING THE FIND ERROR COMMAND

The Find Error command is another option you can use to double-check your work. It is similar to a spell check, but it also identifies possible date errors and other items. To check a Family File using the Find Error command, go to the Family Page view.

1. From the Edit menu, choose Find Error. The Find Error dialog box appears.

2. Select the check boxes for the types of errors you wish to locate:

   ❋ Name Errors

   ❋ Unlikely Birth, Death, and Marriage Dates

Figure 9-15

The Data Entry Checking feature alerts you to possible errors while you enter data.

3. Click on OK. Family Tree Maker searches for errors and displays a Find Error dialog box when it finds one.

4. In the Find Error dialog box, you can do any of the following to respond to the error message:

   ✸ Fix the error manually in the fields in the dialog box.

   ✸ Fix it automatically by clicking on the AutoFix button.

   ✸ Skip it by selecting the Ignore Error check box.

5. Click on the Find Next button to move to the next error. Family Tree Maker displays a message box when it finishes checking the Family File for errors. If you want to quit checking for errors before Family Tree Maker is finished, click on the Close button. Click on Yes when asked if you are sure.

6. Click on OK.

Family Tree Maker can find errors and possible errors with names and dates. If you mistakenly put a title such as Dr. or Rev. in the Name field, it will also show up as an error (see Figure 9-16). In this case, you would click on the AutoFix button, which deletes the "Rev." from the Name text box and places it in the Title text box. Then you can click on the Find Next button to locate the next error.

Creating a Data Errors Report

The Data Errors report is a thorough and efficient way to double-check your Family File. It lists all the potential errors Family Tree Maker can identify, allowing you to sit down at your leisure and figure out what's OK and what needs fixing. You can generate a copy whenever you wish from the Report window. To run a Data Errors report:

Figure 9-16

The Find Error Command checks for errors throughout the Family File.

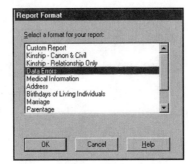

Figure 9-17

Choose a Data
Errors Report

1. Open the Family File and click on the Report button on the toolbar, or from the View menu, choose Report. The Report window appears.

2. From the Format menu, choose Report Format. The Report Format dialog box appears (see Figure 9-17).

3. Select Data Errors in the list box and then click on OK. The Potential Data Errors report appears (see Figure 9-18).

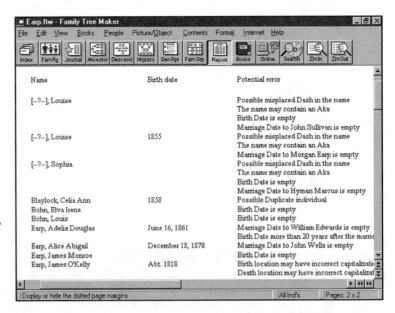

Figure 9-18

The Data Errors Report
helps you locate and
fix possible errors in
your Family File.

❀ **TIP** ❀   *Before sharing your information with others, check out all potential data errors in your files.*

4. Select an individual on the list and note the error in the Potential Error column.

5. Double-click on the highlighted line. The Family Page for the individual appears.

6. Correct the error and then click on the Report button on the toolbar to return to the Potential Data Errors report. You'll see an updated report that reflects corrections you have made.

You may want to print the report so you can refer to it as you check through the Family File for the errors that are listed on the report. Display the report and then from the File menu, choose Print Data Errors Report. In the Print Data Errors Report dialog box, click on OK. (You may need to change Setup options such as orientation to print a more readable report.)

Classes of Errors

Family Tree Maker finds errors involving names and dates, and also some other potential problems. This section gives examples of the items you may see on a Data Errors report. Name errors that may be included are as follows:

❀ Possible misplaced dash in the name.

❀ There may be a title in the name field.

❀ The name may contain an illegal character.

❀ Possibly used married instead of maiden name.

❀ The name may have too many or too few capital letters.

❀ The name may contain a nickname.

As noted earlier, you should always record women by their maiden names. When cousins with the same surname marry, however, it looks exactly like an error.

Family Tree Maker will flag an entry whenever both the husband and the wife have the same surname and let you figure out whether or not it's OK.

If you type an individual's nickname in the Name field instead of using the aka field in the Lineage dialog box, you'll get the nickname error message.

Date errors you might come across include:

* Born when parent was under 13.

* Individual's birth date is after the mother's death date.

* Individual's birth date occurred too long after father's death date.

* Death date is before birth date.

* Individual's marriage occurred before age 13.

* Event date is empty.

* Death date is more than 120 years after birth date.

* Individual's birth date is more than 20 years after the marriage date of parents.

* Individual's birth date is before marriage date of parents.

* Not in birth order in the children list.

* Mother is older than 50 at the time of child's birth.

The Other Errors class is a catch-all category, including:

* **No parents, no children, and no spouses.** You'll get this message when you have inadvertently unlinked someone when you were trying to fix a relationship mistake or have omitted the persons to whom this individual is related.

* **Is this \<name\> the same as \<name\>?** This happens when Family Tree Maker finds two people of the same sex with identical names and birth dates. You need to make sure that they are distinct individuals.

✽ **<Fieldname> may have incorrect capitalization.** This happens when you type information in all caps.

Fixing Relationships

Genealogy is filled with complicated relationships, and if you throw in a few typographical errors or sleepy-eyed misreadings of your data, your Family Files may turn up some really strange combinations. Family Tree Maker provides options that allow you to fix incorrect relationships. These include, in addition to detaching incorrect spouses as you learned earlier, techniques that let you:

    ✽ Detach a child from the wrong parents

    ✽ Link children to their parents

    ✽ Link individuals by marriage

DETACHING A CHILD FROM THE WRONG PARENTS

If you have a child in a Family File that appears with the incorrect parents, use the Detach Child command to separate them. To detach a child:

1. Display the Family Page containing the set of parents and the child that you want to detach from each other. The child must appear in the Children list.

2. Place the cursor on the child you want to detach.

3. From the People menu, choose Fix Relationship Mistakes, and then choose Detach Child.

4. If the child has siblings, you will be asked whether you want to detach the siblings as well. Choose Yes to detach all of the siblings; choose No to detach only the individual. A message box appears, asking if you are sure you want to detach this child from these parents.

5. Click on the Yes button. A message box informs you that the detach is complete.

6. Click on OK.

If you want to move (reattach) this child somewhere else in the tree, follow the instructions in the next section, "Linking Children to Their Parents."

LINKING CHILDREN TO THEIR PARENTS

If an individual and his or her parents are in your Family File, but the individual does not appear on the parents' Family Page, you can use the Attach Child command to fix this problem. To attach a child to his or her parents:

1. Display the Family Page where you want the individual to appear as a child. This is the page that shows the person's parents as spouses.

2. From the People menu, choose Fix Relationship Mistakes, and then choose Attach Child. The Select the Child dialog box appears.

3. Select the child from the list and click on OK. A message box appears, asking if you want to attach this individual as a child on this Family Page.

4. Click on the Yes button. A message box informs you that the attach is complete.

5. Click on OK.

If the child has siblings, Family Tree Maker asks whether you want to associate those siblings with the new set of parents. If you choose Yes, then Family Tree Maker will attach any siblings that have the same preferred parents.

If the child already has another set of parents, Family Tree Maker displays the Set Relationship dialog box. Click on the drop-down list next to each parent's name and select the word that describes the relationship between the parent and child. Click on OK after you make the selection.

LINKING INDIVIDUALS BY MARRIAGE

You might run into a situation where both members of a married couple are in your Family File but they are not listed on a Family Page as husband and wife. To correct this problem, use the Attach Spouse command to join them.

☙ **NOTE** ☙   *Before you can attach a spouse, there must be an opening for him or her on the Family Page. If two spouses already appear on the Family Page, you will have to create a place for the new one by clicking on the Spouses button for the appropriate individual, and then clicking on the <u>C</u>reate A New Spouse button in the Spouses dialog box.*

1. To attach two individuals as spouses, display the Family Page where one of them appears in either the Wife or Husband field.

2. From the <u>P</u>eople menu, choose <u>F</u>ix Relationship Mistakes and then choose Attach Spouse. The Select the Spouse dialog box appears.

3. Select the name of the individual you want to attach as a spouse and click on OK. A message box appears, asking if you want to attach this individual as a spouse.

4. Click on the <u>Y</u>es button. A message box informs you that the attach is complete.

5. Click on OK.

Fixing Duplicates

Another error that occurs is the duplication of individuals in a Family File. This can happen when you combine files, append a World Family Tree pedigree to your Family File, or simply enter the same person's data twice by accident.

Genealogical databases have a way of growing rapidly. Your cousins will send GEDCOMs or files with information about their lines, and you will then want to include that information. You also may wind up with several files that you decide to mesh together to create one large Family File. If those files contain overlapping information, Family Tree Maker will automatically combine exact duplicates and then let you compare possible duplicates so you can decide whether they should be combined or not. Unfortunately, no matter how careful you are when merging files, you may accidentally combine two individuals who are not the same person. This is a nuisance but not a disaster—assuming you spot the problem before you close the program. Check your work carefully!

🌿 **NOTE** 🌿   *If you close the program, you'll have to delete the combined "individual" and reenter everything for both parties. Once you quit Family Tree Maker, you can not reverse a merge. If you do quit before reversing a merge, you will either have to reenter the information or use a backup file, if you made one.*

FIXING DUPLICATE FILES ON SAME PERSON

Use the Merge Duplicate Individuals command to help you find duplication in your Family File. Family Tree Maker will give you a report of potential duplicates, so you can merge those individuals that are really duplicates. To merge duplicate individuals:

1. Display any Family Page of the Family File for which you want to merge duplicates.

2. From the People menu, choose Merge Duplicate Individuals. A caution box appears, recommending that you back up your file.

3. Click on OK. The Merge Duplicate Individuals dialog box appears, showing you the file name and number of individuals in the file (see Figure 9-19).

    🌿 **NOTE** 🌿   *If Family Tree Maker cannot find any duplicate individuals, a message box will appear stating that none were found in the files.*

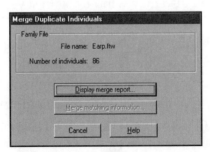

Figure 9-19

The Merge Duplicate Individuals dialog box gives you the Display Merge Report option.

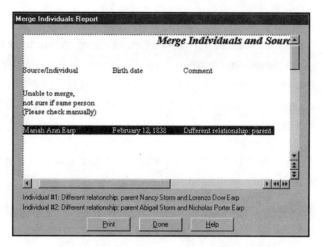

Figure 9-20

A Merge Individuals Report in the Earp Family File reveals that there are different relationships for Mariah Ann Earp—a possible indicator that there are two different individuals by the same name.

4. Click on the <u>D</u>isplay Merge Report button. The Merge Individuals Report dialog box appears, showing individuals in your Family File who are exact or possible matches with others (see Figure 9-20). Read this report carefully.

5. Select entries in the list to view data differences between individuals. You can click on the <u>P</u>rint button to print a copy.

6. Click on the <u>D</u>one button when you finish viewing the merge report. You return to the Merge Duplicate Individuals dialog box.

7. Click on the <u>M</u>erge Matching Individuals button.

❦ **NOTE** ❦   *Family Tree Maker merges two people with no differences automatically, and it gives you the option to merge two people with a possible discrepancy between them.*

❦ **CAUTION** ❦   *When you finish merging, print out some trees and reports to be sure that you didn't make any errors in the process of merging individuals. If you did, you can reverse the merge option by going to the <u>E</u>dit menu and choosing <u>U</u>ndo. You must do this before you exit from Family Tree Maker—you cannot reverse a merge after you have quit the program.*

MERGING SPECIFIC INDIVIDUALS

There may be identical individuals in your Family File that Family Tree Maker does not recognize as duplicates—usually because you have not entered enough information about one of them for the program to ascertain they are the same person. In those instances where you know that two individuals are the same, use the Merge Specific Individuals command.

1. Display the Family Page and put the cursor in the individual's name, birth, or death date field.

2. From the People menu, choose Merge Specific Individuals. The Select the Individual Who Is the Same As dialog box appears (see Figure 9-21).

3. Select the name of the person you wish to merge with the individual already displayed on the Family Page.

4. Click on OK. Family Tree Maker will display message boxes asking you questions about the individuals you are about to merge. Answer Yes or No depending on the situation. The Merge Individuals dialog box appears.

    ⚜ **CAUTION** ⚜   *Check and recheck before merging. Fixing mistakes in your Family File takes some time, but it is something you should do periodically—errors are easy to make and only compound themselves if they are not caught and corrected.*

5. Click on the Merge button.

6. Other dialog boxes may appear—the Set Relationship dialog box, for example. Supply the information requested as best you can, and click on OK. The Family Page will show the merged information.

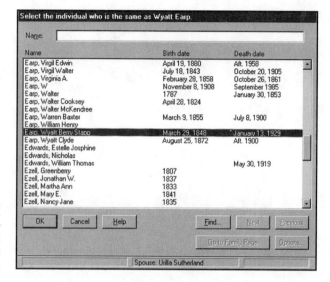

Figure 9-21

Compare details about
the individuals before
clicking on OK.

The following text appears within the photographed book pages:

Ancestors of George Howard Lafferty

- Samuel Lafferty
  1801 - 1873
- Edwin E. Lafferty
  1834 - 1907
- Margaret McDowell
  1803 - 1861
- George E. Lafferty
  1867 - 1936
- Erastus Fowler
  1793 - 1875
- Celia Fowler
  1914
- Temperence Merrill
  1796 - 1871
- Nathan Wescott
  1818 - 1900
- Hiram Wescott
  1820 - 1901
- Sarah Ann McMichael
  1820 - 1901
- Samuel C. Amsden
  1822 - 1899
- Theresa Jerusa Amsden
  1843 - 1934
- Clarissa Hubbard
  1820 - 1870

The History of George Howard Lafferty

George Howard Lafferty was born September 2, 1894 in Lenox township, Ashtabula County, Ohio, to Amber Amelia Wescott Lafferty and George Edwin Lafferty. A sister, Maud Irene, was born May 23, 1892.

A family of farmers, the Laffertys harvested the land where they lived. On May 9, 1919, they moved to Warren, Ohio, to a house on Forest Street NE. They lived next door to their daughter Maud, her husband Jay Rood Webster, and their three beautiful daughters, Reta, Shirley, and Marion.

As a youth, Lafferty went by "Howard" rather than "George" and signed his name as G. Howard Lafferty. After graduating from Lenox Township schools in 1911, he received a Teachers Certificate and became an educator and later a high school Principal. He then switched careers and ventured into banking just before World War I.

As a student at Ohio State University during the war, Howard Lafferty hoped to join the army but was classified 5G due to his glasses and other restrictions. In 1923 he received an L.L.B. degree and passed

---

CHAPTER TEN

Visualizing Your Family Tree

amily Tree Maker creates charts—called *trees*—that give you a visual display of your genealogical data. Most nongenealogists have a difficult time understanding how a person living now connects to someone who lived hundreds of years ago, but such relationships are easy to see on a well-designed tree like the ones Family Tree Maker produces. Family Tree Maker also creates several reports (another way of arranging or formatting data) that are essential to genealogical study.

Viewing Trees

The various trees display different kinds of relationships in graphic formats that make them easy to follow. You can pick any individual and trace his or her ancestors as far back as your Family File goes—and his or her descendants forward to the present day as well, if you wish. Or you can concentrate on descendants in either a graphic or a text-based tree. The upcoming sections give you a taste of each of the options.

Family tree charts have been around a long time, as people have probably always wanted to see how they are connected to others. On the other hand, noble and royal inheritance and power no doubt played a large role in making genealogical charts popular. For example, to make any sense out of English monarchy, which for the most part was a hereditary monarchy in the male line since the 13th century, one needs a large chart to follow all its branches.

Beautiful trees appear in Family Bibles—often printed in color, which was an expensive project years ago. Typically a Bible was given to a young couple as they began their lives together. Many old Bibles have survived, dutifully filled in with the names of the parents and their children, along with birth, marriage, and death dates.

Today, with a computer, a color printer, and Family Tree Maker, you can create your family's trees and charts in a variety of traditional and popular formats.

> ❄ **TIP** ❄   *You can jump to the Family Page of an individual from any of the trees by double-clicking on the name.*

Displaying Ancestor Trees

An Ancestor Tree (also known as a *Pedigree Chart*) shows an individual's direct ancestors: parents, grandparents, great-grandparents, and so on. It does not show your other relatives such as aunts, uncles, and cousins. Those are *collaterals*. Collateral blood relatives are neither descendants nor ancestors in the strictest sense of the word. *Collateral kindred* is the term used to designate brothers, sisters, uncles, aunts, nieces, nephews, and cousins. Collaterals descend from a common antecedent (progenitor; forefather or mother) but can neither ascend to nor descend from other collateral relatives. To display an Ancestor Tree:

1. Select the primary individual whose ancestors you wish to see by highlighting his or her name on a Family Page or in another view. Only the primary individual's *ancestors* will be shown—not the siblings or children.

2. Click on the Ancestor button on the toolbar, or from the <u>V</u>iew menu, choose <u>A</u>ncestor Tree. Using either the button or the menu takes you to a submenu.

3. From the submenu, select either <u>F</u>an or <u>S</u>tandard (see Figure 10-1). The Ancestor Tree appears in the format you choose. (I'll describe the advantages of each.)

FAN FORMAT

The fan format of the Ancestor Tree shows the selected primary individual and his or her ancestors in an attractive design (see Figure 10-2). The fan format is easier to read than the standard (box-style) format once you have several generations of ancestors entered in your database. The fan-format printout of

Figure 10-1

Clicking on the Ancestor button offers the choice of seeing the tree in either Fan or Standard format.

an Ancestor Tree displays ancestors in an expanding circle around the primary person. Each branch of the family tree extends from the center in a pattern similar to the spokes of a bicycle wheel.

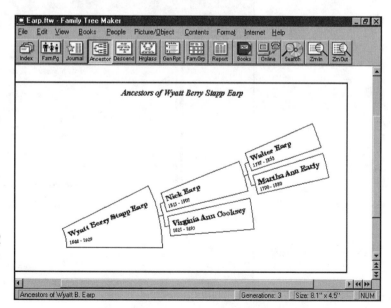

Figure 10-2

Ancestors of Wyatt B. Earp shown in the fan tree format.

❀ **TIP** ❀   *Zoom the tree display in or out by using the Zm In and Zm Out buttons on the toolbar.*

The Fan Tree can be fully customized with various fonts, borders, and colors. You will want to experiment with the many options available. (You can include everything in a Fan Tree that you can include in a Standard Tree, with the exception of images.) A colorful Fan Tree is bound to be a big hit at your next family reunion. Table 10-1 shows the changes you can make to the Ancestor Fan Tree.

❀ **TIP** ❀   *All the features described in Table 10-1 are also available on a shortcut menu. Right-click on any part of a tree view window to display the shortcut menu for that tree and view.*

STANDARD FORMAT

An Ancestor Tree in the standard format offers an attractive display with various choices of fonts, boxes, borders, and colors. You can quickly switch to the standard format by clicking on the Ancestor button and choosing Standard. Figure 10-3 shows an Ancestor Tree of Wyatt Earp in the standard format.

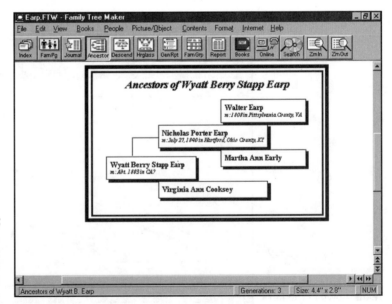

Figure 10-3

Ancestors of Wyatt Earp are shown in the standard format of an Ancestor Tree.

Table 10-1 Formatting the Ancestor Fan Tree

To Use This Feature	Choose This Menu and Option
Change the tree format	Format, Fan Tree Format. Choose Fit to page or Custom.
Change the shape	Format, Fan Tree Format, Shape. Choose one of three shapes.
Change the density	Format, Fan Tree Format, Density. Choose Generous, Condensed, or Squished.
Change width; rotate or flip	Format, Fan Tree Format. Choose any or all three check boxes: Make all boxes the same width, Rotate tree to center, Flip text.
Set a maximum width for each box	Format, Maximum Width for each Box. Set the spin box to a width in inches.
Change box styles	Format, Box, Line, & Border Styles, Boxes. In the Items to format list box, you can choose Females, Males, or Unknown gender and then set a separate Box style, Outline, Fill, and Shadow color for each, if you want. Instead of setting colors for the boxes, you can select the Color By Generation check box to have Family Tree Maker make each generation of the family show up in a different color.
Change border styles	Format, Box, Line, & Border Styles, Borders. Choose a Border style, then change the Border color and Background color.
Change line styles	Format, Box, Line, & Border Styles, Lines. Choose one of three Line style thickness options for the lines around and connecting boxes. Choose a Line color for the lines connecting boxes.
Change the text font, style, and size	Format, Text Font, Style, & Size. In the Items to format list box, choose the item whose text you want to change, and then choose a Font, Size, Style, and Color. You can also choose Underline and see any of these effects in a Sample box before applying them.
Change the items to include in boxes	Contents, Items To Include In Each Box. Choose from many Available items and move them up or down in the order they should appear.
Change the title and footnote	Contents, Title & Footnote. Choose the Automatic title or a Custom title that you type in. Optionally, add a footnote and choose whether you want a box around it.
Change the number of generations	Contents, # Of Generations To Show. In the spin box, choose how many generations the tree will include.

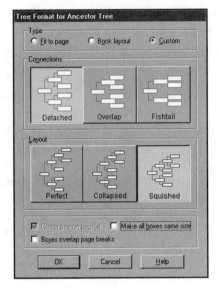

Figure 10-4

Choose from several
Connection and
Layout options for the
standard format of
the Ancestor Tree.

The standard Ancestor Tree has many of the same formatting options on the Format and Contents menus that the fan format offers. To reach them, display a standard Ancestor Tree and then, from the Format menu, choose Tree Format to display the Tree Format for Ancestor Tree dialog box (see Figure 10-4).

If you choose the Custom option button, you will have access to the three Layout options. Try different combinations of these options and click on OK to find out what you think looks best for the Ancestor Tree you are working with. Refer to Table 10-1 to discover other features, which are available for most of the tree types.

Displaying Hourglass Trees

Another tree view is the Hourglass Tree—named because it spreads out from a central individual to show both ancestors and descendants, and winds up looking a lot like an hourglass if you've got similar numbers of generations on both sides. Display the Hourglass Tree by clicking on the Hrglass button on the toolbar, or from the View menu, choose Hourglass Tree and then the format. The Hourglass Tree is available in either Fan (see Figure 10-5) or Standard (see Figure 10-6) format.

Creating Empty Branches

Sometimes you may wish to create blank boxes to help you see where missing names need to be filled in. Often for family reunions people will print family trees with empty branches and hang them on a wall so that others can help fill in the blanks.

To make this work well, you need to change the format of the items in the boxes. By default, if no information exists for an individual for a particular item included in the tree, the label for that item is not included. You'll want to include labels for specific fields so that others can view, and have the opportunity to fill in, the empty spaces.

To add empty branches to standard Ancestor Trees or to the ancestor part of standard Hourglass Trees, choose Options from the Contents menu. Choose Items to Include and highlight items from the right-hand column. Select the Include Empty Branches check box and then click on OK.

Figure 10-5

Displaying an Hourglass Tree in fan format is an attractive way to show both your ancestors and descendants.

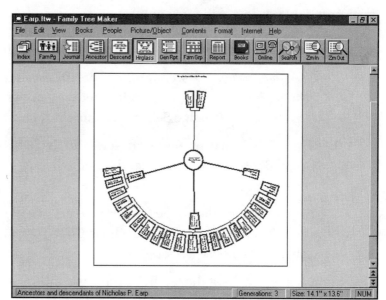

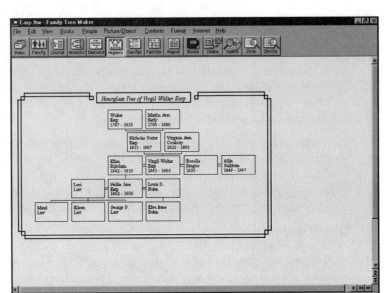

Figure 10-6

The Hourglass Tree in standard format. It can be customized to your specifications.

For either the standard or fan format of the Hourglass Tree, many of the same format and content options are available as for the Ancestor Tree, described in Table 10-1. A difference is that you can choose which individuals to include (for the descendant portion of the tree only).

1. From the Contents menu, choose Individuals To Include.

2. Choose either All Descendants or Direct Descendants Only from the primary individual to a secondary individual (whom you select by clicking on the Change Secondary Individual button).

3. Optionally, you can select or deselect the Include Siblings Of Direct Descendants check box, depending on whether you want to show these siblings.

    You can change the shapes of the two sections in relation to each other. From the Format menu, choose Tree Format, and then on the General tab choose a Shape (see Figure 10-7).

Also on this General tab (of the fan tree), there is a Fit To Page option that gives you a one-page tree. If you choose this option, Family Tree Maker will do whatever is needed to the tree's layout, font sizes, number of generations, and amount

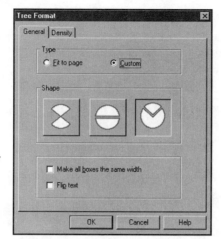

Figure 10-7

You can choose one of three different shapes for the Hourglass Fan Tree.

of information that appears in the boxes to make it fit on one page. The standard format for the Hourglass Tree also offers the Book Layout option, which gives you a tree divided into pages with cross-references to the previous and next page. When you're working on a Family Book (described in Chapter Thirteen), you will want to choose this option.

The Hourglass Tree options allow you to select separate densities—to compact or spread out the boxes—for the ancestor and descendant sections. You can experiment with these options to see which shape looks best for the number of people you are displaying in each section.

To change the density in the fan format of the Hourglass Tree, follow these steps:

1. From the Format menu, choose Tree Format. The Tree Format dialog box appears.

2. Choose the Density tab (see Figure 10-8).

3. In the Ancestor section, select one of the three buttons: Generous, Condensed, or Squished.

4. In the Descendant section, select one of the three buttons—the same choices as in Step 3.

5. Click on OK.

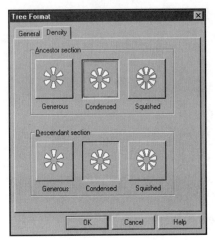

Figure 10-8

Density options for
both ancestors and
descendants can be
chosen for the
Hourglass Fan Tree.

❧ **NOTE** ❧   *You can print any of the trees. From the File menu, choose Print Tree to display the Print dialog box. Or you can right-click on the tree and choose Print Tree from the shortcut menu. In the Print dialog box, be sure to click on the Setup button to select the correct printer, orientation, and other settings to accommodate the printing of the tree. See the section later in this chapter on "Printing Reports and Trees."*

Displaying Descendant Trees

Descendant Trees show a person's children, grandchildren, great-grandchildren, and so on. The primary individual appears at the top and the descendants fill the branches below that person. The Descendant Tree is a popular one that's widely used. You often see it used in historical novels, showing various family connections back to a particular progenitor. I once found a descendant tree sketched by a judge in a probate case. Evidently he needed some graphic help to untangle my ancestors, too.

To display a Descendant Tree and choose its layout:

1.   Select the primary individual by highlighting his or her name on a Family Page or in another view.

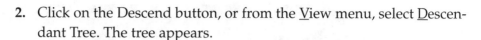
2. Click on the Descend button, or from the <u>V</u>iew menu, select <u>D</u>escendant Tree. The tree appears.

3. From the Forma<u>t</u> menu, choose Tree <u>F</u>ormat (or Fan Tree <u>F</u>ormat). The Tree Format For Descendant Tree dialog box appears. (Or if you are using the fan format, the Format For Fan Tree dialog box appears.)

4. Choose one of the Type option buttons—either B<u>o</u>ok layout or <u>C</u>ustom layout. If you choose <u>C</u>ustom, then click on the <u>L</u>ayout button for the preferred style.

    For the fan format, you can choose the <u>F</u>it To Page option and the same Shape and Density settings and other format settings as the Ancestor Tree uses (refer to Table 10-1).

    ❀ **NOTE** ❀   *Book layout is not available for fan format trees.*

5. Select the Center <u>T</u>ree On The Page(s) check box or the Make All Bo<u>x</u>es Same Size check box if you want these options—you can use either or both.

6. Click on OK. The Descendant Tree appears (see Figure 10-9).

    ❀ **TIP** ❀   *A tip worth repeating: All the options available for the tree you are viewing onscreen can be accessed by right-clicking on the tree (or surrounding area) and choosing from the shortcut menu.*

Displaying Outline Descendant Trees

The Outline Descendant Tree—long a popular style for showing the descendancy from a particular ancestor—is a text version of a Descendant Tree. You get the same type of information that you find in a Descendant Tree, but instead of allocating a box for each individual, the Outline Descendant Tree arranges individuals in an outline format. Each person's information appears on a separate line, with each generation indented slightly more than the one before it. Spouses—identified by a plus sign (+)—show up on the line following the descendant they married. Several generations fit on a single page, which probably accounts

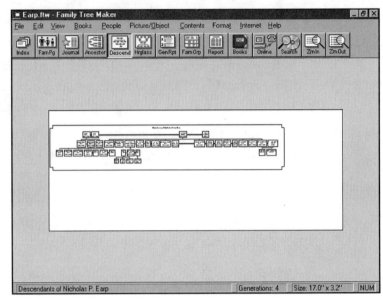

Figure 10-9

The Descendant Tree shows an individual's children, grandchildren, and so on.

for the format's long-time popularity among genealogists. Figure 10-10 is an Outline Descendant Tree of Nicholas Porter Earp, the father of Wyatt Earp. Nicholas is shown as No. 1 and then his first wife and the children and grandchildren (and their spouses) are given. The numbers in front of the names refer to the number of generations.

To display an Outline Descendant Tree and choose its format:

1. Select the primary individual by highlighting his or her name on a Family Page or in another view.

2. From the View menu, choose Outline Descendant Tree. The tree appears.

3. From the Format menu, choose Tree Format. The Tree Format for Outline Descendant Tree dialog box appears.

4. Select the Indentation options you prefer:

   The default is leader dots (. . .) extending from the left margin of the page to each individual's name, in the Indent With Which

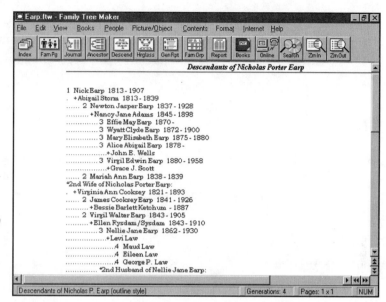

Figure 10-10

Descendants of
Nicholas Porter Earp
shown on an Outline
Descendant Tree.

Character text box. However, you can select some other character if you wish. You can also increase or decrease the size of each generation's indentation by clicking on the up or down arrow in the Indent Each Generation By (In Inches) spin box. Selecting a large number will create a wider tree, a small number creates a narrower one.

5. If you want to use generation numbers, then select the Place A Generation Number Before Each Descendant's Name check box. If you select this check box, then enter a number in the Starting Generation Number spin box.

❧ **NOTE** ❧ *It is usually a good idea to use generation numbers, especially if you have a large tree. Normally 1 is the first generation, but you can enter any number up to 9999 in this field.*

6. Select the Size & Spacing options. These options include the Maximum Height (In Rows) For Each Individual spin box, the Number

Of Blank Lines Between Individuals spin box, and the Always One Page Wide check box. The latter option makes Family Tree Maker reduce the size of the text as much as necessary to fit it on one page.

7. Click on OK.

Using Reports

Reports is a catch-all term for all sorts of lists that you can use as research tools to help you study trends or patterns within your family. Here are the reports available to you with Family Tree Maker:

- 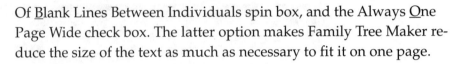 Custom
- Kinship
- Data Errors
- Medical Information
- Address
- Birthdays of Living Individuals
- Marriage
- Parentage
- Documented Events
- Bibliography
- Alternate Facts

To run any of these reports:

1. Open the Family File.

2. Display the Report view by clicking on the Report button, or from the View menu, choose Reports.

3. From the Forma**t** menu, choose Report **F**ormat. The reports are listed in the Report Format dialog box (see Figure 10-11).

4. Select one and then click on OK.

⚜ **NOTE** ⚜   *For some reports, such as the Kinship report, you must select the primary individual before you display the report.*

⚜ **TIP** ⚜   *You don't have to print the reports just as Family Tree Maker presents them. You can export any of them to a word processor or spreadsheet program in a text format.*

To export a report:

1. Create the report.

2. From the **E**dit menu, choose **C**opy Report. Family Tree Maker will copy the report to the Windows Clipboard.

3. Open any word processor or spreadsheet that supports this Windows feature—say, Microsoft Word or Excel—and paste the report into it by opening the other program's **E**dit menu and choosing **P**aste. Once you have exported the data into the other program, you can edit, sort, and print it however you wish.

Figure 10-11

The Report Format dialog box lets you select many Family Tree Maker reports.

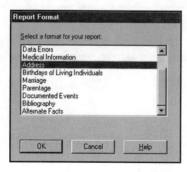

Creating a Custom Report

With Family Tree Maker's standard reports, the program chooses most of the contents for you and allows you to change some of the formatting. While standard reports are handy, you may find a need for a Custom report, which gives you more flexibility in the contents you want to show—you can choose the data fields, formatting, and whom to include on the report. You begin a Custom report the same way as any of the standard reports:

1. Open a Family File.

2. Display the Report Format dialog box (by clicking on the Report button and then choosing Format, Report Format).

3. Select Custom Report and then click on OK. A plain report appears, with an equally plain title: Report (see Figure 10-12).

Now the fun begins—choosing what to add or change on the report. The items you need are accessible on the Contents and Format menus. You should investigate each of the options. The same options are available on the shortcut menu.

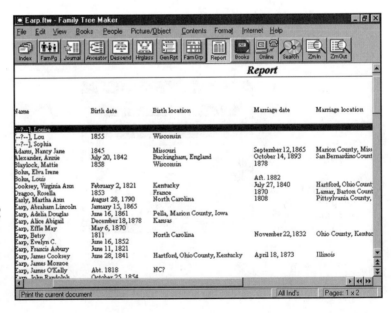

Figure 10-12

Right-click on the plain report to find almost all the custom reporting options on the shortcut menu.

Right-click on the report and you will see the list of reporting features. Each of these menu selections takes you to a dialog box to choose individual options. Table 10-2 shows some of the options available when you access the menu items.

Custom reports can contain up to 100 columns, but you would probably run more than one report instead of trying to put all the fields into a single report. It's important to keep the report readable.

> ❀ **TIP** ❀ *Anything you create in Family Tree Maker (including a custom report) can be saved from the Books menu. This lets you set up templates so that the formatting can be used over and over again. This is very useful for trees, where you can change the primary individual as necessary.*

Table 10-2 Custom Reporting Features

Use This Shortcut Menu Item	To Choose These Options
Items To Include In Report	Each field item to include on the report, and the order in which you want them listed.
Individuals To Include In Report	All individuals or selected individuals, which can include ancestors or descendents, or both.
Title & Footnote	Title, page numbers, and footnote text.
Maximum Width For Each Column	Column widths and spacing, either automatic or manual.
Sort Report	Sort by up to two items: Name, Birth date, or Death date, in ascending or descending order.
Border Styles	Border style, color, and thickness, and also background color.
Text Font, Style, & Size	Font, size, style, color, and underline for selected items: body and endnote text, title, footnote, and page numbers.

Creating Kinship Reports

Kinship reports often come in handy, especially when you are trying to figure out how one individual in your family tree is related either to you to or someone else in your file. Family Tree Maker actually has two kinship reports. One is called the Kinship: Canon & Civil and the other is Kinship: Relationship Only. The latter report lists each individual's name, birth date, and relationship to the primary individual. The Kinship: Canon & Civil report lists the names, relationships, and relationship degrees of the primary individual's blood relatives and their spouses, plus the blood relatives of the primary individual's spouse or spouses (see Figure 10-13).

Degree of a relationship is a legal term, not an exact relationship, and refers to the number of steps (distance) between two individuals who are related by blood. The word "degree" merely indicates that there is a varying distance between relatives. In civil law the degree represents the total number of steps through the bloodline that separates two individuals. Canon law refers to ecclesiastical law or statutes that date back to the 12th, 13th, and 14th centuries. Canon law was observed by most states in establishing rules about who could not marry based on the degree of descent from a common ancestor.

Figure 10-13

The Kinship: Canon and Civil report shows both kinds of relationships to Nicholas Earp, the primary individual. Civil degrees are given in Roman numerals.

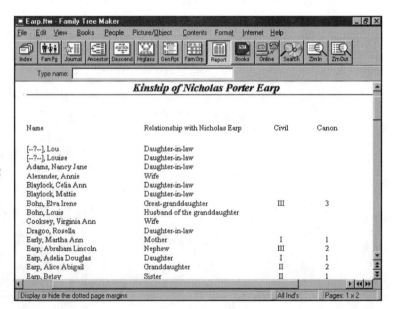

Creating More Reports

Depending on the project you're working on, you will find uses for several other reports listed in the Report Format dialog box:

- ❈ Medical Information
- ❈ Address
- ❈ Birthdays of Living Individuals
- ❈ Marriage
- ❈ Parentage

> ❧ **NOTE** ❧ *Another report in the Report Format dialog box is the Data Errors report, which you learned about in Chapter Nine. Family Tree Maker can also create Genealogy, Bibliography, Documented Events, and Alternate Facts reports—these are covered in depth in Chapter Twelve.*

MARRIAGE REPORT

The Marriage report automatically includes everyone in your Family File, but you can use the Format menu to customize the column width, sorting order, border, and text styles. Arranged by name of the husband, it has an entry for each of his spouses. You can sort by surnames and marriage dates, or choose not to sort. This report can be convenient to print out as a worksheet where you can see if you have entered all the data you have about a particular individual or gotten all the dates correct. It also lets you see if you entered the names of all the spouses of a particular line—it is easy to overlook someone when you are entering data from Family Group Sheets, and it helps to get another view of the resulting file. (See Figure 10-14 for a sample.)

ADDRESS AND BIRTHDAY REPORTS

Other reports you will find handy are the Address and Birthdays of Living Individuals reports. The Address report gives you a simple alphabetical listing of the addresses for people in your file. You can use the Birthdays report to compile a list of the birthdays of your family members—which eliminates paging through a calendar. Left to itself, Family Tree Maker puts everyone in your Family File on

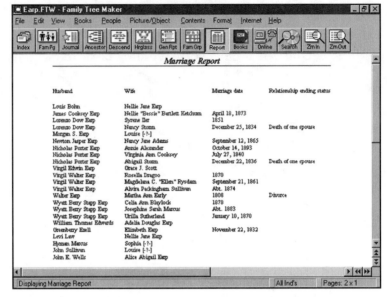

Figure 10-14

The Marriage report is arranged by the name of the husband, with a separate line for each spouse.

this report, as long as they do not have a death date and would be up to 120 years old. However, you can determine the specific individuals to include and customize the report's format.

PARENTAGE REPORT

The Parentage report deals with a family unit, much as the Marriage report does, only from the child's perspective (see Figure 10-15). It is arranged by the child's name, gives the names of the mother and father and their relationship to the child. Information pertaining to relationships can be created in the Lineage window (select the More button next to an individual's name, and then select the Lineage button on the vertical toolbar). The following relationships can be entered:

- Natural
- Adopted
- Foster
- Unknown
- Step

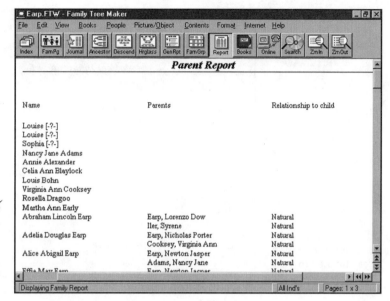

Figure 10-15

The Parentage report shows various relationships, such as adopted, foster, and step connections.

❧ Family member

❧ Private

MEDICAL INFORMATION REPORT

A Medical Information report (see Figure 10-16) can be used to track hereditary health conditions such as diabetes, cancer, or vision problems. This information comes from any notes you have entered in the Medical window. To collect information pertaining to cause of death or diseases suffered, check out death certificates, obituaries, U.S. Mortality schedules, military pension applications, and other family records. You can select the individuals you wish to include in the report.

> ❧ **NOTE** ❧ *You can reach the Medical window by clicking on the More button next to an individual's name in the Family File and then clicking on the Medical button on the vertical toolbar.*

To run a Medical Information report:

1. Click on the Report button.

2. From the Forma*t* menu, choose Report *F*ormat.

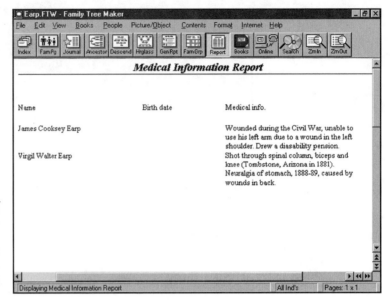

Figure 10-16

The Medical
Information report
can be used to track
hereditary health
problems.

3. In the Report Format dialog box, select Medical Information and then click on OK.

4. To select the individuals you'd like to include in the report, go to the Contents menu and choose Individuals To Include. Of course, only those about whom you have entered medical notes will appear in the actual report.

❋ **TIP** ❋ *You can also personalize this report with a title and footnote: from the Contents menu, choose Title & Footnote. You can further customize the column width and spacing, sorting order, and border and text styles.*

Using the Research Journal

The Research Journal allows you to create a personal To Do list and create a FamilyFinder report. As you enter data or study reports about the information you have compiled on your ancestors, you will often discover that you have overlooked a source or neglected to check for a marriage, obituary, or census

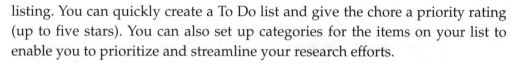
listing. You can quickly create a To Do list and give the chore a priority rating (up to five stars). You can also set up categories for the items on your list to enable you to prioritize and streamline your research efforts.

To create a Research Journal, click on the Journal button on the toolbar; or, from the View menu, choose Research Journal. The Research Journal appears, as shown in Figure 10-17.

> ❧ **NOTE** ❧   *When you first open the Research Journal, a message box prompts you about creating a FamilyFinder report that searches for your relatives on the Internet and Family Archive CDs. Click on No for now to go directly to the Journal.*

USING THE TO DO LIST

You can use the To Do list as a reminder of research that needs to be done. List what census records should be searched; or, if you're missing a marriage record, put it on the To Do list. Give the items priority ratings so you'll know which ones should be done first.

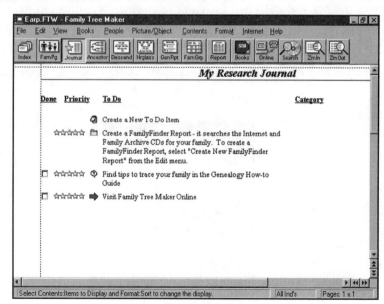

Figure 10-17

The Research Journal allows you to create a To Do list, run a FamilyFinder report, find tips in the Genealogy How-to Guide, or select Visit Family Tree Maker Online.

To create a New To Do Item:

1. In the Research Journal, double-click on Create A New To Do Item, located under the To Do column heading. The New To Do Item dialog box appears.

2. In the To Do text box, type in the records you wish to search.

3. In the Priority spin box, give this task a priority rating of one to five.

4. Fill in the Category (Optional) text box if you want to use categories to keep track of your to-do items (these can be such topics as census or parish records).

5. Fill in the Date (Optional) text box if you wish.

6. Click on OK. The new To Do item is added to the journal.

Figure 10-18 shows a To Do Item pertaining to a check of the 1870 Washington Territory census to search for Magdalena "Ellen" Rysdam, the first wife of Virgil Earp, along with suggestions on conducting the search.

RUNNING THE FAMILYFINDER REPORT

The Research Journal also provides an option called FamilyFinder Report. With this invaluable feature of Family Tree Maker, you can customize a search for one or many individuals in your Family File. Unlike the other reports, this one isn't limited to information you've already collected—it goes out to FamilyFinder

Figure 10-18

A To Do item can include research suggestions for additional records that need to be consulted.

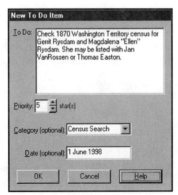

CDs and online records and picks up potential matches for you. The rating of the matches is based on several factors such as spouses and names of other family members, dates, locations, and whether the name is common. Then, using a five-star system, the FamilyFinder Report rates the quality of these matches, placing the best matches at the top of the list. If you had clicked on Yes to the prompt to create the FamilyFinder Report when you opened the Research Journal, it would have started working right then.

You can perform this search later in Research Journal:

1. From the Research Journal, click on the folder in front of the Create a New FamilyFinder Report. The Create New FamilyFinder Report dialog box appears. You have several options pertaining to the names you want to include and whether you search online or in the FamilyFinder Index CDs.

2. Select CD FamilyFinder Index and then choose the individuals you want to include (you've done this a few times before).

3. Put the FamilyFinder Index CD in your CD drive, and then click on OK to start the search.

4. Insert other CDs as prompted. When the search of the index is complete, the possible matches appear in the Research Journal under the FamilyFinder Report entry.

A search in the FamilyFinder Index CD for potential matches for Virgil Walter Earp turns up 10 possible matches, ranging from three stars down to one star (see Figure 10-19). The FamilyFinder report provides the CD number and the volume and tree number of where the possible matches were found.

After you create the initial FamilyFinder report for a Family File, you can keep it updated. Maybe you have some new names in your Family File and want to repeat the search of the CDs. Or if you haven't searched online yet, you can do that now. To update the FamilyFinder report, open the Edit menu and choose Update FamilyFinder Report (see Figure 10-20).

You can select an Online search or a search in the CD FamilyFinder Index, and you can include all or selected individuals in your Family File. (The online

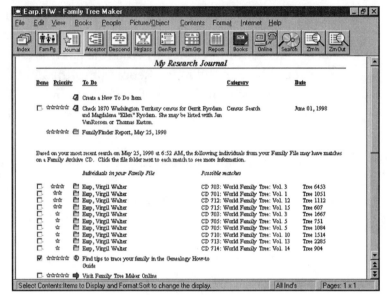

Figure 10-19

Using Research Journal to prepare a FamilyFinder report for Virgil Earp reveals several potential matches on various Family Archive CDs.

report is a much more powerful tool than the CD.) Click on OK after making your choices.

The results of the updated FamilyFinder report show up in the Research Journal along with the possible matches, arranged by the one- to five-star ratings, with the most likely matches for your data on top (see Figure 10-21).

To find out more about a match in the FamilyFinder report, click on the folder icon next to it, which drops down a list of possible matches on the CD. If you

Figure 10-20

The Update FamilyFinder Report dialog box includes options to search online or in the CD FamilyFinder Index for all individuals in your Family File or for selected individuals.

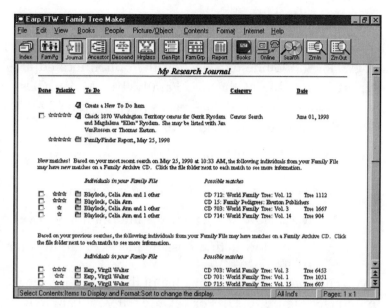

Figure 10-21

The updated
FamilyFinder report
provides possible
matches for selected
individuals in the
Family File, along with
information about
where the information
can be found on
various CDs.

click on a CD location or Tree number in the report, you are taken to the Family Tree Maker Web site, where you can order the Archive CD you selected. If you already have the CD volume for your selection, put the CD in the drive, highlight the item in the report, and then click on the Search button on the toolbar. The World Family Tree Index for the volume appears. From here, you can search the CD using the Search Expert. (Refer back to Chapter Five if you need a refresher on how to search CDs.) If you are running the FamilyFinder report with the Online option, you can go to the location online by clicking on the Online entry in the Possible Matches column.

> ❋ **TIP** ❋ *The check boxes on the left side of the FamilyFinder report allow you to check which items are Done—those you have already looked up or aren't likely matches. After clicking in a check box to mark the item as Done, you can hide the Done items from the list. From the Contents menu, choose Items to Display. In the Items to Display in Research Journal, select the items you want to see: Done, Not Done, or Both Done And Not Done. Selecting Not Done hides the Done items. You also can make selections in this dialog box to refine which matches are displayed and which categories of To Do items are displayed.*

FINDING TIPS IN THE GENEALOGY HOW-TO GUIDE

From the Research Journal you can get tips for tracing your family in the Genealogy How-To Guide by selecting the option located after the FamilyFinder Report item. (One of the two Family Tree Maker CDs—the ones with the FamilyFinder Index on them—needs to be in your CD-ROM drive.) A separate Help window opens (see Figure 10-22).

The Genealogy How-To Guide is arranged in three steps:

* Step 1: How to start collecting information

* Step 2: How to organize the information you've collected

* Step 3: How to find missing pieces of family information

If you click on Step 3, you get a list of the type of information you might want to find (see Figure 10-23). For example, if you want to learn how to locate the date someone died, click on Death Date for tips on how to find this information. Whenever you get stuck in your research, it helps to look at these tips to refresh your memory about possible sources and ideas for locating the material you need.

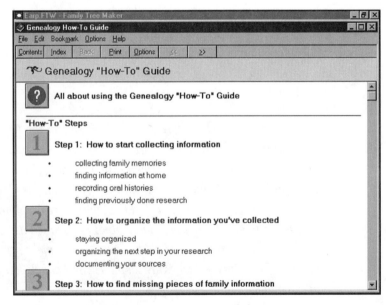

Figure 10-22

Selecting the Genealogy "How-To" Guide in the Research Journal provides easy access to tips on genealogical research.

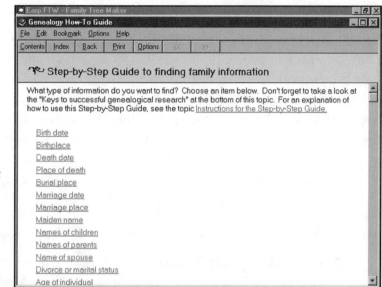

Figure 10-23

Step 3: How To Find
Missing Pieces Of
Family Information
offers quick access to
suggestions for
locating information
about your family.

※ **TIP** ※   *The final item on the Journal Report, Visit Family Tree Maker Online, is a link to the Web site where you can find more research help. You learned about some of the features of the Family Tree Maker Online Web site in Chapter Six.*

Printing Reports and Trees

You will want to print various trees and reports to include with other hard copies of genealogical material. Also, you will want to have some of these reports on paper to share with others and to take with you on field trips to libraries and archives. Once you're set up and ready to go, there are four main steps to printing information in Family Tree Maker.

1. View the document you wish to print.

2. Customize the view so it looks the way you want.

3. Change the print setup

4. Print the document.

Preparing to Print

Family Tree Maker uses the same printer settings as your other Windows programs, so they're probably already OK. You can change them, however, if a particular report doesn't look the way you want it to. When you do change your printer settings from within Family Tree Maker, you are changing them only for a specific view—the rest of the views continue to default to your Windows settings. Use the Print Setup dialog box to adjust printer settings for page margins, paper size and orientation, paper source, whether or not your pages overlap, which printer prints your documents, and other printer-specific options. To change your printer setup:

1. Display the view (such as a report or tree) that you want to print.

2. From the File menu, choose Print Setup. The Print Setup For <View> dialog box appears (see Figure 10-24), where <View> is the name of the specific tree or report you are setting up to print.

3. Select from the following options:

   ❀ **Printer.** Select Default Printer—the one you normally use with your Windows programs—or Specific Printer, if you want to use a different printer for this tree or report.

Figure 10-24

You can adjust Print Setup options to meet your various printing needs for trees and reports.

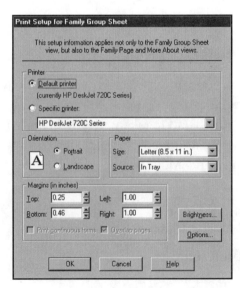

* **Orientation.** Select either Po<u>r</u>trait or <u>L</u>andscape, if available on your printer. Portrait is the way a letter normally prints, while Landscape prints with the long edge of the paper at the top (sideways).

❀ **TIP** ❀ *Ancestor trees usually take fewer pages in portrait orientation and Descendant trees usually take fewer pages in landscape.*

* **Paper.** Choose Si<u>z</u>e (usually letter size, 8 1/2 x 11" paper) and <u>S</u>ource (which paper tray).

* **Margins (in inches).** Select a setting in each box for <u>T</u>op, <u>B</u>ottom, <u>L</u>eft, and Right.

* **Other settings.** Click on the <u>O</u>ptions button if you need to change any special settings for the printer you have selected. You can select Print <u>C</u>ontinuous Forms (if your printer uses a continuous sheet of paper) and O<u>v</u>erlap Pages (if you want information on the edge of one page to be repeated on the edge of the next page so that it is easier to tape pages together). If you are printing color or grayscale images, you can click on the Brigh<u>t</u>ness button to adjust the color level for all the Picture/Objects in the current view. (This setting does not affect black-and-white images).

4. Click on OK. The settings will control printing of the currently displayed tree or report view.

Printing Reports and Trees

Once you're satisfied with the setup for a report or tree document, you can proceed to print it.

1. Display the view (such as a report or tree) that you want to print.

2. From the <u>F</u>ile menu, choose <u>P</u>rint <View>, where <View> is the name of the specific tree or report you're printing. The Print <View> dialog box appears (see Figure 10-25).

3. Be sure the printer named in the dialog box is the one you want to use; if it's not, you can click on the Setup button to change it.

4. For the page range to print, All may be the only selection available. For some views, such as the Research Journal, you can select All or you can print part of the report: select Pages and then type the page range in the From and To text boxes.

5. In the Print Quality drop-down list, you can choose a different print resolution or use the one that appears.

    ✳ **TIP** ✳   *You may want to print in a lower quality to save ink while you output a draft copy so you can test whether you like the appearance of the tree or report.*

6. In the Copies text box, type the number of copies to print, if you want more than one.

7. Select any of these check boxes that apply:

    ☀ **Print To File.** If you want to print the tree or report later or on a different printer, you can save it to a file, which you will be prompted to name (after you click on OK).

    ☀ **Print Empty.** If you want to print an empty tree, perhaps to take with you to fill in when you are away from your computer collecting information, you can print a tree with empty boxes. This option is available for the standard tree format but not the fan format.

Figure 10-25

Print the current view
of the tree or report
using the Print
dialog box.

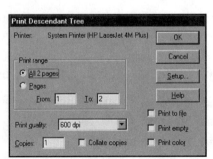

> ❋ **Print Color.** Check this box if you have a color printer or want to print in grayscale on a black-and-white printer. Otherwise, printing will be in black and white.

❋ **TIP** ❋ *If you want to print a tree or report in color, spend some time choosing attractive color combinations for text, boxes, and borders by adjusting the options on the Format menu.*

8. Click on OK. The tree or report should print on the selected printer. If you chose to print to a file, the Print To File dialog box appears, where you can choose the drive, folder, and file name for the file and then click on OK.

You may find out after printing that you need to change some of the content, formatting, or setup options to improve the appearance of the tree or report. Just repeat the steps for changing those features and then try printing again. The Family Tree Maker manual contains many hints for solving problems with tree printing, including what you can do if your tree is too tall or too wide, and how to print on an extra-large piece of paper or on banner paper.

PART IV

Computerizing Your Family Tree

The following text appears within the scrapbook image:

Ancestors of George Howard Lafferty

Samuel Lafferty
1801 - 1873

Edwin E. Lafferty
1834 - 1907

Margaret McDowell
1803 - 1861

George E. Lafferty
1867 - 1936

Erastus Fowler
1792 - 1875

...elia Fowler
...1914

Temperence Merrill
1796 - 1871

Nathan Wescott
1818 - 1900

...iram Wescott

Sarah Ann McMichael
1820 - 1901

...a Wescott
...2 - 1953

Samuel C. Amsden
1822 - 1899

Theresa Jerusa Amsden
1845 - 1934

Clarissa Hubbard
1820 - 1870

The History of George Howard Lafferty

George Howard Lafferty was born September 2, 1894 in Lenox township, Ashtabula County, Ohio, to Amber Amelia Wescott Lafferty and George Edwin Lafferty. A sister, Maud Irene, was born May 23, 1892.

A family of farmers, the Laffertys harvested the land where they lived. On May 9, 1919, they moved to Warren, Ohio, to a house on Forest Street NE. They lived next door to their daughter Maud, her husband Jay Rood Webster, and their three beautiful daughters, Reta, Shirley, and Marion.

As a youth, Lafferty went by "Howard" rather than "George" and signed his name as G. Howard Lafferty. After graduating from Lenox Township schools in 1911, he received a Teachers Certificate and became an educator and later a high school Principal. He then switched careers and ventured into banking just before World War I.

As a student at Ohio State University during the war, Howard Lafferty hoped to join the army but was classified 5G due to his glasses and other restrictions. In 1923 he received an L.L.B. degree and passed

---

CHAPTER ELEVEN

Creating Scrapbooks

*H*ave you ever thumbed through an old family scrapbook—perhaps your childhood scrapbook, or a scrapbook belonging to a parent or grandparent? I'm lucky to have not only my own childhood scrapbook (complete with endless photos of the horses I loved), but access to my mother's scrapbook as well. In it are sketches she made as a child, items from important events in her life (such as a menu from a boat that sailed from Alaska to Seattle), and other memorabilia that offer a glimpse into my mother's childhood. Such items are priceless, and often very fragile.

Computers allow you to share rare and fragile items with others by means of scanning. You can scan your mother's love letters to your father, your great-grandfather's baby photo, or even a piece of lace made by your grandmother. You can send copies of the scanned images to other relatives and interested researchers, or you can include them in your genealogy database.

Family Tree Maker's Scrapbook function is the ideal place to include all of the items from your family archives. This chapter will show you how to create a Scrapbook from information you already have entered in Family Tree Maker, and you will also learn how to add photos, sounds, and other items to your Scrapbook for a specific individual or for a marriage. As with prior chapters, you'll be working with the Earp family, but this time you will be adding files instead of information.

The Scrapbook allows you to be creative beyond traditional paper scrapbooks. You can do all sorts of nifty things, such as:

> ❧ Create an electronic slide show of family photos, complete with captions.

> ❧ Print your Scrapbook to share with family and friends.

> ❧ Create a Scrapbook for a child or grandchild, and include a video of his or her first steps.

> ❧ Create a tribute to a relative or ancestor and include sound files.

> ❧ Keep scanned copies of important documents.

Deciding What to Include

Family Tree Maker's Scrapbook feature can handle four different types of items: graphic images such as photos and clip art—including Kodak Photo CD pictures—and also sound clips, video clips, and OLE objects. Before you begin working on a Scrapbook, you should familiarize yourself with the items you can include.

Working with Graphic Images

Graphic images can be photos, documents, hairpins, medallions, artwork; anything that you can scan or digitize, you can include in your Scrapbook. Graphic images, also called *graphics,* are electronic records of an item. Most graphics are obtained by scanning an item, but you can still include graphics if you don't have a scanner.

> ❧ Photo developers such as Kodak will place your undeveloped film, slides, negatives, and old photos on disk or CD (at an additional cost). Kodak can also make your photos available online for you to download and use on your computer.

> ❧ Your local print shop may be able to scan any existing photos.

> ❧ Companies such as Seattle FilmWorks will develop your film and make electronic copies available online to be downloaded and used on your computer.

> ❧ You can also include graphics from another program simply by copying the image to the Clipboard and pasting it into the Scrapbook (more about that in a bit).

You are not just limited to including photos in a Scrapbook! There are many records and documents that are valuable to genealogists that would make a great addition to your Scrapbook. For instance, I have several old letters from my husband's ancestors. They were immigrants from Luxembourg, and sent home many accounts of their life in America. I've scanned the images of the letters, and included them in each individual's Scrapbook. Signatures are especially nice to have in a Scrapbook—be it an "X" on a formal document, or a signature on a letter to a loved one. Other items I've included in Scrapbooks are images from scanned maps of Luxembourg, newspaper articles, pictures of headstones, immigration records, and a ship's passenger list entries.

Working with Sound Clips

Sound clips are recorded sound files, such as music, digitized recordings of someone speaking (captured with a microphone connected to a computer), or other computer sound files.

Have you ever thought of creating a talking family tree? Imagine bringing a laptop to a family reunion and displaying a family tree that has sound files for each individual—you can do that by including sound clips in the Family Tree Maker Scrapbooks. To create a talking tree:

1. Record short sound clips for individuals in your family. Have family members tell short stories, sing songs, recite poetry, or explain momentous events in their lives.

2. Add the sound clips into each individual's Scrapbook (instructions on adding sound clips are found below).

3. Go to the Family Page and select your primary individual by clicking on his or her name.

4. Go to the Yiew Menu and select the type of tree you want. (Outline-style trees will not work with this project.)

5. Once the tree is displayed, from the Contents menu, select Items to Include.

6. Select Picture/Object from the list on the left, then click on the Add button.

7. The Options: Picture/Object dialog box will be displayed. To include a sound file, click on the By Category button, then select Any in the left drop-down box, and Sound Clip in the right drop-down box.

   ❧ **NOTE** ❧ *Family Tree Maker will select the first sound clip it finds in each individual's Scrapbook. If you have multiple sound clips for an individual, and you wish to select another one, you must assign a different category to the item, then include that category.*

8. Click on OK once you have the sound files you want.

9. Finish formatting your tree, and return to the tree view. You can listen to each person's sound file by clicking on the sound icon—a "talking tree."

Working with Video Clips

Video clips are moving images created by the use of video capture software and hardware (which allows you to connect a video camera or VCR to your computer). Video capture software lets you select portions of video and save them as video files on your computer.

If you have the proper hardware (a video capture peripheral), or even just a scanner, you can have some fun with videos. I used my video camera to videotape my house and property as it was being developed. Brief excerpts from the video were made with a video capture device called Snappy and are included in my own Scrapbook. (Video and sound files tend to be hard drive space hogs, so you'll probably want to use short clips unless you have a large hard drive.) Using a scanner, I scanned a photo of my great-grandfather when he was a boy, and another photo when he was in his 60's, and morphed the two images together to create a video clip showing how he had aged. You can add other photos to a morph to show how an individual has changed over the years.

   ❧ **TIP** ❧ *A morph is a video clip that starts with one image and ends with another. Many video capture peripherals have some sort of morphing software included, but you can purchase it separately as well. Resulting morphs are always video files.*

If you create an OLE sound clip in one program, you can include the clip in your Scrapbook. You can still edit the OLE object even if you delete the original object file. Other OLE items you might want to include are text from a word processor, or tables, graphs, and drawings from a spreadsheet or database. For instance, if you use a database program to store your census extracts, you could include the OLE census information (object) in your Scrapbook.

Using the Scrapbook

You can open a Scrapbook for an individual or a marriage. This allows you to create a custom Scrapbook for just one person or for an entire family. To open a new or existing Scrapbook for an individual or marriage:

1. Go to the Family Page that contains the individual or marriage whose Scrapbook you want to open.

2. Place your cursor on any one of the individual's fields or the marriage fields.

3. From the <u>V</u>iew menu, choose <u>S</u>crapbook. The Scrapbook for the individual or marriage appears.

A fast way to open a Scrapbook for an individual or marriage is to click on the Scrapbook button for each individual or marriage. The Scrapbook button changes to look like an open book when there are items in a Scrapbook for that individual or marriage (see Figure 11-1).

The first time you open a Scrapbook, it will be empty and you will be at the first page (see Figure 11-2). You can begin adding items at that point, or go to a different view using the menu or toolbar at the top.

> ❧ **NOTE** ❧   *The number of "places" (empty spots) you see in a Scrapbook depends on your monitor's resolution; the higher your resolution, the more places you will see in a Scrapbook. Family Tree Maker supports 2,000 places for each Scrapbook, so you can have 2,000 Scrapbook objects per person and marriage.*

Open Scrapbook ——————

Closed Scrapbook ——————

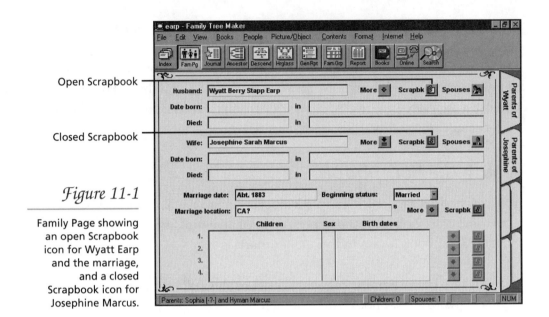

Figure 11-1

Family Page showing
an open Scrapbook
icon for Wyatt Earp
and the marriage,
and a closed
Scrapbook icon for
Josephine Marcus.

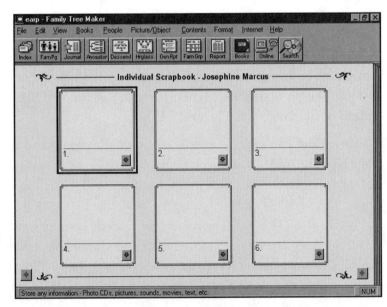

Figure 11-2

An individual's
Scrapbook begins with
empty pages.

If you open a Scrapbook that you have worked on previously, you will start at the last page you were working on when you closed the Scrapbook. Notice that the Scrapbook reflects the name of the individual or the partners in the marriage (see Figure 11-3). You cannot customize the Scrapbook title onscreen, but later in this chapter I'll show you how to change it when you print a Scrapbook.

You can open a Scrapbook from any view in Family Tree Maker, but if you open the Scrapbook from any view *other* than the Family Page, the Scrapbook will default to the primary individual. If you find yourself with a Scrapbook open for an individual you do not want, simply go to the View menu and click on Index Of Individuals (or click on the Index button), then select the individual whose Scrapbook you want to open and choose OK.

Inserting Scrapbook Items

Once you are familiar with the Scrapbook, you'll want to begin putting stuff in it. The first step is to learn how to insert the many types of objects a Scrapbook can hold. How you insert an item depends on what type of file or object you wish to include. Table 11-1 shows the Scrapbook items and the menu and option

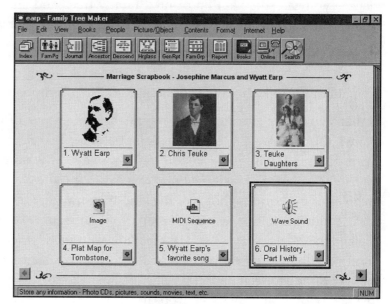

Figure 11-3

An existing Scrapbook for a marriage displays graphic images and sound clips.

Table 11-1 Inserting Scrapbook Items

To Insert This Object	Choose This Menu and Option
Graphic file	Picture/Object, Insert Picture From File
OLE object	Picture/Object, Insert Object
Objects from the Clipboard	Edit, Paste or Paste Special (Paste Special applies only to OLE objects)
Pictures from a Kodak Photo CD	Picture/Object, Insert Photo CD Picture

you choose to insert various objects in the Scrapbook. Most of the object types are inserted using dialog boxes accessed from the Picture/Object menu.

INSERTING A GRAPHIC IMAGE

Graphics are the most common item included in a Scrapbook, because they are visual—you can see them on printed family trees and charts—as opposed to sounds and video clips, which can only be utilized on a computer.

You've heard the saying, "a picture is worth a thousand words." The same is true when dealing with a family history project, although, as I said above, you are not limited to including just photographs in a Scrapbook.

Perhaps you have ancestors who migrated west on one of the famous wagon trains? You might want to make a Scrapbook for that marriage with graphics (scanned images) of the migration trail, an image of what type of wagon they traveled in, photos of historical markers existing today, images from historical archives of the period, photos of the land they traveled through, or journal entries detailing the arduous trip. Perhaps your ancestors homesteaded once they reached their destination—you can include a scanned image of the land bounty grant describing their property. Maps, records, certificates, historical images—they can all add to your understanding of your ancestors. Don't just limit yourself to a few photographs; visit your local library or archives for historical images, plot a migration trail on a map, create a customized genealogy atlas showing houses and important locations—anything you can include will bring you that much closer to understanding their lives.

> ❊ **TIP** ❊   *The Scrapbook will accept four standard graphic file formats supported by most graphics programs:*
>
> ❊ *Windows Bitmap (.bmp)*
>
> ❊ *JPEG Interchange Format (.jpg, *.jff)*
>
> ❊ *Tagged Image Format (.tif)*
>
> ❊ *Zsoft Image (.pcx)*

To insert a graphic image such as a photo you have scanned, follow these steps:

1. Open the Scrapbook of the individual or marriage where you want to put the graphic file, and select the area where you want to place the image.

    > ❊ **NOTE** ❊   *You can't select a page beyond the first area. However, it's OK to select an area that already has an object in it. Family Tree Maker will insert the new object in that position and move the existing areas over to make space for it. This way, you can't accidentally overwrite the contents of an area.*

2. From the Picture/<u>O</u>bject menu, choose Insert Picture From <u>F</u>ile. The Insert Picture dialog box appears (see Figure 11-4).

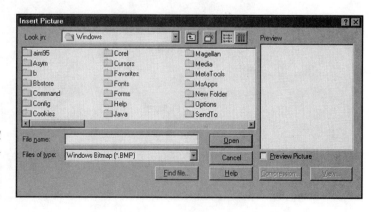

Figure 11-4

Locate the graphic file you want to place in the Scrapbook.

3. In the Look In dropdown list, select the drive where the graphic file is located. Then double-click on the folder that contains the file.

4. In the Files Of Type dropdown list, All Graphics Files may already be selected. If you want to narrow the list of files displayed to a particular type of image file, select it from the list. Files of the type you have selected (or All Graphics Files) appear in the list box.

5. Select the file you want to insert into the Scrapbook.

   ❋ **TIP** ❋ *If you can't find the file you want, click on the Find File button in the Insert Picture dialog box. In the Find File dialog box, select the File Format (select All Files if you aren't sure) and drive to Search, and then click on the Search button. When the file name appears in the Found Files list box (scroll the list if needed), select it and then click on the Open button. The graphic image appears in the Edit Picture dialog box. Skip to Step 8 below.*

6. Click on the Preview Picture check box to get an advance look at the image before you select it.

7. Click on the Open button. The picture appears in the Edit Picture dialog box (see Figure 11-5).

Figure 11-5

Rotate, crop, or flip the picture before placing it in the Scrapbook.

8. Edit the picture (optional) by rotating, cropping, or flipping. You can click on the <u>H</u>elp button to find out more about these features, or refer to the "Editing Pictures and Objects" section of this chapter.

9. Click on OK. The picture is placed in the Scrapbook. You can move items if you want to rearrange your Scrapbook. You learn how in "Enhancing the Scrapbook," later in this chapter.

❄ **TIP** ❄ *You can double-click on a graphic object page in the Scrapbook to see a closer view of the picture in the View Picture box. Use the Zm In and Zm Out buttons to further change the view (temporarily). Click on OK to close the View Picture box.*

INSERTING A SOUND CLIP

Sound clips, like graphics, can enhance a Scrapbook by letting you hear an individual speak, sing, or (in the case of a baby) cry. Doting grandparents have been known to create Scrapbooks upon the birth of their grandchildren, often starting with video and sound clips of the newborn. It's wonderful to be able to hear the voice of a loved one who is no longer with you, or the song of a child who is now grown.

My husband has an audiotape of his grandfather who died many years ago. The tape gives my husband an opportunity to hear his grandfather telling the story of what life was like in Italy before he immigrated to the U.S. Although very nostalgic, the tape also has information useful to genealogists, so I've included Grandpa Louie's stories in his Scrapbook to be preserved even if the audiotape is destroyed. To add a sound clip to a Scrapbook:

1. Click on the Scrapbook icon to open an individual's Scrapbook.

2. From the Picture/<u>O</u>bject menu, select Insert <u>O</u>bject.

3. In the Insert Object dialog box, select the Create from <u>F</u>ile button, and enter the path to the sound file you want to include (use the <u>B</u>rowse feature if you don't know where the file is).

4. Once you find the file, you can display the file itself (it shows up as a sound icon), or choose another icon by selecting the <u>D</u>isplay As

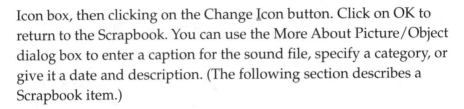

Icon box, then clicking on the Change Icon button. Click on OK to return to the Scrapbook. You can use the More About Picture/Object dialog box to enter a caption for the sound file, specify a category, or give it a date and description. (The following section describes a Scrapbook item.)

TIP *You can double-click on a sound object page in the Scrapbook to play the sound file.*

Entering Information about Scrapbook Objects

Once you have placed your objects in the Scrapbook, you can begin to label and document them to explain what they're about. Just as you might do with a traditional paper Scrapbook, you can enter object captions, descriptions, and dates. Unlike a traditional Scrapbook, Family Tree Maker makes it easy to categorize objects and sort objects as well; if you want to organize an individual's Scrapbook chronologically, you can sort by date. If you want to organize that same Scrapbook by subject, you can sort it by category—and you can also move items around manually if none of the preset sorts will do what you want, all without touching a bottle of rubber cement!

In my husband's Family File, I have several Scrapbooks for his relatives. Sometimes it gets confusing when there are so many items, so I use Family Tree Maker's Scrapbook category function to organize items into specific categories:

- Photos: Adults
- Photos: Children
- Photos: Groups
- Maps
- Vital records (birth, marriage, and death certificates)
- Immigration records (includes naturalization certificates)
- Wills and Deeds
- Census images

- Sound files: stories

- Sound files: songs

- Sound files: oral history

- Video files

- Letters

- Journals

- Signatures

- Textiles

- Headstones

- Migration trails

- Houses

❈ **TIP** ❈   *You'll want to put some thought into your categories. The Family Tree Maker user's manual has some excellent suggestions that will allow you to conduct precise searching of the items through categories.*

The more information you record about each object, the more valuable the Scrapbook becomes. Record names, dates, and any comments you have about the object. If you print or share your Scrapbook with others, they might need help to identify the people or places in the pictures, voices, or other items you include. Enter as much information as you can about each object in the More About Picture/Object dialog box (see Figure 11-6). To access this dialog box for each object, click on the down arrow below an object in the Scrapbook.

❈ **NOTE** ❈   *Another way to open the More About Picture/Object dialog box is to select the page in the Scrapbook. From the Picture/Object menu, choose More About. Still another method is to select the page and then press Ctrl+m.*

Using the More About Picture/Object dialog box, you can do several useful (but optional) things:

Keep the caption short.

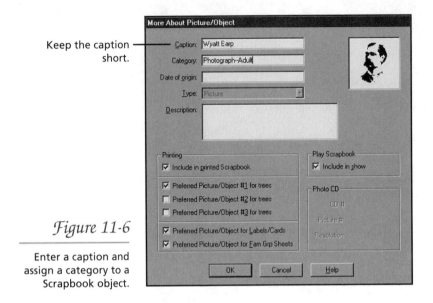

Figure 11-6

Enter a caption and assign a category to a Scrapbook object.

→ Enter a caption for the object. Make it short; only the first few words show below the object in the Scrapbook.

→ Assign a category to the object, such as anniversary photos, childhood photos, family portraits, and birth certificates. Be descriptive when you choose category titles so you can locate them easily when you have accumulated a large number of objects.

→ Enter information about the date of origin of the object.

→ Select the type of object. Family Tree Maker will recognize a picture automatically. Use the Type dropdown list to select other types.

→ Enter a full description of the object. If you want to name multiple individuals in a photo, or wish to enter facts about a scanned document or record, this is the area to do it! Use the Description text box to enter facts about the object, the object's source, and any comments about the information the object contains (especially useful when you have scanned records). See Figure 11-7.

→ You can create a slide show of specific Scrapbook objects. I describe this feature later in this chapter in "Playing the Scrapbook."

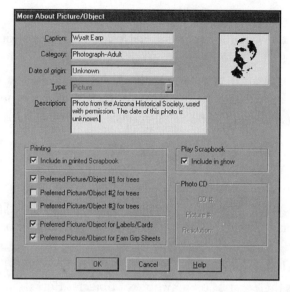

Figure 11-7

Enter a date of origin
and a description of
the photograph. Note
that Family Tree
Maker automatically
recognizes this object
as a picture.

✷ Specify the three pictures or objects you want designated as Preferred Pictures/Objects for printing in trees. Although Family Tree Maker specifies only three Preferred Pictures/Objects, you can include any other Scrapbook item in a tree by the use of categories.

   ❧ **NOTE** ❧   *Family Tree Maker makes it easier to select which pictures to put in trees by allowing you to choose three pictures (or other objects) that you want to print for each individual. Those three choices are designated by using the Preferred Picture/Object for trees check box. So, if you picked each individual's birth certificate as the Preferred Picture/Object #3 for trees, every time you print a tree that includes a Preferred Picture/Object #3 for trees, the tree will include each individual's birth certificate.*

✷ Specify the picture or object you want designated as the Preferred Picture/Object for printing on labels or cards.

✷ Specify the picture or object you want designated as the Preferred Picture/Object for printing on Family Group Sheets.

✷ Display information (CD #, Photo #, and Resolution) about a Kodak Photo CD picture.

When you finish entering the information in the More About Picture/Object dialog box, click on OK. Notice in the Scrapbook that a caption, if entered, shows below the object. The down arrow button changes to show three horizontal lines under the arrow icon if you have entered any data in the Category, Date Of Origin, or Description text boxes. This indicator informs the viewer (you) that information has been entered for this object.

Enhancing the Scrapbook

After you've inserted your pictures, scanned images, graphs, charts, sounds, videos, and miscellaneous OLE objects into the Scrapbook, you can manipulate and modify some objects. This is your chance to change any of the items included in your Scrapbook. Don't like the order your pictures are in? Move them! Is a photo too big, small, light, or dark? Edit it! Can't find a particular item? Search for it! Is the Scrapbook a jumble of objects? Sort them!

Family Tree Maker gives you the option of changing the order of items included in the Scrapbook. You may want to think about how you want the Scrapbook arranged. Do you want objects displayed chronologically, or sorted by subject? Would you like the photos separated from the sound files, or do you want objects to follow a certain pattern?

Rearranging Scrapbook Objects

If your Scrapbook items are not in an order pleasing to you, you can move, copy, or delete them.

MOVING OBJECTS

To move a picture, select it (see Figure 11-8), and then from the Edit menu, choose Cut Picture/Object. Select the page in the Scrapbook where you want to place the picture, then go back to the Edit menu and choose Paste Picture/Object (see Figure 11-9).

COPYING OBJECTS

You can copy and paste an item between Scrapbooks as well. To copy an item, select it and then open the Edit menu and choose the Copy Picture/Object

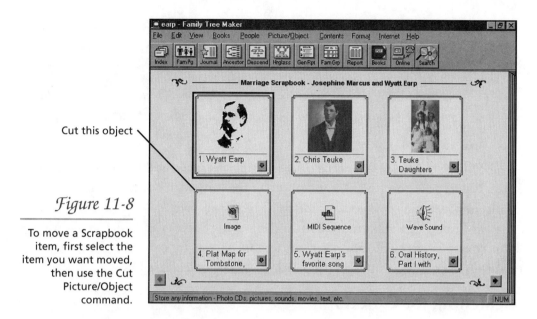

Cut this object

Figure 11-8

To move a Scrapbook item, first select the item you want moved, then use the Cut Picture/Object command.

command. Then select the individual whose Scrapbook will receive the copied graphic. Open up the Scrapbook and use the Paste Picture/Object command from the Edit menu.

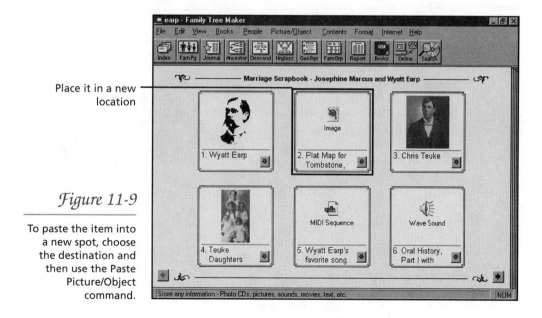

Place it in a new location

Figure 11-9

To paste the item into a new spot, choose the destination and then use the Paste Picture/Object command.

> ❧ **TIP** ❧ *The Cut (Ctrl+x), Copy (Ctrl+c), and Paste (Ctrl+v) options are also available on the shortcut menu that appears when you right-click on the object.*

> ❧ **NOTE** ❧ *If you want to delete a Scrapbook item, simply select it and press the Delete key, or from the Edit menu, choose Cut Picture/Object.*

SORTING OBJECTS

One of the very useful functions of the Scrapbook is the ability to sort objects by category. If you don't want your photos mixed in with sound files, images of wills, and drawings of your grandchild, you can sort the objects quickly and easily by opening the Format menu and choosing Sort Scrapbook (see Figure 11-10). You can select an option button to sort objects by categories, captions, or date—in ascending or descending order—and then choose OK.

Searching for Objects

Once you begin to gather a number of Scrapbook items, you may need to search the collection for a particular treasure. Family Tree Maker will allow you to search the Scrapbook for text in a number of fields. To search for an object:

1. From the Edit menu, choose Find Picture/Object.

2. Click on the Search dropdown list and choose the name of the field you want to search (see Figure 11-11). The For text box changes to accommodate the allowed values for the field you chose to search.

3. In the For text box, type the text you are searching for or select a value if there is a dropdown list.

Figure 11-10

The Sort Scrapbook feature can be used to arrange your Scrapbook by category, caption, or date.

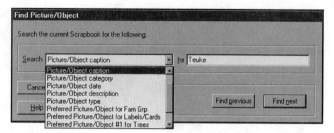

Figure 11-11

Search the Scrapbook
for a specific item.

4. Click on the Find <u>N</u>ext button to begin the search. The first object that matches the search conditions is selected in the Scrapbook.

5. Continue clicking on the Find <u>N</u>ext button until you are finished searching, or click on the Find <u>P</u>revious button to return to previous matches. Then click on Cancel to close the dialog box.

Editing Pictures and Objects

When you add a graphic object to the Scrapbook, you have the option of editing the picture at that time. The Edit Picture dialog box allows you to rotate, flip, or crop the image before you put it in the Scrapbook. You also have the option of editing graphic files already in the Scrapbook, but Family Tree Maker recommends that you work from the original graphic file instead. Family Tree Maker's compression and decompression routines can reduce the quality of the graphic if you try to play with the Scrapbook copy.

You can easily edit an existing picture or graphic. From the Picture/<u>O</u>bject menu, choose the <u>E</u>dit command to open the Edit Picture dialog box. You can also right-click on the item and choose Edit.

> ❧ **NOTE** ❧   *When you use the Edit Picture command for the first time on a graphic, a message box appears, asking if you want to get the original of the picture (to maintain better picture quality). If you choose <u>Y</u>es, the Insert Picture dialog box appears. Use the same steps as in the "Inserting a Graphic Image" section of this chapter to insert the picture again, which will also open the Edit Picture dialog box. If you choose <u>N</u>o, the Edit Picture dialog box appears (see Figure 11-12).*

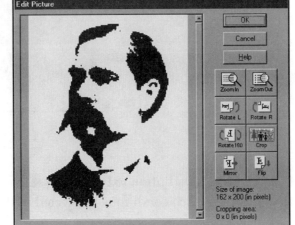

Figure 11-12

The Edit Picture dialog box allows you to do a number of things to your pictures.

✳ **TIP** ✳ *You can click on the Zm In button to get a closer look at a picture, or Zm Out to view more of the picture again—these buttons don't change the way the graphic appears in the Scrapbook.*

In the Edit Picture dialog box, you can rotate a picture 90 degrees to the left or right, or 180 degrees (see Figure 11-13). You can flip a graphic that is upside-down by clicking on the Flip button, or create a mirror image of the graphic by

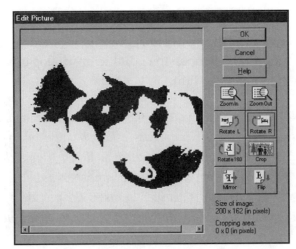

Figure 11-13

Rotate a picture 90 degrees to the right— but only if it will look better that way.

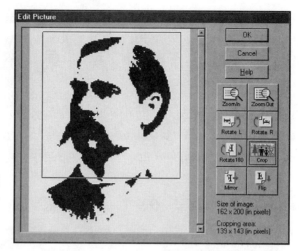

Figure 11-14

Select the area of the
picture you want
to crop.

clicking on the Mirror button. You can also crop a graphic or photo to include
just the area you want. First, drag the mouse pointer (shaped like crosshairs)
across the picture to select the area you want to crop (see Figure 11-14).

Click on the Crop button. The area you selected becomes the new picture object
(see Figure 11-15). If you aren't satisfied with the way it looks, click on Cancel to
discard the changes you made in the Edit Picture dialog box. If you are finished
editing the picture and want to keep the changes, click on OK.

Figure 11-15

The cropped picture
allows you to show a
close-up view.

Family Tree Maker can't edit OLE objects, but the Edit command is still available. If you use the Edit command with an OLE object, it will send you to the object's source software for any edits you may want to make.

> ❧ **NOTE** ❧ *You can control the brightness and contrast of a color image (a non-OLE object) easily. To change the contrast, select the Picture/Object you wish to change, and then from the Picture/Object menu, select Contrast. Adjust the contrast as you desire in the Contrast dialog box.*

Presenting the Scrapbook

After you've raided your family archives, visited the library for historical photos and images (be sure they are copyright free), recorded family members, videotaped your grandchild's first step, and carefully scanned your grandmother's bridal quilt, you'll probably want to share your Scrapbook with others. You may just want to produce a finished product for family members or friends, or you might want to publish it in a family history book.

Family Tree Maker offers you two ways to share your Scrapbook: you can display the Scrapbook items in a Slide Show, or print the Scrapbook to be shared with friends and family.

Printing a Scrapbook

One of the best things about a Scrapbook is the ability to share it with others; Family Tree Maker allows you to print your Scrapbook in an attractive format. You can even select a group of Scrapbooks (printed in a batch) if you want to create a family album. However, there may be some items that you may not want printed. Sound and video files will show up only as icons (see Figure 11-16), and it just teases your readers to hand them a family album or book that includes things they can't get at.

> ❧ **TIP** ❧ *You can include Scrapbook items in a Family Tree Maker book by using the Text Item feature (see Chapter Thirteen for more information on this feature). If you wish to include an entire Scrapbook in a family history book you create elsewhere, you can print the Scrapbooks normally, and manually add them to your book later.*

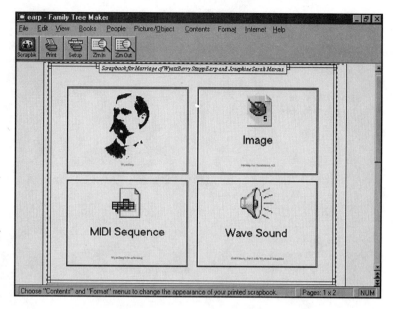

Figure 11-16

A Scrapbook Print
Preview shows icons to
represent sound files.

Family Tree Maker lets you customize your Scrapbook quite a bit. You can choose the border, color, font, and layout, so it's best to think about what your goal is in printing the Scrapbook. Do you want to include it in a formal family history book? If so, you might want subdued fonts and borders. Do you want to make a family album to share with your children? If so, you can be creative and daring with colors, backgrounds, and layout design. Will you be showing the album to relatives at a family reunion? If so, you need to include captions and descriptions for each picture—and if you have relatives who are getting on in years, make sure those labels are big and easy to read.

Before you print your Scrapbook, you should use the preview feature to see what the Scrapbook will look like when printed. You can preview a Scrapbook by opening the File menu and choosing the Print Preview command.

CHANGING THE SETUP

Once in preview mode, you can specify margins, orientation, and brightness of the images. Click on the Setup button on the toolbar to open the Print Setup For Scrapbook Print Preview dialog box. Click on the Brightness button to open the Brightness dialog box (see Figure 11-17). (Choose OK to keep the settings and close the dialog boxes.)

Change orientation here.

Change margin settings here

Move this slider to change the brightness

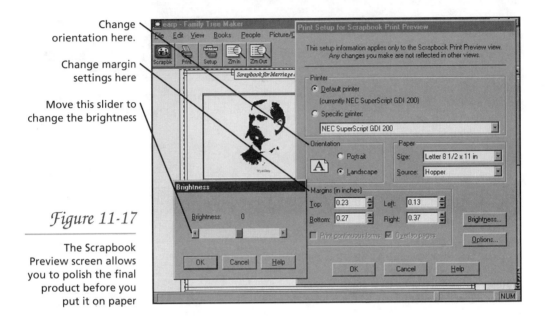

Figure 11-17

The Scrapbook Preview screen allows you to polish the final product before you put it on paper

CHOOSING WHAT TO PRINT

You can also choose what items you would like to include in your printed Scrapbook: Picture/Object caption, category, date, description, and the object's number on the Scrapbook page. From the Contents menu, choose Items To Include With Each Picture/Object to open the Items To Include In Printed Scrapbook dialog box (see Figure 11-18).

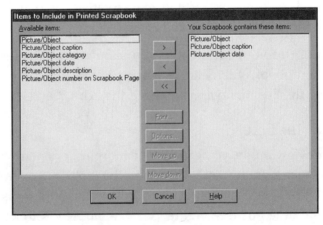

Figure 11-18

Select the items to include in your Scrapbook.

Automatic title ⟶
Enter a custom title ⟶

Figure 11-19

Customize to create a
more interesting title.

Start on a different
page number if you
are continuing from
other sets of
Scrapbooks.

The items already selected to print appear in the Your Scrapbook Contains These Items list box on the right side. To add additional items, select an item in the Available Items list box on the left, and then click on the > button to add it to the list box on the right. To remove an item from printing, select it in the right list box and click on the < button to remove it from the list. Click on the Font button if you want to change the font for an item's printed text.

If you would like to customize the title page numbers of the printed Scrapbook, you can do so by opening the Contents menu and choosing Title & Footnote. You can keep the standard title or enter your own (see Figure 11-19). Use the check boxes to choose whether to print the title on every page and whether to include page numbers.

CHANGING THE APPEARANCE

You can do more to customize the way your Scrapbook prints by choosing the layout. From the Format menu, choose the Scrapbook Format command. In the Format For Printed Scrapbook dialog box, you will have the choice of selecting an existing layout design or creating your own (see Figure 11-20).

Once you have the layout you want, you can choose which box, line, and border colors and styles you want. From the Format menu, choose the Box, Line & Border Styles command to open the relevant dialog box (see Figure 11-21). Choose styles from a variety of illustrated buttons and choose colors from the dropdown lists.

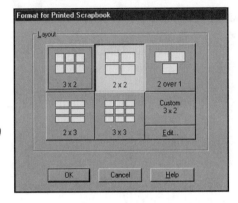

Figure 11-20

Select the Scrapbook layout—or you can customize your own.

If you want to change the font of the Scrapbook text, you can do so by opening the Format menu and choosing Text Font, Style & Size to open the relevant dialog box. Choose an item in the Items To Format list box and then change the settings in the dropdown lists, observing the appearance in the Sample box.

CHOOSING WHICH SCRAPBOOKS TO PRINT

To print all of the items in an individual or marriage Scrapbook, go to the Scrapbook view. From the File menu, choose Print Scrapbook to open the Print Scrapbook dialog box (see Figure 11-22). You can choose to print your Scrapbook in color if you have a color printer.

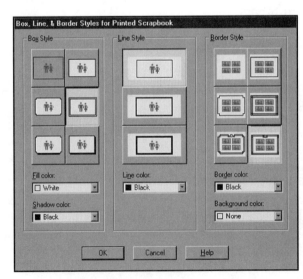

Figure 11-21

Customize the Scrapbook's appearance by choosing colors, lines, borders, and boxes.

Figure 11-22

Select your print range, print quality, and number of copies

If there are several individuals for whom you want to print Scrapbooks, you can use the batch printing options (from the File menu, choose Batch Print Scrapbook). Batch printing allows you to specify which individuals' Scrapbooks you want to print. The Individuals To Include In Batch Print dialog box lists everyone in your database (see Figure 11-23). You can select individuals to include by selecting names and clicking on the appropriate button. You can move people back and forth from the Available Individuals box on the left side to the You Have Included These Individuals box on the right side of the dialog box.

If you are unable to locate a person, or want to include people who match specific criteria, you can use the Find command to search for individuals by name or birth information, or Scrapbook items (see Figure 11-24).

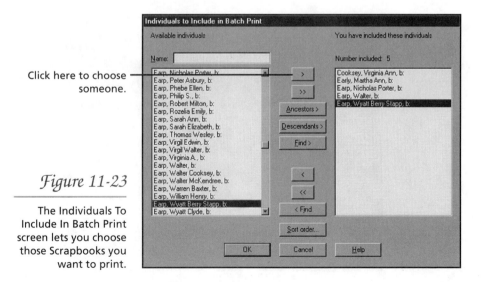

Click here to choose someone.

Figure 11-23

The Individuals To Include In Batch Print screen lets you choose those Scrapbooks you want to print.

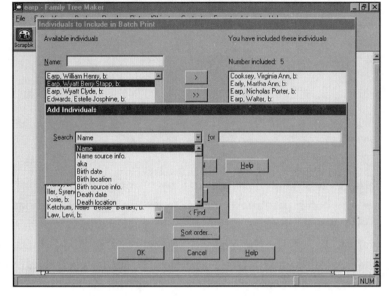

Figure 11-24

Find individuals to include by name, birth, or death information, or a variety of other criteria.

Family Tree Maker also gives you the ability to limit your list to just the ancestors or descendants of an individual. To include the ancestors or descendants, click on the individual's name first, then on the <u>D</u>escendants or <u>A</u>ncestors button. Family Tree Maker will send all the appropriate people to your list of individuals to include (see Figure 11-25).

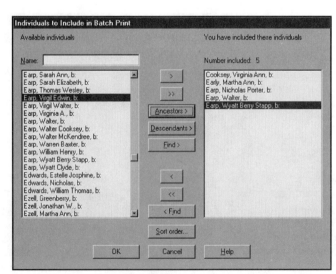

Figure 11-25

You can specify the ancestors of an individual to be included in the print list.

Batch Print Scrapbook Print Preview

Printer: System Printer (NEC SuperScript GDI 200)

Print quality: 800 dpi

Page Numbering

○ Don't number pages

● Number pages consecutively for entire printout (e.g., 1, 2, 3, 4)

○ Number pages separately for each individual (e.g., 1, 2, 1, 2)

Starting number: 1

OK

Cancel

Setup...

Help

☐ Print color

Figure 11-26

You can use continuous page numbers for the Scrapbook batch.

After you choose OK in the Individuals To Include dialog box, the Batch Print Scrapbook Print Preview dialog box appears (see Figure 11-26). Select Page Numbering options. Optionally, select the Print Color check box if you are printing on a color printer. Choose OK to print the batch of Scrapbooks.

Playing the Scrapbook

One of the fun things to do with your Scrapbook is to make a slide show for your family and friends. Family Tree Maker will display the objects you designate sequentially when you play the Scrapbook onscreen; a slide show can include scanned images, sounds, videos, and OLE objects as well as photos, making it a lot livelier than a printed Scrapbook. If you have a laptop computer, you can take your slide show on the road and share it with people outside your home office. To create a slide show:

1. Display the Scrapbook you want to play. Family Tree Maker will show the items you choose in the order it finds them in your Scrapbook, so make sure everything is where you want it before you play the Scrapbook—in chronological order, sorted by object type, or whatever. See "Rearranging Scrapbook Objects" earlier in this chapter if you need to refresh your memory on this trick.

2. Click on the down arrow next to a Scrapbook object. The object's More About Picture/Object dialog box appears.

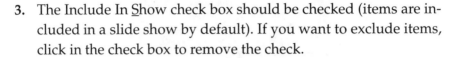

3. The Include In Show check box should be checked (items are in-cluded in a slide show by default). If you want to exclude items, click in the check box to remove the check.

4. Click on OK to close the More About Picture/Object dialog box for this object.

5. Repeat Steps 2 through 4 to deselect any items you do not want in the slide show.

Now that you have placed the Scrapbook "slides" in order, you can play the Scrapbook like a slide show. Slide shows are great fun at family gatherings, holidays, and family reunions. You can create themed slide shows (Grandma Teuke's Quilts) that focus on a particular aspect of an individual's life, or create your own version of This Is Your Life, complete with photos, sound, and video clips. To play the Scrapbook:

1. Display the Scrapbook you want to play.

2. From the Picture/Object menu, choose the Play Scrapbook command. The Play Scrapbook dialog box appears (see Figure 11-27).

3. In the Time Between Picture/Objects spin box, choose how many seconds you want each object in the slide show to stay on the screen. Each item appears for the same number of seconds, and sound and video clips play all the way through.

4. Click on OK, and then you can sit back and enjoy the slide show. If you want to skip an item in the show, simply click on the screen and you'll jump to the next Scrapbook item.

Figure 11-27

Specify the time to display each slide show object.

❈ **TIP** ❈   *Remember that sound files are played sequentially in the Scrapbook. However, you can use Family Tree Maker to play music while you are playing the Scrapbook:*

1. *Make sure the audio file (music, poetry, etc.) is not included in the Slide Show.*

2. *Open the Scrapbook, and double-click on the sound file to start playing it.*

3. *As the sound file plays, from the Picture/Object menu, select Play Scrapbook. The first sound file will continue to play as you view your Scrapbook slide show.*

Creating Special Scrapbooks

Not only can you include sounds, videos, and interesting OLE objects along with the photos in your Scrapbook, but you can create themed Scrapbooks for an individual or a whole family. Here are a few ideas on fun ways to use your Scrapbook:

❊ Create a slide show of family and ancestors to show at a family reunion.

❊ Print a Scrapbook for a family member's anniversary, with photos of the spouses from birth to present time—and of their children and grandchildren. Give the Scrapbook as an anniversary present.

❊ Print a detailed family history book and include a photo Scrapbook section, a scanned document section, or charts and graphs from OLE objects.

❊ Print Scrapbooks for your immediate family members, and share them at holidays or family get-togethers.

❊ Let children create their own electronic or print Scrapbooks, including items such as photos, drawings, letters they've written, stamps, and scans of favorite objects.

❊ Print a child's Scrapbook and send it to the grandparents!

❧ Create an electronic library of your research documents and records. You can use the Scrapbook as a backup of your hard-copy documents, and easily print them to share with other researchers.

❧ Use the Scrapbook to store images of family memorabilia such as maps, cards (postcards, funeral cards, calling cards, business cards), fabrics and textiles (quilts, needlework, lace, homespun material), signatures, and other ephemera (passports, membership cards, ribbons and medals, small jewelry, sketches).

❧ Create a biography of an individual's life in photos, sound, and video—perhaps your own autobiography.

❧ If you are printing a family history book with Family Tree Maker, include maps and other geographic items in your Scrapbook for a marriage; you can create migration trail map Scrapbook sections for each family showing maps, locations, and houses they lived in.

CHAPTER TWELVE

Creating Genealogy Reports

hile charts are pretty and provide graphic looks at your ancestors, they are unable to tell the full and rich story of a family as well as a narrative can. Moreover, you'll probably want to publish—if only for your immediate family—your family history at some point. Additionally, you might wish to have your work, or some of it, published by one of the scholarly genealogical periodicals. To accomplish either of these goals, you need to learn how genealogies are organized for publication.

Genealogy Reports Explained

In preparing ancestral charts, you start with yourself (usually) and work backward to parents, grandparents, etc. But when organizing a genealogy for publication, you work in the opposite direction, beginning with the first known progenitor of the family (frequently this is the immigrant ancestor to the country—also called a "gateway ancestor") and tracing his descendants to the present. This is a *descending* genealogy and is the method most often used to prepare genealogical articles for journals (periodicals) and books.

So why a particular format? Why not create your genealogy in any style or format you wish? Well, back in the mid-nineteenth century, when American genealogy was in its infancy, that's what everyone did. The results were a bewildering variety of formats. Albert H. Hoyt, editor of *The New England Historical and Genealogical Register*, in 1870 said that "everyone who compiles a genealogy has his own plan for arranging his matter, hence there are as many plans as there are volumes." To reduce the confusion, Hoyt devised a system that subsequently became known as the Register Plan or Register Form. Now it is simply called *Register*.

Later, in 1912, the Register format was refined by the National Genealogical Society and is known today as the *NGS Quarterly System.* These are the most commonly used formats for descending genealogies.

The two formats are very similar, and some of the differences are simply stylistic ones. The basic arrangement of each family—head of household, his/her spouse(s), and their children—are treated as a discrete unit, with each generation of the family featured in a single chapter. In order to show how each head of household is descended from earlier generations and from the immigrant ancestor, a special numbering system is used. The immigrant ancestor, or progenitor, is assigned the number 1 and given a superscript 1 (the latter indicates first generation) after his first name. The Register format then follows the children who marry and in turn leave children of their own who marry, numbering them consecutively 2, 3, 4, etc., in order of birth. The children then receive superscript number 2, indicating they are part of the family's second generation. The placement of superscript generation numbers immediately after a given name and before any punctuation mark alerts the reader that a generation is being identified rather than referencing a footnote or endnote. For example, in a published genealogy, when you see a reference to "John^3," the superscript three refers to John's generation rather than to a footnote or endnote pertaining to him.

What about children who did not marry or have families, or those who died young? In the Register style those individuals are not carried forward to the next generation. This was the major reason for the creation of the NGS Quarterly System. The latter format includes the children who did not marry or have children, and those who died young.

Genealogy Reports, as Family Tree Maker refers to them, are narratives of genealogical information in distinctive formats. While they are based upon particular numbering systems, they are much more than that. These reports include basic facts about each family member, plus any biographical information you have included. Family Tree Maker creates its Genealogy Reports in three formats, or styles:

- Register (Descendant Ordered)
- NGS Quarterly (Descendant Ordered)
- Ahnentafel (Ancestor Ordered)

Comparing the Register, NGS Quarterly System, and Ahnentafel Formats

The first two—Register and NGS Quarterly System—are widely used in scholarly genealogical periodicals. They enable you to follow several lines of a family easily because they adhere to established formats and precise numbering patterns. These reports also can, and should in most instances, include the endnotes or inline notes that cite the sources you've used to establish the pedigree and compile your family tree.

> ❦ **NOTE** ❦   *Next time you're at a library that has some books of compiled family histories or genealogies, take a closer look at their formats. It's likely you'll discover that some of the authors devised their own numbering systems—and sometimes they are so complicated that only the authors can figure them out. It is not necessary to invent a numbering system for your genealogy as authors in olden times thought they had to do. While even the leading formats have certain drawbacks, they work well and are widely used. There simply is no perfect numbering system for all genealogies, and chances are that if you make one up, its only advantage will be that you understand it perfectly—but nobody else will share that advantage. Your communication— which is what this is all about—will be better if you take the time to get comfortable with the standard systems.*

Both Register and the NGS Quarterly System are descending genealogies, meaning they start with a particular ancestor and show his or her descendants. The Ahnentafel is an ascending genealogy, and presents all the ancestors of a more recent individual. *The Register* is a journal that originated in 1870 by the New England Historic Genealogical Society (NEHGS) in Boston. If you have any New England roots, particularly early ones, you are probably familiar with America's oldest genealogical society and its periodical. *The NGS Quarterly* is the journal of the National Genealogical Society, and the NGS Quarterly System has been in use ever since the society began publishing its journal in 1912. The major differences between the Register and NGS Quarterly System formats are in the numbering of children who are not carried forward in the compilation as adults, and the fact that the NGS Quarterly System follows all the children. Following are summary definitions of the three Genealogy Reports in Family Tree Maker:

- **Register format.** Gives an identifying number only to those individuals about whom there is more information later in the article.

- **NGS Quarterly System format.** Assigns a number to each child, regardless of the presence of additional information in the compilation or whether or not the child is known to have left progeny. To distinguish between individuals who are carried forward and those who are not, a plus sign (+) precedes the number of those who are treated separately.

- **Ahnentafel format.** An ascending genealogy based upon the following numbering system: An individual is given the number 1, his/her father is 2, his/her mother is 3, the paternal grandparents are 4 and 5, and the maternal grandparents are 6 and 7. Men are always even numbers and the women odd numbers (except that individual 1 can be either female or male). Wives are always one number larger than their spouses in this format.

There are some other differences in the Register and NGS Quarterly System formats, but most of these are typographical or editorial style variants. For example, in both formats, when an individual is introduced in his or her separate sketch, some form of typographical emphasis is placed upon the first usage of that person's name and upon the first reference to the spouse. The NGS Quarterly System uses boldface for this purpose, while the Register uses small capitals in lieu of lowercase letters. The NGS Quarterly System format does not use abbreviations in the text, but the Register uses them in the genealogical data—for example, b. for born and d. for died.

Genealogists using typewriters or writing in longhand found it nearly impossible to create superscript, small caps, italics, and boldface in the same way that typographers could. This is no longer a problem since today's software and computer printers can handle these typographical functions. Genealogical format styles do change, especially regarding typography. If you submit material to a scholarly genealogical journal for consideration, you'll want to follow its current guidelines on style matters.

The following sections present examples of the same genealogical material, created with Family Tree Maker in its Register, NGS Quarterly System, and Ahnentafel formats.

REGISTER EXAMPLE

This is how material looks in Register format. Note the use of small capital letters for all names. However, documents printed in the NEHGS *Register* now put the first reference to a person in boldface capitals and the parenthetical outlines of ancestry in italics in upper and lower case. Moreover, the Register style puts the lists of children of each treated individual in a smaller font size.

Earp Genealogy

Generation No. 1

1. NICHOLAS PORTER[2] EARP *(WALTER[1])*[1]. He married (1) ABIGAIL STORM[2] December 22, 1836 in Ohio County, Kentucky. He married (2) VIRGINIA ANN COOKSEY July 27, 1840 in Hartford, Ohio County, Kentucky. He married (3) ANNIE ALEXANDER[3] October 14, 1893 in San Bernardino County, California.

Children of NICHOLAS EARP and ABIGAIL STORM are:

2.   i.   NEWTON JASPER[3] EARP.
     ii.   MARIA H ANN EARP.

Children of NICHOLAS EARP and VIRGINIA COOKSEY are:

     iii. JAMES COOKSEY[3] EARP[4,5,6,7,8], m. NELLIE "BESSIE" BARTLETT KETCHUM[9], April 18, 1873, Illinois[10].
3.   iv.   VIRGIL WALTER EARP.
     v.   MARTHA ELIZABETH EARP[11].
     vi.   WYATT BERRY STAPP EARP, m. (1) URILLA SUTHERLAND, January 10, 1870, Lamar, Barton County, Missouri; m. (2) CELIA ANN BLAYLOCK, 1878; m. (3) JOSEPHINE SARAH MARCUS, Abt. 1883, California?[12].
     vii. MORGAN S. EARP, m. LOUISE [--?--].
     viii. WARREN BAXTER EARP.

ix.   VIRGINIA A. EARP.

4.   x.   ADELIA DOUGLAS EARP.

Endnotes

1. Jean Whitten Edwards, *Earp Family Genealogy*, (Breckenridge, Texas: Breck Printing, 1991), p. 139, References to material about Nicholas Earp is given as coming from "Data on the Earp Family," by Mrs. William Irvine, where it was copied from a newspaper article, from Vallejo, Calif. [dates not provided]. Under "Notes and References" for material about this generation, No. 17 lists: "Mrs. William Irvine, Data on the Earp Family Frank Waters, "The Earp Brothers of Tombstone," a Bison Book, B978.020924.

6. Stuart N. Lake, *Wyatt Earp: Frontier Marshal*, (New York: Pocket Books (reprint), 1993).

7. Frank Waters, *The Earp Brothers of Tombstone: The Story of Mrs. Virgil Earp*, (New York: Framhall House, 1960).

8. Glenn G. Boyer (collected and edited by), *I Married Wyatt Earp: The Recollections of Josephine Sarah Marcus Earp*, (Tucson, Ariz.: University of Arizona Press, second printing, 1979, copyright, 1976).

17. *U.S. census, Barton County, Missouri, population schedule, Lamar township, Barton post office, page 830B, (written page number 28), family numbers 212, 213 and 214,* National Archives micropublication M593, Roll 757.

NGS QUARTERLY EXAMPLE

Descendants of Nicholas Porter Earp

Generation No. 1

    1. Nicholas Porter2 Earp (Walter[1])[1]. He married **(1) Abigail Storm**[2] December 22, 1836 in Ohio County, Kentucky. He married **(2) Virginia Ann Cooksey** July 27, 1840 in Hartford, Ohio County, Kentucky. He married **(3) Annie Alexander**[3] October 14, 1893 in San Bernardino County, California.

Children of Nicholas Earp and Abigail Storm are:

+   2   i.   Newton Jasper[3] Earp.

     3   ii.   Mariah Ann Earp.

Children of Nicholas Earp and Virginia Cooksey are:

     4   i.   James Cooksey[3] Earp[4,5,6,7,8]. He married Nellie "Bessie" Bartlett Ketchum[9] April 18, 1873 in Illinois[10].

+   5   ii.   Virgil Walter Earp.

     6   iii.   Martha Elizabeth Earp[11].

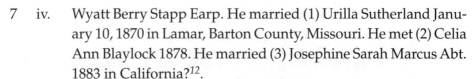

7	iv.	Wyatt Berry Stapp Earp. He married (1) Urilla Sutherland January 10, 1870 in Lamar, Barton County, Missouri. He met (2) Celia Ann Blaylock 1878. He married (3) Josephine Sarah Marcus Abt. 1883 in California?[12].
8	v.	Morgan S. Earp. He married Louise [--?--].
9	vi.	Warren Baxter Earp.
10	vii.	Virginia A. Earp.
+ 11	viii.	Adelia Douglas Earp.

Endnotes

1. Jean Whitten Edwards, *Earp Family Genealogy*, (Breckenridge, Texas: Breck Printing, 1991), p. 139, Reference to material about Nicholas Earp is given as coming from "Data on the Earp Family," by Mrs. William Irvine, where it was copied from a newspaper article, from Vallejo, California. [dates not provided]. Under "Notes and References" for material about this generation, No. 17 lists as the source: "Mrs. William Irvine, Data on the Earp Family, Frank Waters, *The Earp Brothers of Tombstone*, a Bison Book, B978.020924.

6. Stuart N. Lake, *Wyatt Earp: Frontier Marshal*, (New York: Pocket Books (reprint), 1993).

7. Frank Waters, *The Earp Brothers of Tombstone: The Story of Mrs. Virgil Earp*, (New York: Framhall House, 1960).

8. Glenn G. Boyer (collected and edited by), *I Married Wyatt Earp: The Recollections of Josephine Sarah Marcus Earp*, (Tucson, Ariz.: University of Arizona Press, second printing, 1979, copyright, 1976).

17. *U.S. census, Barton County, Missouri, population schedule, Lamar township, Barton post office, page 830B, (written page number 28), family numbers 212, 213 and 214*, National Archives micropublication M593, Roll 757.

AHNENTAFEL EXAMPLE

The other format available for Family Tree Maker's Genealogy Reports is the *Ahnentafel* (German for *ancestor table*), which is ancestor-ordered rather than descendant-ordered as are the other two styles. The Ahnentafel format lists both the maternal and paternal lines by generation in the same report.

You may be more familiar with the traditional Ahnentafel, which is a condensed genealogy format—a continuous list of ancestors instead of a chart. The Ahnentafel format created by Family Tree Maker starts with the specified individual, but shows both the descendants and the ancestors of that person.

Ancestors of Nicholas Porter Earp

Generation No. 1

1. Nicholas Porter Earp[1]. He was the son of **2. Walter Earp** and **3. Martha Ann Early**. He married **(1) Abigail Storm**[2] December 22, 1836 in Ohio County, Kentucky. He married **(2) Virginia Ann Cooksey** July 27, 1840 in Hartford, Ohio County, Kentucky. He married **(3) Annie Alexander**[3] October 14, 1893 in San Bernardino County, California.

Children of Nicholas Earp and Abigail Storm are:

    i.   Newton Jasper Earp, married Nancy Jane Adams September 12, 1865 in Marion County, Missouri.

    ii.   Mariah Ann Earp.

Children of Nicholas Earp and Virginia Cooksey are:

    i.   James Cooksey Earp[4,5,6,7,8], married Nellie "Bessie" Bartlett Ketchum April 18, 1873 in Illinois[9].

    ii.   Virgil Walter Earp[10], married (1) Magdelana C. "Ellen" Rysdam September 21, 1861 in Knoxville, Marion County, Iowa[10]; married (2) Rosella Dragoo 1870 in Lamar, Barton County, Missouri[11]; married (3) Alvira Packingham Sullivan Abt. 1874.

    iii.   Martha Elizabeth Earp[12].

    iv.   Wyatt Berry Stapp Earp, married (1) Urilla Sutherland January 10, 1870 in Lamar, Barton County, Missouri; met (2) Celia Ann Blaylock 1878; married (3) Josephine Sarah Marcus Abt. 1883 in California?[13].

    v.   Morgan S. Earp, married Louise [--?--].

    vi.   Warren Baxter Earp.

    vii.   Virginia A. Earp.

    viii.   Adelia Douglas Earp, married William Thomas Edwards.

Generation No. 2

2. Walter Earp. He married **3. Martha Ann Early** 1808 in Pittsylvania County, VA.

3. Martha Ann Early.

Children of Walter Earp and Martha Early are:

       i.   Lorenzo Dow Earp[14], married (1) Nancy Storm December 25, 1834 in Ohio County, Kentucky; married (2) Syrene Iler 1851 in ?.

1   ii.   Nicholas Porter Earp, married (1) Abigail Storm December 22, 1836 in Ohio County, Kentucky; married (2) Virginia Ann Cooksey July 27, 1840 in Hartford, Ohio County, Kentucky; married (3) Annie Alexander October 14, 1893 in San Bernardino County, California.

     iii.   James O'Kelly Earp.

     iv.   Elizabeth Earp[15], married Greenberry Ezell November 22, 1832 in Ohio County, Kentucky.

     v.   Josiah Jackson Earp.

     vi.   Francis Asbury Earp.

    vii.   Walter Cooksey Earp.

   viii.   Jonathan Douglas Earp.

     ix.   Sarah Ann Earp.

Endnotes

1. Jean Whitten Edwards, *Earp Family Genealogy*, (Breckenridge, Texas: Breck Printing, 1991), p. 139, Reference to material about Nicholas Earp is given as coming from "Data on the Earp Family," by Mrs. William Irvine, where it was copied from a newspaper article, from Vallejo, Calif. [dates not provided]. Under "Notes and References" for material about this generation, No. 17 lists: "Mrs. William Irvine, Data on the Earp Family Frank Waters, "The Earp Brothers of Tombstone," a Bison Book, B978.020924.

6. Stuart N. Lake, *Wyatt Earp: Frontier Marshal*, (New York: Pocket Books (reprint), 1993).

7. Frank Waters, *The Earp Brothers of Tombstone: The Story of Mrs. Virgil Earp*, (New York: Framhall House, 1960).

8. Glenn G. Boyer (collected and edited by), *I Married Wyatt Earp: The Recollections of Josephine Sarah Marcus Earp*, (Tucson, Ariz.: University of Arizona Press, second printing, 1979, copyright, 1976).

17. *U.S. census, Barton County, Missouri, population schedule, Lamar township, Barton post office, page 830B, (written page number 28), family numbers 212, 213 and 214*, National Archives micropublication M593, Roll 757.

Endnotes Explained

For the previous examples, the endnotes are the same in all three formats, since they come from the same sources and database. You can use the E_dit Master

Sources option (on the <u>E</u>dit menu) to enter detailed information about your sources. (You learned about this option in Chapter Four, "Editing Sources as You Go.") You'll want to study the printed version of your endnotes to be sure they are in the proper form. If you'd like to change the way notes for your sources appear within the Genealogy Reports (as endnotes, inline notes, or not to appear at all), select Options from the Contents menu, then make your choice from the Source Information area of the Options for Genealogy Report dialog box.

Family Tree Maker repeats the full name of a source every time instead of using "ibid"—the Latin abbreviation for ibidem, meaning *in the same place.* This abbreviation shows up frequently in genealogies because it saves space—the same source, a census or parish record, for example, often provides information for several members of the family who appear in the record. If you really want to use the abbreviation, you can export all three Genealogy Reports in Rich Text Format (.rtf, a file type that preserves the formatting) and then open the resulting file in your word processor to edit further. On the other hand, you may prefer the longer Family Tree Maker format.

Running Genealogy Reports in Family Tree Maker

Before you generate a Genealogy Report, you'll first want to select the primary individual for the report by clicking on the name on the Family Page (or in any other view where you can select an individual). You can then run a Genealogy Report by clicking on the Gen Rpt button on the toolbar, or from the <u>V</u>iew Menu, Select G<u>e</u>nealogy Report. The Genealogy Report then appears in the format that was last selected (Register, NGS Quarterly, or Ahnentafel).

Choosing a Style

From within the Genealogy Report, select Forma<u>t</u>, Genealogy Report <u>F</u>ormat to open the Genealogy Report Format dialog box (see Figure 12-1). This is where you can select the format for your Genealogy Report.

If you haven't previously run this report, then <u>R</u>egister is probably selected; the one you see selected when you first open the dialog box happens to be the report already shown onscreen. To switch to one of the other styles, click on its option button. Notice the sample of the style in the lower half of the dialog box. Click on OK. If you changed the style option, the new style of report appears.

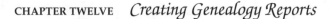

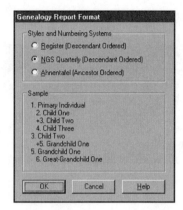

Figure 12-1

Three Genealogy Report formats are offered: Register, NGS Quarterly, or Ahnentafel.

Formatting the Text

You have just a few formatting options for Genealogy Reports. You can change the font, style, and size of text, but you can't change its color—it's designed to be shown and printed in black text. From the Format menu, choose Text Font, Style, & Size to open the relevant dialog box (see Figure 12-2). There are six different text items you can format, shown in the Items To Format list box.

In the Items To Format list box, select an item, and then select options from the Font, Size, and Style drop-down list boxes. Do this for each item for which you want to change the text format, and then click on OK. The text formatting changes are applied to the report.

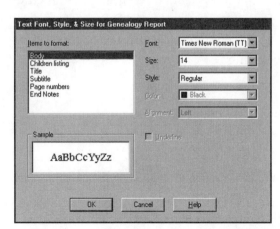

Figure 12-2

Choose your font, size, and style on each of the formattable items for the Genealogy Report.

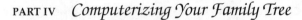

Figure 12-3

Choose a custom title
or use the automatic
title for your
Genealogy Report.

Adjusting the Title and Page Numbering

You can make choices about the title and page numbers for the Genealogy Report. From the <u>C</u>ontents menu, choose Title & Footnote to open the Title & Footnote For Genealogy Report dialog box (see Figure 12-3). If you don't want to keep the <u>A</u>utomatic title, then click on the <u>C</u>ustom title option button and type a new title in the text box. If you want to use page numbers, keep the Include <u>P</u>age Number check box selected and use the <u>S</u>tarting Number spin box to change the starting number if necessary. Click on OK; the changes are applied to the report.

Changing the Number of Generations

Another option you have to choose from is the number of generations to show in the Genealogy Report. From the <u>C</u>ontents menu, choose # Of <u>G</u>enerations To Show. The dialog box that appears (see Figure 12-4) includes a spin box labeled Select <u>N</u>umber Of Generations To Show. Select a number (the default is 4) and then click on OK. If you changed the number of generations, the report changes to reflect the new setting.

Figure 12-4

You can decide the
number of
generations to show
in your Genealogy
Report.

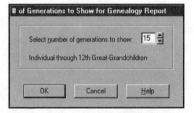

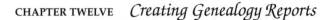

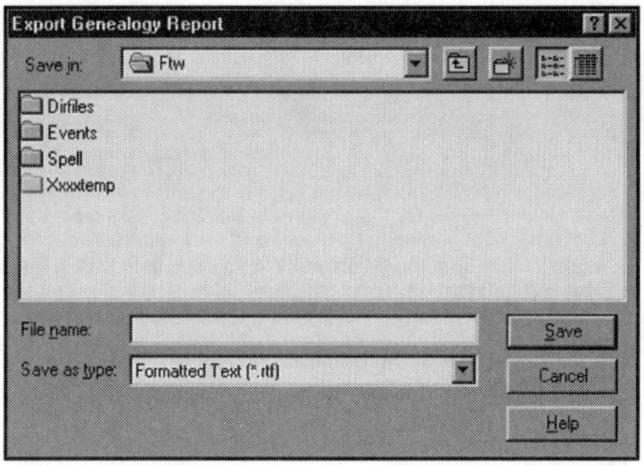

Figure 12-5

Choose a folder and file name where you want to export the Genealogy report.

Exporting the Report

Genealogy Reports can be exported in Rich Text Format (.rtf), making the information easy to import into a word processor for additional editing or polishing. Reports can also be exported in plain text format (.txt), but this will not preserve any of the formatting. From the File menu, choose Export Genealogy Report to open the Export Genealogy Report dialog box (see Figure 12-5). Choose a folder in which to save the report, and type a file name. Keep the Save As Type setting as Formatted Text (*.rtf) if you want to preserve the formatting you see in the existing report.

Choose Save to export the Genealogy Report to the selected folder. Now you can open the exported file in a word processor or other program, where you can further edit it as desired.

Including Notes and Other Options

In addition to the standard Genealogy Report formats, you can also produce these reports with all the material you've input into the Notes window. If you have family stories that you've compiled in another Windows program, you can copy them to the Clipboard, then paste them into the appropriate Notes window (see Figure 12-6) to later include them into a Genealogy Report. (Also see Chapter Eight for more information on importing and exporting text to and from the Notes window.)

You can also include information from the Facts and Medical windows in a Genealogy Report by choosing the appropriate settings in the Options For

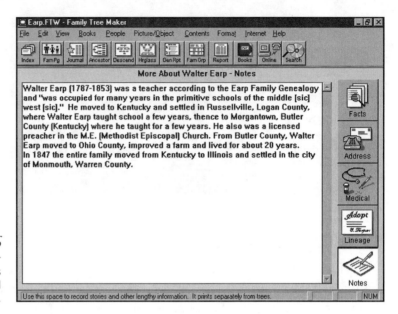

Figure 12-6

Text from a Notes window can be added to a Genealogy report.

Genealogy Report dialog box. To select these and more Genealogy Report options, follow these steps:

1. On the Family Page, click on an individual for whom you have entered information in the Notes, Facts, or Medical windows (except for height and weight, which do not appear on the report). Alternatively, select an individual for whom you have entered notes, facts, or medical information for any of his or her *descendents*. (Or for the Ahnentafel format, use information on *ancestors*.) The purpose is to show how these notes and facts appear in a Genealogy Report so that you can decide whether to include or exclude them.

2. Run a Genealogy Report, as described earlier. The report appears onscreen.

3. From the Contents menu, choose Options. The Options For Genealogy dialog box appears (see Figure 12-7).

    ❀ **TIP** ❀   *Another way to display all the options available for the Genealogy Report is to right-click on the report to open the shortcut menu. Each*

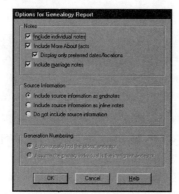

Figure 12-7

Set which options to include or exclude for a Genealogy Report.

item on the shortcut menu opens a dialog box. Selecting Options here is another method of opening the Options For Genealogy Report dialog box.

4. To include the contents of the Notes window for the primary individual and descendants on the Genealogy Report, select the Include Individual Notes check box. To include marriage notes, select the Include Marriage Notes check box. Notes and facts for ancestors will not be shown, even though their names appear on the report. The exception is the Ahnentafel format, which does show ancestor notes and facts.

    ❄ **TIP** ❄   *What if you want some of the notes to show, but not everyone's? Family Tree Maker must include all or none, so go ahead and include all of them, export the report to a file (as explained in the previous section), then open the file in a word processor and edit it to remove any notes you don't want to show on this copy of the report.*

5. To include the contents of the Facts and Medical windows (excluding height and weight) for the primary individual and descendants, select the Include More About Facts check box. If you select this option, then you can also decide to select the Display Only Preferred Dates/Locations check box to display only those facts that have the Pref'd check box selected in the Facts window. The facts and medical information appear on the Genealogy Report in a paragraph for the individual, beginning with the words "More About."

✢ **NOTE** ✢   *By default, the facts in the Facts window have the Pref'd check box already selected. Only if there is a duplicate fact type is one or more of the Pref'd check boxes not selected. For example, if you have two facts labeled Born because you don't know which is correct and want to keep both until the dates and locations are verified, you can choose to show only the preferred one (the one you have checked as Pref'd) in the Genealogy Report. To show all facts—even the not preferred ones—uncheck the Display Only Preferred Dates/Locations check box in the Options For Genealogy Report dialog box. See the sidebar "Locating Conflicting Facts" later in this chapter to learn how to locate all the conflicting facts in the Family File.*

Because the Include Source Information As Endnotes option button is selected by default, source information is normally included as endnotes in the Genealogy Report. You can change this or exclude sources from the report.

6. To show sources within the report instead of at the end, select the Include Source Information As Inline Notes option button. To exclude sources from the report, select the Do Not Include Source Information option button.

   You can also change the way generations are numbered in the report. By default, Genealogy Reports use Automatically Find The Oldest Ancestor (Male)—that's the method that is selected in the Generation Numbering area of the dialog box until you change it.

   ✢ **TIP** ✢   *In the example "**NICHOLAS PORTER² EARP (WALTER¹)¹.**" the superscript 2 after Nicholas Porter shows that he is the second generation in this particular genealogy. His father, Walter, has a superscript 1 after his name, which shows he is the first generation in this genealogy. Any superscript numbers that occur after punctuation marks are endnote references.*

7. To change the generation numbering so that the report begins with a generation number of "1," regardless of how many generations precede the primary individual, select the Assume The Primary Individual Is The Immigrant Ancestor check box.

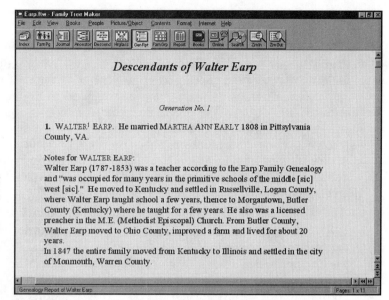

Figure 12-8

The Register
Genealogy Report
showing information
from the Notes
window for Walter
Earp, father of
Nicholas Porter Earp.

8. Click on OK. The changes are applied to the Genealogy Report (see Figure 12-8).

    ❧ **NOTE** ❧ *Every time you run a different Genealogy Report—that is, switch between the Register, NGS Quarterly, or Ahnentafel formats—you must go into the Options for Genealogy Reports dialog box and choose the options you wish to include.*

    ❧ **NOTE** ❧ *After you finish setting options for a Genealogy Report, you can print it much the same as other reports. From the File menu, choose Print Genealogy Report. Click on the Setup button if you want to change any print setup options. Click on OK to print.*

Genealogical Source Reports

Family Tree Maker offers you two other reports that are important to a good genealogy: the Bibliography and the Documented Events reports. You access these reports the same way you accessed the reports in Chapter Ten—in the Report Format dialog box (see Figure 12-10). That is, click on the Report button

Locating Conflicting Facts

Family Tree Maker allows you to enter pieces of information in the Facts window that seem to conflict with each other. There is a good reason for this: as you do your genealogical research, you're bound to find different accounts of the same event, and you'll want to store them all while you're investigating further. Some of these inconsistencies won't ever be resolved, but you may want to check on them periodically. Then you can add reminders in your Research Journal To Do list to look for more evidence. Some of these apparently conflicting facts could be data entry errors, too—in that case you can clean them up so they won't appear on your Genealogy Reports.

The tool you can use to help locate these inconsistencies is the Alternate Facts report, accessed from the Report Format dialog box. It can cover the entire Family File or just selected individuals. First click on the Report button on the toolbar, and then from the Format menu, choose Report Format. In the Report Format dialog box (see Figure 12-9), select Alternate Facts and then click on OK. The Alternate Facts report appears.

To go to the individual's Facts window to examine or correct the alternate facts, select the individual's name in the report and then from the View menu, choose More About, then Facts. The Facts window appears. If you need to keep the alternate fact for now, be sure the one you regard as more likely to be correct has a check mark in its Pref'd check box—that's the one that will show up in certain reports that allow you to show the preferred data.

Figure 12-9

Run the Alternate Facts report to double-check for discrepancies in the file.

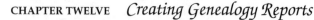

Figure 12-10

You can find the
Bibliography report in
the Report Format
dialog box.

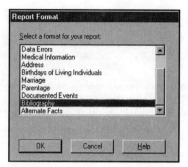

on the toolbar. From the Format menu, choose Report Format. You'll have to scroll to the bottom of the list box to find the Bibliography and Documented Events reports. Select the one you want and then click on OK.

Creating a Bibliography Report

The Bibliography report can be helpful as you research, giving you a quick overview of the references you've already consulted or letting you provide precise information to your cousin Sherril when she wants to obtain a copy of a particular book, for example.

The Bibliography report is available in two formats: standard and annotated. From the Contents menu, choose Options to open the Options For Bibliography Report dialog box. The Standard Bibliography format is the default report; it lists master sources which have been referenced with a citation and includes such information as author, title, and publisher for each source. If you want an annotated bibliography, which displays everything you entered about your sources, select Annotated Bibliography and then click on OK. Figure 12-11 shows an annotated bibliography.

> ❊ **NOTE** ❊   *The Options For Bibliography Report dialog box has a check box labeled Include Footnotes Without Referenced Sources. Check this box to include source entries from a previous version of Family Tree Maker. These entries will not have a title until you enter one in the Master Source dialog box.*

The annotated version is the one in which your explanatory notes or commentary regarding the material will show up. This will be the text you have entered in the Comments text box of each of the Master Source citations (shown in Figure 12-12).

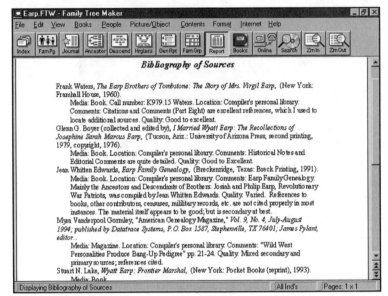

Figure 12-11

Bibliographies can be
annotated (like this
one) or in the
standard format
(without the extra
commentary).

✽ TIP ✽   *You learned in Chapter Four about entering master sources, in the section "Entering Sources as You Go." Click in the data field, then from the* View *menu, choose* Source, *and then click on the* Edit Master Source *button. You can also go directly to the Master Source dialog box: from the* Edit *menu, choose* Edit Master Sources.

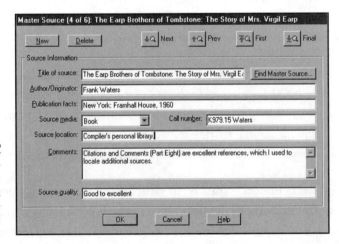

Figure 12-12

The contents of the
Comments text box
will appear in the
annotated
bibliography.

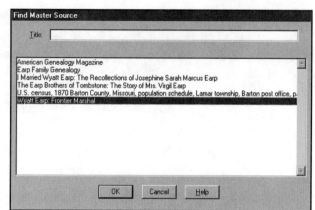

Figure 12-13

Use the Find Master
Source dialog box to
locate the name of the
source you want to
edit or delete.

No matter how carefully you document sources, you will probably make a mistake or two along the way; this is easily fixed by editing the Master Source. To locate a Master Source, choose Edit Master Sources from the Edit menu. Click on the Find Master Source button and then, in the Find Master source dialog box (see Figure 12-13), select the source that needs editing and click on OK. In the Master Source dialog box, make the correction (or click on the Delete button if you need to delete the source entry) and then click on OK.

> ❀ **TIP** ❀ *As with other reports that are selected in the Report Format dialog box, you can add formatting and select which individuals to include. Right-click on the displayed Bibliography report to select from the available options on the shortcut menu (the same options, except printing, are available on the Format and Contents menus).*

Creating a Documented Events Report

The Documented Events report (see Figure 12-14) lists individuals in your Family File for whom you have entered sources to document events. It can come in handy when you're trying to figure out what really happened to someone in your family.

You can choose from a number of options to restrict the individuals and events shown on the report. First run the report (available in the Report Format dialog box) and then from the Contents menu, choose Options. In the Options For Docu-

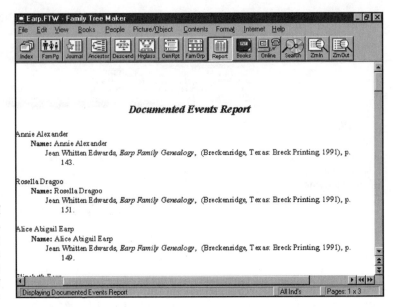

Figure 12-14

The Documented
Events Report reveals
what sources you have
for individuals in your
Family File.

mented Events Report dialog box (see Figure 12-15), select the options you want for the Whom To Report, What To Report, and Printed Format areas. Then click on OK to apply these options to the report.

It's helpful to use all of Family Tree Maker's reports—they have distinct functions. Don't be afraid to experiment with them. You can always change your mind with just a click here and there.

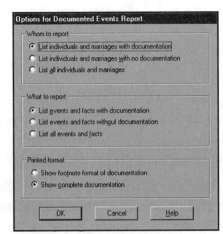

Figure 12-15

Select options to
define which
individuals and events
will appear on the
Documented
Events Report.

Ancestors of George Howard Lafferty

Samuel Lafferty
1801 - 1871

Edwin E. Lafferty
1834 - 1907

Margaret McDowell
1803 - 1861

George E. Lafferty
1867 - 1936

Erastus Fowler
1793 - 1875

lelia Fowler
1914

Temperence Merrill
1796 - 1871

Nathan Wescott
1818 - 1900

ram Wescott
1820 - 1901

Sarah Ann McMichael
1820 - 1861

an Wescott
1963

Samuel C. Amsden
1822 - 1899

Theresa Jerusa Amsden
1845 - 1934

Clarissa Hubbard
1820 - 1870

The History of George Howard Lafferty

George Howard Lafferty was born September 2, 1894 in Lenox township, Ashtabula County, Ohio, to Amber Amelia Wescott Lafferty and George Edwin Lafferty. A sister, Maud Irene, was born May 23, 1892.

A family of farmers, the Laffertys harvested the land where they lived. On May 9, 1919, they moved to Warren, Ohio, to a house on Forest Street NE. They lived next door to their daughter Maud, her husband Jay Rood Webster, and their three beautiful daughters, Reta, Shirley, and Marion.

As a youth, Lafferty went by "Howard" rather than "George" and signed his name as G. Howard Lafferty. After graduating from Lenox Township schools in 1911, he received a Teachers Certificate and became an educator and later a high school Principal. He then switched careers and ventured into banking just before World War I.

As a student at Ohio State University during the war, Howard Lafferty hoped to join the army but was classified 5G due to his glasses and other restrictions. In 1923 he received an L.L.B. degree and passed

CHAPTER THIRTEEN

Creating a Family History Book

ou've collected data on your ancestors, checked sources, scanned photos, copied tombstone inscriptions, located deeds, wills, and naturalization records . . . now what? If you are itching to share your information with friends, family, and even the interested public, it's time to publish a family history book. Most family historians don't spend the long hours researching their families solely for their own enjoyment. Who doesn't want to share the results of their research with children, grandparents, cousins, and interested researchers? Fortunately, Family Tree Maker gives you the tools to create an entertaining, informative, and valuable family history book.

Don't be intimidated by the thought of creating a book! Anyone can do it. A family history book does not have to be a formal genealogy published in hardback and sold to other researchers. Your book can be a simple collection of family data, photos, and stories that you want to share with your immediate family during the holidays or give as a birthday or anniversary gift. Grandparents may want to create a book for their grandchildren with information about their ancestors. You can create separate books for each of your parents' families, or each of your eight great-grandparents' families! Of course, if you wish, you can create a detailed, documented, thoroughly researched family history featuring several generations, with reports, charts, sources, and analytical writing.

Planning Your Family History Book

Whichever type of book you choose to create, you should have a specific goal in mind before you begin. Your goal will influence the format of the book, and having a particular focus will keep you on track when you begin collecting the various charts, reports, text, and custom book items. I'll get into the details on how to use Family Tree Maker to create a book later in this chapter—but planning has to come first.

Choosing a Book Format

Family history books vary a lot, but they all fall into two basic categories: ancestor and descendant formats. Ancestor-format books are ideal gifts for family members (parents, grandparents, siblings, children, and grandchildren). The ancestor format shows an individual's family history generation by generation, starting with a specific person, and working backward. You can create an ancestor-format book with yourself as the primary individual, books for each of your parents, for your grandparents, great-grandparents . . . you choose how specific you want the book's focus to be by designating the starting individual.

Descendant-format books are great for family reunions, family gifts (Christmas and birthdays), and for exchange with other interested researchers. The descendant format shows how everyone fits into a family tree by starting with distant ancestors, and working forward to the current generation. Direct descendant-format books can show a particular line, and how a particular person is related to a specific ancestor (a *direct descendant* format shows only a single line of descents between an ancestor and an individual). You may want to keep a copy of a direct descendant line with you when you are researching as a reminder of important individuals and information.

Deciding on the Contents

The first step to creating a successful family history book, be it solely for sharing information with your immediate family or for taking a critical look at several generations, is to plan what items you want to include in the book.

For Immediate Family Members

Perhaps you want to create a book to share with your children, parents, brothers and sisters, and other immediate family members. For such an audience, you may not want to detail information about distant ancestors, and instead might celebrate living family members. Books for a small family circle (or large circle if you'd like to include cousins) can be great fun at family gatherings and holidays. If you want to create a book featuring immediate family members, you might want to include:

- Family Group Sheets for each family to remind everyone "who belongs where."

- Themed photos (childhood, birthdays, holidays, weddings) or family portraits.

- Family stories and interviews about different family events, traditions, and places.

- A Calendar showing everyone's birthday and anniversary dates.

- A Kinship report to settle relationship issues regarding distant cousins. (No more arguments about cousin Joan being a second cousin once removed, or a first cousin twice removed.)

- A Custom report showing different family features (eye colors, years of education, age at marriage, or whatever).

ANCESTOR EMPHASIS

You may want to create a book about you and your ancestors for your children or grandchildren. Who could resist a book written by parents or grandparents, sharing their joys, their sorrows, and detailing all of the major events of their lives? If you want to create such a book for your descendants, you might want to include:

- Family Group Sheets to show which relatives made up what family.

- Photos for as many major events as you can find (births, marriages, graduations, first car, first new home, etc.). Photos of distant ancestors are probably much harder to come by, which makes them that much more valuable. Include photos for every individual when possible. You may want to include a descriptive text pointing out some feature (notice that Grandma Teuke had the same widow's peak that her mother and sisters have), or information about the event depicted in the photo. (This is Uncle Bob's first new car—he worked all summer in an ice-cream shop to buy it.)

❋ Your autobiography or family memories. This is your moment to shine—spend some time collecting your memories and writing them down as they occur to you. You might even want to take a class in writing your life history! Your memories and family stories help your children to understand your life. Don't be shy about a variety of topics (births, deaths, world events, good times, bad times, etc.).

❋ A calendar to show the birth dates and anniversaries of your ancestors. Some families have a tradition of taking flowers to a relative's grave on his or her birthday, or remembering a special day in an ancestor's life.

❋ A timeline to remind your audience of the events that might have had an influence on you and your ancestor's lives: how old you were when World War II broke out, how your family made it through the depression, how you thrived through Reagan's trickle-down economics.

❋ An Ancestor Tree (or Ancestor Fan Tree) to graphically display your ancestors.

❋ An Hourglass Tree to show graphically how the generations, both ancestors and descendants, are connected.

❋ An Ahnentafel report to show your ancestors by generation.

❋ A Custom report showing different ancestral family facts (age at marriage, age at death, medical information, and so on).

❋ An Index to sort all the individuals in your book.

DESCENDANT EMPHASIS

There may come a time when you want to create a more formal family history that shows the descendants of a particular ancestor. If you were creating a book for your family or other researchers about the descendants of specific ancestors, you might want to include:

❋ A title. Pick an appropriate one for the entire family—"Our Jones Family" is not the best title for a detailed family history;

"Descendants of William Jones and Hannah Price" gives more information, and "William Jones and Hannah Price of Jonesville, Iowa" gives researchers a better idea of what Jones family you are featuring.

* A table of contents (automatically generated by Family Tree Maker)

* An Introduction or Foreword to explain your purpose and research.

* Family Group Sheets to show nuclear families.

* Photos (always include photos and scanned images of documents and records whenever possible).

* A calendar to show ancestors' birth and anniversary dates.

* A timeline to show readers what world and local events would have had an influence on the individuals.

* A Kinship report to keep those relationships understandable.

* A Descendant Tree (or Descendant Fan Tree) to graphically display the descendants of an individual.

* An Hourglass Tree if you want to show the descendants and ancestors on the same tree.

* A Genealogy Report in NGS Quarterly or Register format to present the results of your long hours of research. Most formal family histories have information presented in such a format.

* An Outline Descendant report to show at a glance how everyone was related to the primary individual.

* Custom reports showing different ancestral family facts (migration information, ages at specific events, and so on).

* Biographies of individuals to flesh out otherwise dry ancestors.

* A Bibliography of sources to allow other researchers to find out where you found your information.

* And finally, an Index so readers can locate anyone you mention in the book.

Remember that your goal influences the items you want to present in your book! Be creative and play with different reports and charts before deciding on the items to include.

Fleshing Out Those Bones

You probably have lots of people in your Family Tree Maker database, but how much information beyond names and dates do you have for those people? Re-read "Basics of Research" and "Putting Flesh on Bare-Bones Genealogies" in Chapter One if your collection seems dull. Dry facts only (names, dates, and locations) can make poor reading; the key to a successful and interesting family history is to make those skinny ancestors plump with information! Dig through those shoeboxes of family memorabilia and pull out items that might tell you something about your ancestors. Search your family archives for items such as:

- Family journals or diaries
- Photos, tintypes, silhouettes, drawings, and portraits
- Letters and postcards
- School report cards or yearbooks
- Birth, death, and marriage certificates
- Immigration and naturalization records
- Deeds and wills
- Funeral cards, obituaries, and funeral notices
- Artwork and creative writings
- Textiles (clothing, quilts, needlework)
- Newspaper clippings
- Information from published sources (biographies or genealogies)

You may also want to develop oral histories by talking with family members and transcribing the results. Oral histories, which you learned about in earlier chapters of this book, can be about a specific individual, or they can be general family memories. Some topics you may want to interview family members about are:

- ⚜ Reminiscences of parents and grandparents
- ⚜ Holiday traditions
- ⚜ Major world events and how they affected the individual
- ⚜ Childhood
- ⚜ Teenage years
- ⚜ Employment
- ⚜ Death of family members

Once you have gathered additional data about your ancestors, you can enter the information into Family Tree Maker or create separate text documents (notes) for each individual, to be included later in your book. You can include your notes in the Family Tree Maker Notes window for each individual, or you may want to keep your notes separate if you are writing a detailed biography or autobiography. Scanned records such as wills and deeds can be included in an individual's (or a marriage's) Scrapbook, or you can create a written extract of the important information contained in those records and include it in an individual's Notes (or your own research notes).

A word about horse thieves, cattle rustlers, pirates, and other black sheep: don't be afraid to mention ancestors who might have been on the wrong side of the law. Many family histories from years ago turned a blind eye to the misdeeds of some family members in an attempt to make the family more presentable. Remember that you are not responsible for the actions of your ancestors, you are just recording their information. Tact is required, however, when dealing with present situations where family members may not desire publication of delicate information. Before you include a fact that might cause distress, discuss the situation with the individuals in question—and remember that it's a really bad idea

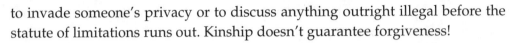

to invade someone's privacy or to discuss anything outright illegal before the statute of limitations runs out. Kinship doesn't guarantee forgiveness!

Organizing your book before you begin creating it is such an important point, it's a good idea to review the key steps:

- ☀ Set a goal for the purpose of the book
- ☀ Consider your intended audience
- ☀ Choose ancestor or descendant format
- ☀ Pick the items to include
- ☀ Do your research first
- ☀ Flesh out the bones
- ☀ Don't censor facts, but be aware of sensitive areas

Creating a Book in Family Tree Maker

Once you've made all the planning decisions for your book, you're ready to move on to the actual creation. Before you begin, you should keep in mind that Family Tree Maker allows you to create up to 32 books per Family File (each book can contain 500 items). Here are some of the items you can include in a book:

Type of item	Available items
Front Matter	Title Page, Copyright Notice, Dedication, Preface, Foreword, Introduction
Trees	Ancestor Tree, Ancestor Fan Tree, Descendant Tree, Descendant Fan Tree, Hourglass Tree, Hourglass Fan Tree, Outline Descendant Tree
Reports	Kinship, Genealogy Report (in Register, NGS Quarterly, or Ahnentafel format), Medical Information, Address, Birthdays of Living Individuals, Marriage, Parentage, Documented Events, Alternate Facts, Bibliography

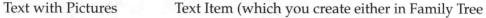

Text with Pictures	Text Item (which you create either in Family Tree Maker's Book text editor or copy and paste from your own word processor). You can insert Scrapbook pictures.
Other Views	Family Group Sheets, Calendar, Timeline
Generated for the Book	Table of Contents, Index

Book Project #1

Now that you've done all of the groundwork, you're probably ready to get started on a book. If you are new to creating a book with Family Tree Maker, you'll want to follow the two book projects detailed below.

Of course, your own family books are what you want to make—but it may be a good idea to start out by returning to the Earp family data so you can follow along with the examples for this project. You can substitute your own files if they're ready to work up into a book, of course. For the purposes of this example, I'll assume that you are Nellie Jane Earp (daughter of Virgil Earp and Magdalena Rysdam) and you want to create a book starting with your father, Virgil Walter Earp, and work back three generations. You want to share the books with your immediate family, and decide to include an Ancestor Tree, a Kinship report, and some text and photos, Calendars, and Family Group Sheets. To create the book for your father's family:

1. In Family Tree Maker, display the Family Page showing your father and click on his name.

2. From the <u>B</u>ooks menu, choose <u>N</u>ew Book. The New Book dialog box appears (see Figure 13-1).

Figure 13-1

When you name a new book, don't forget to enter the author's information.

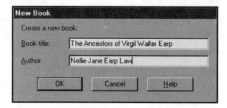

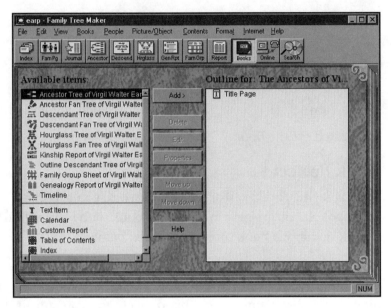

Figure 13-2

The Books window
shows the available
items and the current
outline for your book.

3. Enter a title for the book in the <u>B</u>ook Title text box, and your name in the <u>A</u>uthor text box.

4. Click on OK.

The Books window appears (see Figure 13-2). In the Books window you'll see an outline of items you can include in your book in a list box on the left side of the screen (under Available Items), while the items you have chosen appear in the list box on the right (under Outline For).

A Title Page is the first item in the Outline list on the right; Family Tree Maker adds it automatically when you fill in the book title and author information. To add items to your book, click on an item's name in the Available Items list, and then click on the Add button. Now, go ahead and add an Ancestor Tree and then a Kinship Report to the book. Figure 13-3 shows these items added to the outline.

> ❊ **TIP** ❊ *Don't worry right now whether the items you add are in order. You can rearrange them later. Also, it's OK to add items you aren't sure that you want, because you can remove them later.*

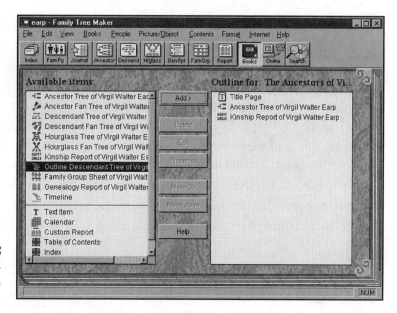

Figure 13-3

Continue to add items
to your outline.

When you click on the Text Item entry on the Available Items list, the Add Text Item dialog box appears, allowing you to select the type of text item you want (see Figure 13-4). You have a number of choices:

* <u>N</u>ew Text

* <u>I</u>ntroduction

* <u>P</u>reface

* <u>F</u>oreword

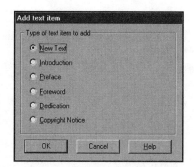

Figure 13-4

The Add Text Item
dialog box offers a
variety of text choices.

✶ Dedication

✶ Copyright Notice

In this case, since you want to add some free-form text and photos, click on the New Text option button and then click on OK. The New Text item appears in the outline. Since the title "New Text" isn't very descriptive, you may want to change it to something more personal. To change the section title, select Text Item in your outline, and then click on the Properties button to open the Item Properties dialog box. You can customize the title to something more descriptive by typing in the Item Name text box. If you're following this example, type **About Virgil Walter Earp.** Figure 13-5 shows the Item Properties dialog box.

Notice that the Item Properties dialog box has other options. You can specify whether you want an item to begin a chapter (this keeps its heading aligned to the left edge in the Table of Contents; unchecking this box causes the item to be indented in the Table of Contents, thus belonging to the item above it that is not indented). You also can choose to start on an odd-numbered page, and include a header or footer. Click on OK to return to the Books view.

Add the Calendar and Family Group Sheet items. When you finish, you should see Title Page, Ancestor Tree, Kinship Report, About Virgil Walter Earp, Calendar, and Family Group Sheet in the Outline list box (see Figure 13-6).

Now you have reports pertaining to your father (remember, we're using Virgil Walter Earp as your father for this example) in your book . . . but what about his father and grandfather? Since Virgil is your primary individual, the report that features only Virgil is the Family Group Sheet. Since you want to add Family

Figure 13-5

The Item Properties dialog box gives you a number of choices.

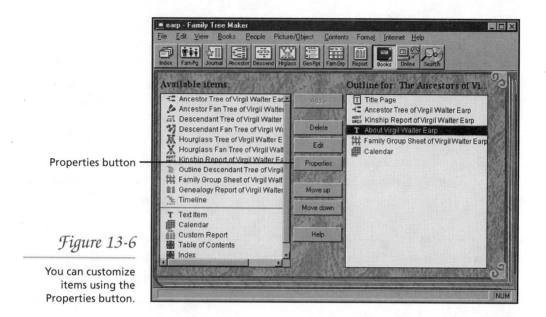

Properties button —

Figure 13-6

You can customize
items using the
Properties button.

Group Sheets for two generations of Virgil's ancestry, you'll need to add a Family Group Sheet for his father and grandfather (spouses will be automatically included in the reports). To add reports for other individuals:

1. In the Books window, click on the Index button.

2. Select your new primary individual (the individual for whom you want to create reports and trees), and click OK.

3. Family Tree Maker will take you back to the Books window, and all of the reports and trees will be for your new individual.

4. For our example, you'll want to select Nicholas Porter Earp (Virgil's father), select the report you want to include, and click on the Add button. In this example, add a Family Group Sheet for Nicholas Earp.

5. Add any additional reports, and then repeat these steps for Virgil's grandfather, Walter Earp. Add Walter's Family Group Sheet.

   ❧ **NOTE** ❧   *Notice in your book outline that any report featuring a primary individual has that person's name in the report title.*

You can rearrange items in the book outline by clicking on an item and dragging it up or down to a new position. A horizontal line indicates what the new position will be. When you release the mouse button, the item appears in the new position. Another way to move items is to select an item and then use the Move Up and Move Down buttons.

> **TIP** *Generate a table of contents by adding the Table of Contents item at the top of the outline (after the Title Page) and clicking on the Edit button. Generate an index for the book by adding the Index item at the bottom of the outline. Click on Edit to create and update it.*

Once you've included all the items you want in your book outline, you can go back and add text and photos—as described in the next section—and format the other items.

Adding Text and Photos

To add your own free-form text, select the text item you added (in this example it's called All About Virgil Walter Earp). Click on the Edit button in the center of the screen; Family Tree Maker displays the Text Item window. You can enter, paste, and format your text here just as you would in a word processor. You can also add photos or other images from any of the Scrapbooks connected with an individual by clicking on the Insert Scrapbook Picture button at the right end of the toolbar, or by choosing Scrapbook Picture from the Insert menu (see Figure 13-7).

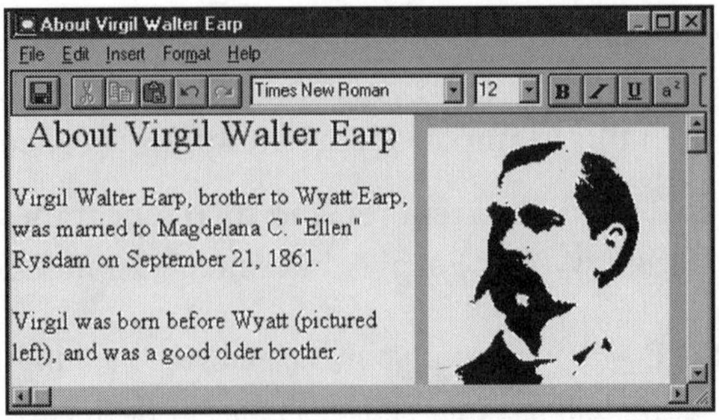

Figure 13-7

You can enter your own text and photos from any Scrapbook in the Text Item window.

Once you have a photo or other Scrapbook item added, you can move it around the page by clicking on it and dragging it, and you can format your text to be centered, left, right, or fully justified. You can also specify which font and style you want to use, and spell check your text once you finish writing. When you finish entering text and adding photos, save the file and return to the Books window.

FORMATTING REPORTS

Formatting trees and reports for your book involves the same procedure you learned in Chapter Twelve. The only difference is that you access the reports from the Books window, and that trees are automatically formatted in "Book Layout" (for instance, an Ancestor Tree is divided across multiple pages, each page with cross-references to the previous and following pages).

To format the Ancestor Tree, first click on that report name in the book outline, and then click on the Edit button. The Ancestor Tree view appears, allowing you to make changes to the tree using the Format and Contents menus.

Once you've finished formatting your tree, save the changes to this book item (from the Books menu, choose Save Custom Book Item) and then return to the Books view by clicking on the Books button.

> ❧ **NOTE** ❧   *You don't have to save your changes as a Custom Book item—after you edit a report that is included in a book, clicking on the Books button will cause Family Tree Maker to ask you if you want to save the changes to that particular item. The report will not be saved as a separate Custom Book item.*

You can format your Kinship report, Calendar, and Family Group Sheet in the same manner:

1. In the Books window, select the tree or report you want to format.

2. Click on the Edit button. The tree or report view appears.

3. Format the report using the Format and Contents menus.

> ❧ **TIP** ❧   *Remember, you can right-click on a report or tree to access its formatting and contents options on the shortcut menu.*

4. From the <u>B</u>ooks menu, choose <u>S</u>ave Custom Book Item.

5. Click on the Books button to return to the Books window.

> ❧ **NOTE** ❧   *You can delete an item from the book by selecting it in the outline and then clicking on the Delete button. If you don't like your book and want to start over, you can delete the entire book. From the <u>B</u>ooks menu, choose <u>D</u>elete Book. In the Delete Book dialog box, select the book you want to delete, and then click on <u>D</u>elete. Click on <u>Y</u>es when Family Tree Maker asks if you're sure, or click on <u>N</u>o if you change your mind.*

After you've formatted the reports, you're ready to print your book! Make sure you're in the Books window for the book you want to print, and then from the <u>F</u>ile menu, choose <u>P</u>rint Book. The Print Book dialog box appears (see Figure 13-8). You can print in color, print to a file, print more than one copy, or just print a section of your book. The Books print setup is controlled by individual items in the book—if you need to change the print setup, do that while you are formatting the items (after clicking on the Edit button).

This example has shown you how to create a book using the Earp Family File. To create one for your own family, choose a primary individual as your cornerstone. If you want to print a book for your mother's side of the family, follow the examples above with your mother as the primary individual. You can also create books for each grandparent, great-grandparent, and so on by selecting a primary individual for each book, and then adding reports and trees for that person's ancestors or descendants.

Figure 13-8

The Print Book dialog box allows you to print just a section of your book, or the entire book.

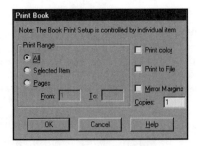

Book Project #2

For this example, assume you want to create a detailed family history featuring a distant ancestor as the primary individual, and work forward in time to his present descendants. Like the previous example, we'll use the Earp family for this project: Walter Earp will be the distant ancestor, and we'll pretend you are the child of Walter's great-grandaughter, Nellie Jane Earp. Feel free to work with your own family instead of the Earps; I've chosen to use the Earp family simply to demonstrate the technique of creating a book.

For this project, assume you want to create a comprehensive family history. You choose to include a large number of reports, trees, and customized items. Since you're excited about sharing the results of your long, hard hours of research, the contents you choose are:

- Title Page
- Copyright notice
- Dedication
- Table of Contents
- Introduction
- Ancestor Tree
- Ancestor Fan Tree
- Descendant Tree
- Descendant Fan Tree
- Hourglass Tree
- Hourglass Fan Tree
- Kinship Report
- Outline Descendant Tree
- Family Group Sheets
- Genealogy Report in NGS Quarterly format
- Timeline

- ✻ Text items (research notes)
- ✻ Documented Events Report
- ✻ Calendar
- ✻ Bibliography
- ✻ Index

LIMITING THE VOLUME OF MATERIAL

That's a lot to include in a book! If you don't organize it so that the material flows from one chapter to another, you'll end up with a confusing book few people will enjoy reading. Since that list has some duplication, here's a plan to prune it down to something a little more reasonable.

First of all, narrative information about an individual and his descendants is a useful item to have in a book. The Genealogy Report captures all the key points people are most interested in, and should therefore be the main section of information in the book. It's a good idea to move it up so it's the first item after the Introduction. Your research notes contain valuable information, insight, and discussions of the material, so place that next.

Trees show information graphically, and give the reader a better idea of how families fit together. Since the bulk of the information is presented in the Genealogy Report, and the rest in the notes, move the Trees behind the narrative section where readers can consult them as needed. An Ancestor tree might be useful, but you don't need two versions; cut the Ancestor Fan Tree. On the other hand, the Descendant Fan Tree is more elegant; keep it and drop the Descendant Tree.

The Hourglass Tree looks visually interesting, and you can also include a Kinship report to help sort out the family relationships. Note that you don't really need three trees in a book, but for the purposes of explaining the various items, we'll include it here.

The Outline Descendant Tree shows descendants at a glance, so move that useful tree up where it can be referred to often (directly after the research notes).

Family Group Sheets are always helpful, so move them in front of the tree section. The Timeline, Calendar, and Documented Events Report are less useful but are still interesting items to include; let them follow the trees. A Bibliography and Index are always found at the end of a book, so that's where they'll stay. Once you've got things organized, the newly revised list of contents looks like this:

- **Front Matter:** Title Page, Copyright notice, Dedication, Table of Contents, and Introduction
- **Narrative:** Genealogy Report in NGS Quarterly format, text items (research notes), and Outline Descendant Tree (which is really a sort of report, even though it's called a tree)
- **Family Group Sheets**
- **Trees:** Ancestor Tree, Descendant Fan Tree, and Hourglass Fan Tree
- **Miscellany:** Kinship Report, Timeline, Calendar, and Documented Events Report
- **Bibliography**
- **Index**

CREATING THE BOOK

Begin creating the book by going to the Family Page of your primary individual; remember that for this example we are pretending you are a child of Nellie Jane Earp, and the primary individual is your pretend great-great-grandfather, Walter Earp. Click on the Index button and select Walter Earp from the list, and from the Books menu, choose New Book.

Enter a title for the book in the Book Title text box, and your name in the Author text box. Click on OK; in the Books window, you'll see the available items you can include in your book. Using the same process mentioned for Book Project #1, select and add to the outline the items that you have decided to include in the book (see Figure 13-9).

Be sure to add in reports and trees for all the individuals you want to include in the book! For instance, if your book featured four generations of the Earps, you would want to include Family Group Sheets for all the Earp families in those four generations. Some reports and trees will display the entire family (for instance, the Outline Descendant Tree), but you should be aware of those reports that feature only one family, and be sure to include reports for other families as needed.

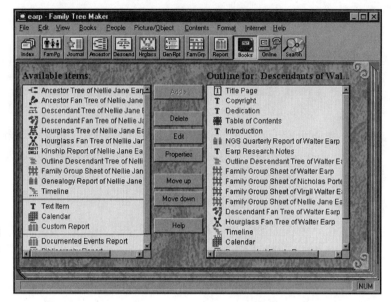

Figure 13-9

You can add to, delete from, and move items around your outline.

As I mentioned earlier, you get the Title Page automatically when you fill in the book's title and author's name. If you want to edit the title page, select the Title Page entry on your outline and click on the Edit button (see Figure 13-10). You can edit the Title Page text, change the font, the page formatting, and include any items from a Scrapbook.

The next three items on your outline are created by selecting Text Item from the Available Items list, clicking on the Add button, and then making a choice (of New Text, Introduction, Preface, Foreword, Copyright Notice, or Dedication) in the Add Text Item dialog box. To edit any of those items, select the item title and click on the Edit button in the center of the Books window.

The Copyright Notice is a short statement about who owns the copyright of the material in the book. This statement traditionally consists of "Copyright 1998 *Your Name*. All rights reserved." You can edit that statement to contain any text you want.

A Dedication is generally a short statement of thanks and appreciation to those people who have helped you, and to whom you would like to dedicate your work (see Figure 13-11).

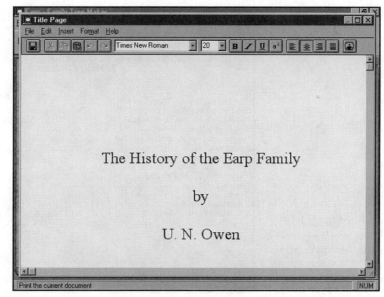

Figure 13-10

The Title Page contains the title of your book and the author's name.

The Table of Contents is automatically updated when you add items to your outline. You must position the Table of Contents near the top of the outline because it only generates headings and page numbers for items located after it in the list (see Figure 13-12). You can change only the title and formatting of the Table of Contents.

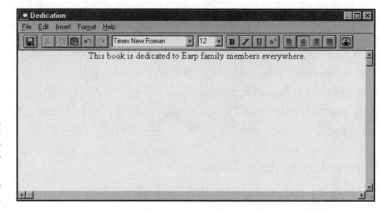

Figure 13-11

You can dedicate your book to an individual, group of people, or an entire family.

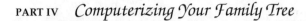

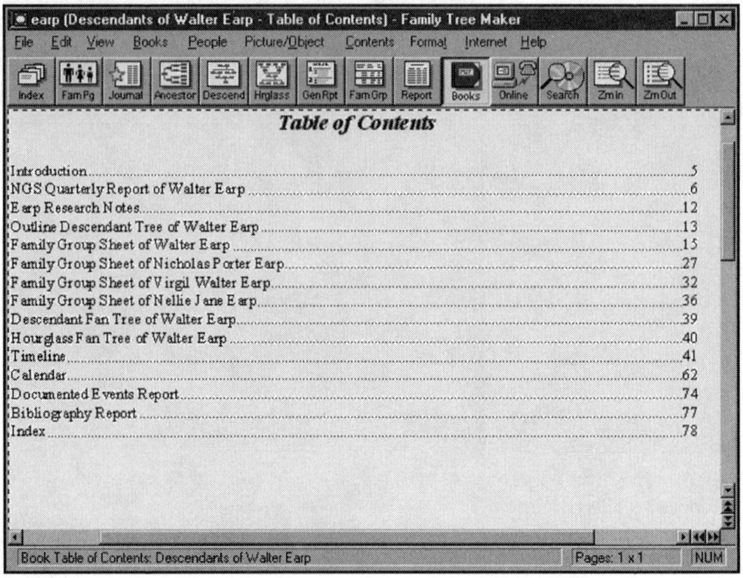

Figure 13-12

The Table of Contents is automatically generated from items in your outline.

※ **TIP** ※ *You can indent a Table of Contents item by choosing the item in the outline and clicking on the Properties button. Remove the check mark in the This Item Begins A Chapter check box. This is how you can subordinate items below a chapter heading. You may also want to check the Start This Item On An Odd Numbered Page box, since that is how chapters traditionally begin.*

The Introduction is where you can explain the purpose and intent of the book, describe your research, give a brief introduction to the family, and so on.

As with other trees, when you create one for a book, Family Tree Maker puts it in "Book Layout," which divides the tree across multiple pages. Each page of a report has the book's title, page numbers, and a chapter title (if you so specify in the book properties); trees in "Book Layout" are also cross-referenced to prior and next pages.

ADDING CUSTOMIZED ITEMS

You may wish to add customized, free-form text and graphics to your book. The New Text feature, mentioned earlier in this chapter, allows you to enter text and pick up graphics from any Scrapbook. Using the New Text feature, you can include items such as:

- ❈ Research notes or comments
- ❈ A biography of an individual or family
- ❈ Extracts from wills, deeds, and other legal documents
- ❈ Explanations and discussions of sources
- ❈ Arguments for or against conflicting information
- ❈ Census extracts
- ❈ Birth, marriage, and death record extracts
- ❈ Military information
- ❈ Obituary and cemetery transcripts
- ❈ Immigration information
- ❈ Family stories and oral traditions
- ❈ Details about locations (houses, towns, cemeteries, and so on) important to an individual or family
- ❈ A list of relatives' names and addresses
- ❈ A list of related Web site URLs
- ❈ Oral history interview transcripts
- ❈ Migration trail maps and descriptions

> ❈ **TIP** ❈   *You may find that some of the items you want to include in the list above are already in your Family File as an individual's Notes or items in your Scrapbook. If you want to format text from Notes in a different manner, you can copy and paste it into a Text Item. You may also paste in graphics from an individual's Scrapbook to augment the text. For example, if you had a Note detailing an individual's homestead, you might want to copy that information into a Text Item so you could include an image of the Land Bounty Grant given to the homesteader.*

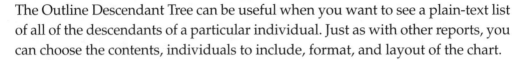

The Outline Descendant Tree can be useful when you want to see a plain-text list of all of the descendants of a particular individual. Just as with other reports, you can choose the contents, individuals to include, format, and layout of the chart.

Family Group Sheets are useful because they show you a single family (parents and children) and the names, dates, and locations for important events. Family Tree Maker allows you to include a graphic, such as a picture, for each person, and one for each marriage.

The Ancestor Tree gives you a graphical view of a primary individual and his or her ancestors. Just as it does for other Book reports and trees, Family Tree Maker uses the "Book Layout" for Ancestor Trees. If you want to change the look of the tree (connections and layout), you can select those options in the Tree Format dialog box.

If you are interested in a different type of tree, you may want to include the Descendant Fan Tree. Although similar to a Descendant Tree, the Fan Tree is used more for decorative purposes than as a display of information. You can include a variety of information in the tree by using the Items To Include In Each Box feature (from the Contents menu).

Another unique chart is the Hourglass Tree, where both ancestors and descendants of the primary individual can be seen on one page (ancestors appear above the primary individual, and descendants below). Just as with other trees, if you edit the Hourglass Tree from the Books window, Family Tree Maker will create the tree in "Book Layout."

All family researchers should be aware of history when they are tracing ancestors' lives; people living years ago were affected by local, national, and world events just as we are today. Knowledge of historical events helps researchers determine events that might have influence over ancestors' lives. A timeline can assist by showing where an individual's life falls in relation to important historical events. The Family Tree Maker Timeline allows you to select contents, format the timeline, and choose what sorts of historical events will appear (such as arts, economics, military, religion, and technology for locations such as Europe, Asia, the United States, or the world).

As a reminder to yourself and to help other researchers, you might want to include a report showing events that you have traced to reliable sources—and perhaps those you're still trying to trace. The Documented Events report allows you to display individual and marriage events for which you have a source, individual and marriage events that do not have a source, or all individual and marriage events. The Documented Events report is one of the standard reports from which you can create a custom book item that will appear in the Available Items in the Books window. To create a custom book item:

1. Click on the Report button on the toolbar, and then from the Format menu, choose Report Format. The Report Format dialog box appears.

2. Select Documented Events (or another standard report in the list), and then click on OK. The report appears.

3. From the Books menu, select Create Custom Book Item. The Create Custom Book Item dialog box appears.

4. Type a name for the report and then click on OK.

5. Click on the Books button. The Books window appears. You'll see the report name listed on the Available Items side of the Books window.

After you create a Custom Book Item, select and add it to the outline as you would any of the available items. You can edit the Documented Events report (see Figure 13-13) as you would any other (you may specify format and content). You can select the types of individuals to include, how events should be listed, and the event format (footnote or complete documentation).

> ❋ **TIP** ❋   *A list of events that haven't been documented can be used as a reminder of what you still need to research.*

A bibliography (see Figure 13-14) is generally considered to be a list of writings on a specific subject; Family Tree Maker offers users the ability to create a list of sources used in the database via the Bibliography report. You can add a Bibliography

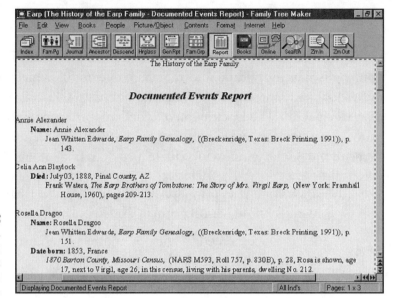

Figure 13-13

The Documented
Events report shows
sources for individual
and marriage events.

report to the Available Items list in the same way you added the Documented
Events report—by creating the report and then using the Create Custom Book
Item command to add it to the outline in the Books window.

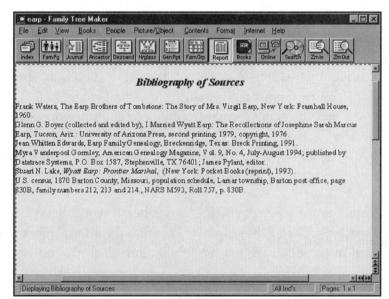

Figure 13-14

The Bibliography
report in standard
format

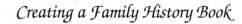
❀ **TIP** ❀   *If you are creating a family history to share with other research-ers, it is recommended that you include every source.*

Every family history book should include an index! Family Tree Maker gives users an Index feature (see Figure 13-15) that will automatically generate an index of individuals found on the trees and reports in your book. You have the ability to change the format and layout (you can choose between one, two, or three columns), but you cannot edit the index yourself. If you add items to your book outline after you have included an index, don't worry; the index will auto-matically maintain page numbers and individuals' names as you add and subtract items from your book.

❀ **NOTE** ❀   *The index will automatically check for new individuals or changes before it prints.*

FINISHING YOUR BOOK

Every item included in your book has a name (or title) and certain other proper-ties, which determine:

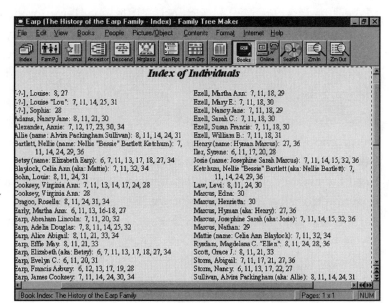

Figure 13-15

Like the Table of Contents, the Index is automatically generated from items included in the outline.

- If the item begins a chapter.
- If the item starts on an odd-numbered page.
- If a header should be included for the item.
- If a footer should be included for an item.

You can choose the properties of each item from the Books window by selecting the item, and then clicking on the Properties button.

> **TIP** *The first page of each chapter generally appears on the right-hand side (the page with an odd number). You can select which items you'd like to start a chapter by adjusting the item properties.*

> **NOTE** *Many book chapters begin with introductory text. You may choose to do the same by including a Text Item (with or without pictures) at the beginning of each chapter. Think of it as a chapter title page. You can introduce chapters made up of trees, chapters of family group sheets, chapters of miscellaneous items, etc.*

A header is a line of text that appears at the top of every page. Family Tree Maker headers can include the book's title, chapter number, or page number. A footer is a line of text that appears on the bottom of every page. Family Tree Maker footers can include the book's title, chapter number, or page number. You can choose to have a header, a footer, or both appear on an item's pages by changing its properties.

To set what should appear in the header and footer for a book, from the Books menu, choose Book Header, Footer. In the Book Header And Footer dialog box (see Figure 13-16), choose what items should appear in the header by selecting from the Header drop-down list. Choose what should appear in the footer by selecting from the Footer drop-down list. Change the font, size, style, color, underline, and alignment of the header and footer by clicking on the Set Font button.

> **NOTE** *The book header and footer settings apply to the entire book—for an item, you can set properties to include or exclude the book's header and footer, but not change the content for an individual item's header and footer.*

Figure 13-16

Choose the header
and footer that will
appear throughout
the book, except on
items where you tell
Family Tree Maker not
to include them.

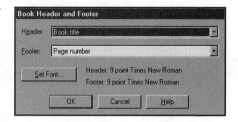

You can change the book's properties (title, author, and page numbering) from the Books menu, by choosing Book Properties. In the Book Properties dialog box (see Figure 13-17), you can change the book title, author, starting page number, and whether to use Roman numerals (ii, iii, iv) as page numbers for the table of contents and preceding items. Choosing this option also causes those preceding items *not* to appear in the table of contents, so you should consider that in your decision and perhaps change the position of the table of contents too.

As you learned in Book Project #1, you can change the order in which items appear in your book by dragging the item to another position. You can also move an item by selecting it and then clicking on the Move Up and Move Down buttons until the item is in the desired position.

Before you actually print the final copy, verify that all the items in the outline are in the order you want and that you have made any changes to the reports and trees from the Contents and Format menus. Then check your header and footer to make sure the book's properties are set the way you want, and update the index one last time. Once you've printed your book, you can take the master

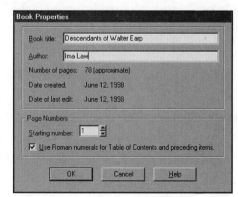

Figure 13-17

Change the properties
for the book here.

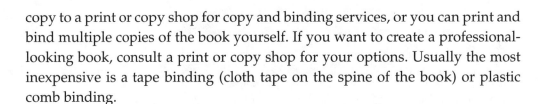
copy to a print or copy shop for copy and binding services, or you can print and bind multiple copies of the book yourself. If you want to create a professional-looking book, consult a print or copy shop for your options. Usually the most inexpensive is a tape binding (cloth tape on the spine of the book) or plastic comb binding.

> ❀ **TIP** ❀   *By clicking on the Mirror Margins option, you can have a larger margin on the inside edge if you want to copy the pages back to back.*

> ❀ **NOTE** ❀   *Be sure to retain several copies of your book for yourself, and consider donating copies to your local genealogy society and library.*

> ❀ **TIP** ❀   *You can include photos or other graphics in free-form text (Text Items), reports, and trees only if they have first been added to an individual's Scrapbook.*

Other Book Ideas

Your book is limited only by your creativity! You can mix and match all the reports, trees, and other items Family Tree Maker supports to create your own personalized family history, a book about just one ancestor, or a family album to be enjoyed with close family members. Here are a few more book ideas you may want to experiment with:

A bound Calendar with each month displaying a different photo (and descriptive text). If you have a color printer and some scanned photos, you can create a lovely gift for your immediate family or distant cousins. Items to include: 12-month Calendar report (living individuals only, or living and deceased individuals), and Text Items with photos from a Scrapbook.

A biography featuring a parent, child, or grandchild. Another excellent gift idea, biographies can show the life and times of an ancestor long gone or a beloved grandchild. Items to include: Family Group Sheets, Ancestor Tree, Text Items with photos from a Scrapbook, and a Timeline.

An autobiography that you can present to family members. Consult a book of oral history questions and write your memories and experiences to share with other generations. Items to include: Family Group Sheets, Ancestor Tree, Descendant Tree, Kinship report, autobiographical Text Items with photos from a Scrapbook, and an Index.

A research book to take with you when you visit libraries, archives, and Family History Centers. Instead of bringing bulky (and valuable) files, binders, and notes, create a book of just the information you need for a specific family. Items to include: Outline Descendant Tree, Family Group Sheets, Documented Events (print a list of events which you need to document), Alternate Facts report, Kinship report, Genealogy Report (in Register or NGS Quarterly format), and an Index.

CHAPTER FOURTEEN

Branching Out: Sharing Your Files

enealogists tend to be generous people when it comes to learning about a family's past. Most are delighted to exchange information and share the results of their years of research with you. Computers make it easy to compile genealogical data and share the results electronically, especially with family members you're familiar with. But how do you find and exchange data with all those distant cousins out there that you may not know about?

Genealogists are setting the Internet ablaze as they search for near and distant relatives—by relationship degrees and miles. They're using e-mail, Web pages, mailing lists, newsgroups, and electronic bulletin boards, hoping to find that cousin who has solved the family mysteries. What was your great-great-grandmother's maiden name? Where in Italy was grandpa born? Who has the family Bible? Are there any pictures of your ancestors stashed in a trunk at a cousin's house in New Zealand or Germany? Most of your cousins—the ones who might have the genealogical treasures—bear surnames other than that of the ancestor of interest. You have to explore the many branches of your family tree in hopes of untangling its roots.

Joining the World Family Tree Project

In 1995, Brøderbund (the producer of Family Tree Maker software) launched the World Family Tree Project in response to its customers' many requests for some way to share their research data. The result is an immense CD-ROM database that includes thousands of family trees and millions of individuals. Participation in this project is open to genealogists worldwide—including you, once you have material to share. The World Family Tree Project offers many rewards, including:

* ❊ Helping others who are seeking the information you have.

* ❊ Extending your family tree when those with connecting lines find you.

* ❊ Preserving your family history so your descendants will be able to access it.

* ❊ Protecting your family history data from loss or damage. Through the World Family Tree project, your collection will become part of a readily accessible database, to be archived at the Library of Congress in Washington, D.C.

But what if your genealogical research is incomplete? There is a maxim recited by longtime researchers: *I think that I shall never see—a completed family tree.* Family history is usually a lifelong avocation, and you will probably never finish the project. However, that does not mean you can't share what you have compiled thus far, whether it is a couple of generations or 12 or 15 generations for several different lines. It is not the size of your database that is important for sharing with others via the World Family Tree Project. Your great-grandfather just may be the missing ancestor that someone else has long sought.

To make your contributions to the World Family Tree Project of greatest value to others, make sure you document and cite your sources, double-check for errors in your database, weed out confusing or misleading information, and verify your sources before you send anything. Do not contribute anything that invades the privacy of living family members, infringes on the copyrights of others, or is defamatory or profane in any way.

Regarding Privacy

Before you contribute your material to the World Family Tree Project, reexamine it one more time to ensure that no information in your Family Files is, or should be, confidential. Perhaps Aunt Cynthia told you about a family scandal involving another family member; it's sitting in the More About Notes even though you have been unable to substantiate it. Don't publish family gossip.

Make a copy of your Family File, delete the confidential information, and contribute a new, edited version of your file to the World Family Tree Project. Invasion of privacy is a serious matter, and just because people are kin to you does not give you the right to publish genealogical or biographical information about them without their permission.

The World Family Tree Project helps protect living individuals by listing only name, sex, and family links for them on its CDs; it replaces other information about living individuals with the word *private*. But there may well be family stories that would cause pain to the living even though the central figures have died, so use your judgment about what to include.

> ❧ **NOTE** ❧   *If no death date appears, Family Tree Maker assumes an individual is living up to 120 years after their birth.*

And just because Johnny, your third cousin once removed, shares his years of research on the O'Kelly family with you, does not give you the right to share it with others or publish it—in print, on a CD, or on your home page on the Web. Be sure you have his written permission to use it—and give credit where credit is due. Also, find out where your cousin's material originated—you do not want to infringe on someone else's copyright, even inadvertently. Most genealogists are more than willing to share their work and give permission to others to use it, but don't assume anything. Always ask first.

Contributing Your Files

Family Files can be contributed to the World Family Tree Project through Family Tree Maker Online or via a floppy disk.

ONLINE CONTRIBUTIONS

To contribute a file to World Family Tree Project online:

1. Start Family Tree Maker and open the Family File you want to contribute.

2. From the File menu, choose Contribute to World Family Tree. (It's OK—all they want is information; they won't hit you up for a cash

Figure 14-1

There are two ways to contribute to World Family Tree.

donation.) The Contribute to World Family Tree dialog box appears, asking how you would like to contribute your file (see Figure 14-1).

3. Click on the Online button. Family Tree Maker opens the Your Rights As a Contributor to the World Family Tree dialog box (see Figure 14-2).

4. Read the information carefully, then click on the Yes button if you agree to the terms. If you click on No, the contribution process ends.

5. Type in the requested contributor information (see Figure 14-3), which includes your name and address in case there is a problem with the file. Your phone number is optional. Family Tree Maker uses the date from your computer's internal calendar. However, if that date is incorrect, be sure to change it—it is important to have the correct date on your Family File in case you send in updated versions. If you wish to be contacted by e-mail, provide your e-mail address.

6. Click on OK. If your modem is not already connected to your Internet Service Provider, the connection is dialed. Once connected,

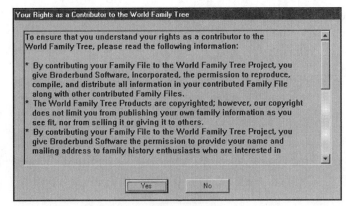

Figure 14-2

Read about your rights as a contributor to the World Family Tree and respond accordingly.

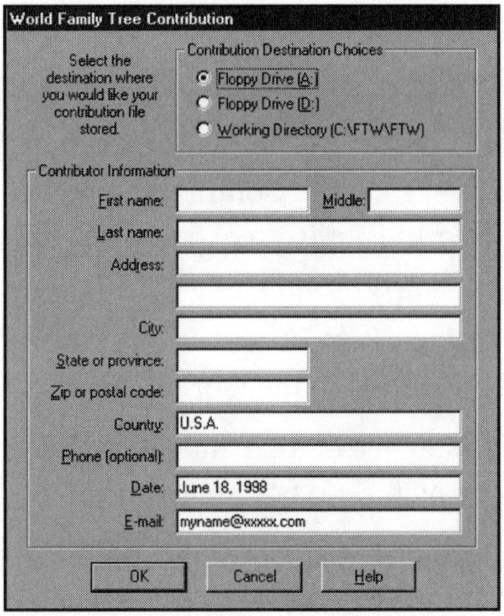

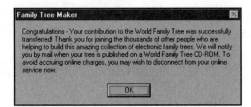

Figure 14-3

Completing the contributor information is a requirement for contributions to the World Family Tree Project.

you'll see a progress indicator as Family Tree Maker uploads the Family File. This process can take a few minutes, depending on the size of your file, the speed of your modem, and the traffic jams on the Internet.

7. When a message appears saying the transfer is done (see Figure 14-4), just click on OK. You can disconnect from the Internet.

DISK CONTRIBUTIONS

Be sure to check your Family File for any errors or confidential information, then prepare an empty, formatted, floppy disk. Label the disk with your name, address, phone number (optional), e-mail address (optional), name of the Family File, and the present date. Use a standard disk label sticker, if you have one. To contribute a file to World Family Tree Project by floppy disk:

Figure 14-4

When the transfer of your Family File to the World Family Tree is complete, this message appears.

Family Tree Maker

Congratulations - Your contribution to the World Family Tree was successfully transferred! Thank you for joining the thousands of other people who are helping to build this amazing collection of electronic family trees. We will notify you by mail when your tree is published on a World Family Tree CD-ROM. To avoid accruing online charges, you may wish to disconnect from your online service now.

OK

1. Put a blank, formatted disk in your floppy disk drive.

2. Start Family Tree Maker and open the Family File you want to contribute.

3. From the File menu, choose Contribute to World Family Tree. The Contribute to World Family Tree dialog box appears, asking how you would like to contribute your file.

4. Click on the Diskette button. Family Tree Maker opens the Your Rights As a Contributor to the World Family Tree dialog box.

5. Read this information carefully and then click on the Yes button (if you agree) or on the No button if you change your mind about contributing.

6. In the Contribution Destination Choices section, click on the option button corresponding to the drive that contains your blank disk (for example, Floppy Drive A:), or select Working Directory to store the file in the same folder (directory) and drive as your Family File.

7. Type in the requested contributor information: name, address, phone number (optional), date, and e-mail address. (The same information as requested for an online submission.)

8. Click on OK. Family Tree Maker copies your Family File to the disk (you will be prompted to insert additional blank disks if the file is too large for a single one) and then displays a message telling you how to label and mail it in.

9. After the file has been copied, remove the floppy disk from the drive and be sure that your name and address are on the label affixed to the disk. Put the disk in a sturdy envelope (bubble-style is best) and mail it to:

Brøderbund Software
Banner Blue Division
Attn: World Family Tree Project
P.O. Box 760
Fremont, CA 94537-9924

Exchanging GEDCOM Files

GEDCOM stands for Genealogical Data Communication. In simple terms, it works for genealogy databases the same way ASCII (a standard text character set) works for word processor text. The GEDCOM standard was developed by the Family History Department of the Church of Jesus Christ of Latter-day Saints to allow people to exchange genealogy databases regardless of what genealogy software program they use. For example, if you want to give your Family Tree Maker file to a cousin who uses Personal Ancestral File (PAF), you can export your file to a GEDCOM (familyname.ged) file. Then your cousin can import your familyname.ged file into his or her software program, which converts it to a format that program can read and use.

> ❧ **NOTE** ❧   *Back in B.C. (Before Computers), cousins would exchange typed or handwritten Family Group Sheets and Pedigree Charts. To import any of the information required retyping the data or filling out new charts by hand. Computers and genealogy software have taken the drudgery out of working with genealogical data. However, there are some pitfalls into which eager genealogists can fall. Always remember to double-check your files for errors and private notes before you send copies to others.*

Importing a GEDCOM File

If a relative sends you a GEDCOM file on disk or as an attachment in e-mail, you can import it into Family Tree Maker. To import a GEDCOM file:

1. From the File menu, choose Open Family File. The Open Family File dialog box appears (see Figure 14-5).

2. In the Look In drop-down list, select the drive (A, B, C, D, or whatever) where the file you want to open is located. Family Tree Maker displays a list of all the files and folders on the selected drive.

3. Double-click on the folder that contains your file. If you're having trouble locating the file you want to import, read "Locating a File" on the following page.

4. In the Files of type drop-down list, select GEDCOM (*.GED).

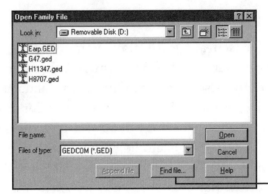

Figure 14-5

The Open Family File dialog box lists all the GEDCOM files on the disk drive you select.

— Find file button

5. Select the GEDCOM file name in the list box, and then click on Open. The New Family File dialog box appears (see Figure 14-7). You must save the imported file as a Family File.

6. In the Save In drop-down list, select the drive and folder where you want to store the Family File you are creating from the imported

Locating a File

To locate an existing file, either in GEDCOM or FTW (Family Tree Maker for Windows) format, there is a nifty Find File option in the Open Family File dialog box (shown in Figure 14-5). Click on the Find file button to open the Find File dialog box. In the File format drop-down list, select a file type, such as GEDCOM (*.GED), as shown in Figure 14-6. Notice that this places *.GED in the File Name text box.

To search for all GEDCOM files, which have an extension of .ged, you can keep *.GED in the File Name text box. To narrow the search, type a file name in the File Name text box—or whatever part of the file name you happen to know. You can use any valid file name and an asterisk (*) or question mark (?) as *wildcard* characters (both are commonly used in operating system and application file management procedures).

In the Search drop-down list, select a drive for Family Tree Maker to search and then click on the Search button. If several file names appear in the Found Files box, you can use the scroll bar to scan the list for the file name you seek. To open a file in the list, either select the file name and click on Open, or double-click on the name in the list.

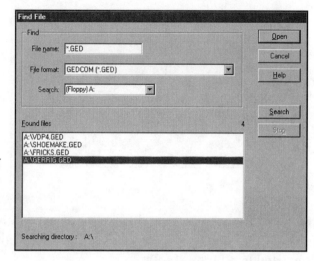

Figure 14-6

The Find File option enables you to locate files and narrow the search to specific file formats.

GEDCOM information. Family Tree Maker cannot create a file on a disk (or other removable medium); therefore you must choose a location on your hard drive.

7. In the File Name text box, type a new name or accept the name suggested. Then click on Save.

❦ **NOTE** ❦   *If your relative has sent you his GEDCOM file of his Pierson family and named it PIERSON.GED, and you already have a file of this name, Family Tree Maker will advise you that a file with this name already exists and will ask you to enter a different name.*

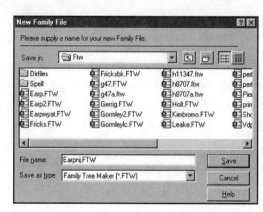

Figure 14-7

Supply a name for the new Family File when you import a GEDCOM into Family Tree Maker.

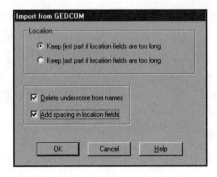

Figure 14-8

Select the options to
format the data
imported from a
GEDCOM file.

Some programs format information differently than Family Tree Maker; the
Import from GEDCOM dialog box provides options for reformatting information as it's imported (see Figure 14-8).

   8.   Choose from these options:

      ➤ **Location.** Some programs such as PAF (Personal Ancestral
         File) have longer location fields. You can elect to keep either
         the first part or the last part if location fields are too long.

      ➤ **Delete Underscore From Names.** Some programs add an un-
         derscore between compound names (for example,
         St._Germaine). Select this check box to replace the under-
         score with a space.

      ➤ **Add Spacing In Location Fields.** Some programs do not put
         any space between the city, county, and state in the location
         fields. Select this check box to add the normal space between
         these words, if necessary.

   If Family Tree Maker encounters any difficulties while importing the
   GEDCOM file, it will offer you a chance to view a list of warnings
   and errors. If the data was imported without errors or warnings, a
   message box informs you that the import is done.

   9.   Click on OK in the message box. The GEDCOM file is imported
      and displays in a Family File.

Exporting to a GEDCOM File

You can export a Family File in GEDCOM file format, which allows you to share your information with others who may not have Family Tree Maker. To export a Family File in GEDCOM format:

1. From the File menu, choose Copy/Export Family File (see Figure 14-9).

2. In the Save In drop-down list, select the drive where you want to place the file.

3. Double-click on the folder (if there is one) where you want to place your file.

4. In the Save As Type drop-down list, select GEDCOM (*.GED).

5. In the File Name text box, type a name for the file or accept the suggested name.

6. Click on the Save button. The Export To GEDCOM dialog box appears (see Figure 14-10).

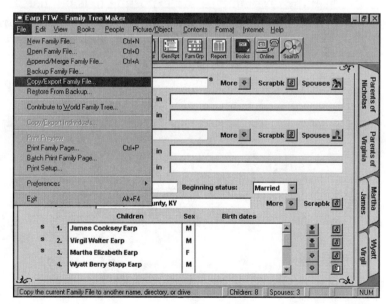

Figure 14-9

Exporting a Family File from the Copy/Export option in the File menu.

Figure 14-10

Choose the File Type
and other options in
the Export To
GEDCOM dialog box.

The Export To GEDCOM dialog box shows File Type options. The Destination drop-down list selections allow Family Tree Maker to check for requirements of the program that will read the GEDCOM file.

7. In the Destination drop-down list, select the type of export file that best meets your requirements (or the software your cousin uses). See Table 14-1.

    If the program you are exporting to is not listed, choose PAF. When you make a selection in the Destination drop-down list, Family Tree Maker makes suggestions for the GEDCOM and Character Set selections. However, you can override these if you need to do so. It is best to select Version 5.5 in the GEDCOM drop-down list, when

Table 14-1   Destination File Types

Select This	To Create This Type of File
ANSTFILE	Ancestral File of LDS Church
FTM	Family Tree Maker for DOS
FTW	Family Tree Maker for Windows
TempleReady	Temple submission to LDS Church
PAF	Personal Ancestral File, version 2.1 or later
ROOTS	Roots II, III, IV, V, or Visual Roots

possible, because it offers the best export. However, when you do not know what file type to use or when you are exporting to PAF version 2.31 or earlier, select Version 4.

8. Choose from the other options in the Export To GEDCOM dialog box if they are available for the file type you chose:

   ⚹ **Indent Records.** Select this to make a file more readable in a word processor. However, some programs cannot read indented records, so in most instances it is best not to select this option.

   ⚹ **Abbreviate Tags.** Most programs use abbreviated tags (labels for fields of information in the GEDCOM file), so it is usually best to select this check box.

9. After selecting your choices for the options in the Export To GEDCOM dialog box, click on OK. The GEDCOM file is created. You can find it in the folder you selected in Step 3.

Exporting a Group of Individuals

You can send your cousin a copy of your entire Family File, if you wish. However, most cousins are interested only in the lines you have in common. In other words, if you and cousin Diane are related through your Henderson branch, which is one of your paternal lines, then she probably is not interested in your maternal lines. Or perhaps you want to send only the new information you have collected on the Mahaffeys to uncle Don. You can do this using the Copy/Export Individuals command. To export a group of individuals:

1. Display an Ancestor Tree, Descendant Tree, Outline Descendant Tree, Hourglass Tree, Kinship Report, Timeline or Custom report that contains the group of individuals you want to export.

2. Review the tree or report to be sure it has the correct individuals.

3. From the File menu, choose Copy/Export Individuals In <View>, where <View> is the view of the tree or report (see Figure 14-11). The Copy/Export Individuals In <View> dialog box appears (see Figure 14-12).

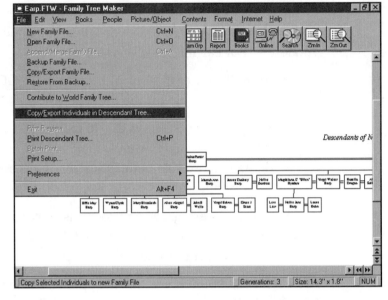

Figure 14-11

You can select certain individuals to export to a new file by using the Copy/Export Individuals option.

4. In the Save As Type drop-down list, select a file format for the new file.

5. Type in a name for the file in the File Name text box.

6. In the Save In drop-down list, select the drive where you want the new file to be created.

7. Double-click on the folder where you want to store the new file.

8. Click on the Save button. Family Tree Maker then creates a new file that contains a copy of the information for the individuals you selected. The original Family File is not affected.

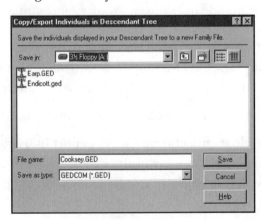

Figure 14-12

Saving a group of individuals in a new Family File using the Copy/Export Individuals option

The History of George Howard Lafferty

George Howard Lafferty was born September 2, 1854 in Lenox township, Ashtabela County, Ohio, to Amber Amelia Wescott Lafferty and George Edwin Lafferty. A sister, Maud Irene, was born May 23, 1892.

A family of farmers, the Laffertys harvested the land where they lived. On May 9, 1919, they moved to Warren, Ohio, to a house on Forest Street NE. They lived next door to their daughter Maud, her husband Jay Rood Webster, and their three beautiful daughters, Reta, Shirley, and Marion.

As a youth, Lafferty went by "Howard" rather than "George" and signed his name as G. Howard Lafferty. After graduating from Lenox Township schools in 1911, he received a Teachers Certificate and became an educator and later a high school Principal. He then switched careers and ventured into banking just before World War I.

As a student at Ohio State University during the war, Howard Lafferty hoped to join the army but was classified 5G due to his glasses and other restrictions. In 1923 he received an LL.B. degree and passed

Ancestors of George Howard Lafferty

- Samuel Lafferty 1801 – 1873
- Edwin E. Lafferty 1834 – 1907
- Margaret McDowell 1803 – 1861
- George E. Lafferty 1867 – 1936
- Erastus Fowler 1793 – 1875
- ...lia Fowler ...1914
- Temperence Merrill 1796 – 1871
- Nathan Wescott 1818 – 1900
- ...ram Wescott
- ...ma Wescott
- Sarah Ann McMichael 1820 – 1901
- Samuel C. Amsden 1822 – 1899
- Theresa Jerusa Amsden 1845 – 1934
- Clarissa Hubbard 1820 – 1870

CHAPTER FIFTEEN

Home on the Web: Creating Your Home Page

ome pages of genealogists are popping up like wildflowers in that colossal cyber garden known as the World Wide Web. Genealogists have been pioneers in adapting computer technology to their needs, so it is not surprising to find them working so diligently to build home pages where they can publish their family histories, post queries about those "difficult lines," share research data, announce family reunions, and tell about family associations and publications.

Publishing Your Genealogy on the Internet

Family histories, lovingly researched and compiled, tend to be expensive to print in the traditional way. Web publishing offers an alternative, but it does not replace the more permanent method. Publishing on the Web allows you to share your research with others, letting them see the lines you are working on or have information about.

Remember, anyone with Web access can see your data. This increases the possibility that some relative who can be helped by your information or could help you will see and contact you. Search engines, like the Internet FamilyFinder, can increase your chances of connections. One of the great pluses of Web publishing is that it is easy to revise the material. As your research progresses, you can update your genealogy publications.

Creating Your Home Page

If publishing in general—and Web publishing with its HTML requirement in particular—intimidates you, relax. You can create your own home page with

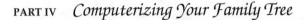

Family Tree Maker Online, and you do not have to worry about learning another language or studying page-layout design and graphics. To create your home page on Family Tree Maker Online, follow these steps:

1. Click on the Online button on the toolbar, or from the Internet menu, choose Go Online. This will take you to Family Tree Maker Online (see Figure 15-1). (Your computer will connect to your Internet Service Provider and your Web browser will start, if it is not already running.)

    ❧ **NOTE** ❧   *If you haven't yet registered with Family Tree Maker Online, you will see a Welcome page instead of the main home page shown in Figure 15-1. Click on the New Family Tree Maker Online User link at the bottom of the Welcome page. Fill in the registration form and click on the Submit button. On the Thank You page that confirms your registration, click on Create Your Home Page Now. The Create Your Own Home Page page appears, as shown in Figure 15-2. You can skip to Step 4.*

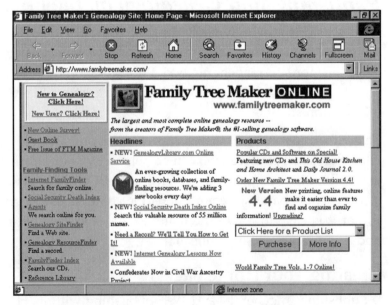

Figure 15-1

You can create and edit home pages from Family Tree Maker Online.

2. Under Genealogy Community in the left column, click on
    Home Pages. The Family Tree Maker Online User Home Pages
    page appears.

    Be sure to click on the Agreement of Use link and take time to read
    the User Home Page Agreement of Use, paying close attention to
    "User Guidelines and Rules." (Then click on the browser's Back but-
    ton to return to the previous page.)

3. Click on the Create a new home page or edit an existing home
    page link. The Create Your Own Home Page page appears
    (see Figure 15-2).

4. In the Title field, type in the title that you want to appear at the top
    of your home page. It is better to be specific. For example, "Earps of
    Finney County, Kansas" tells more about your family of interest
    than "My Earp Family" does.

5. In the Contact Information fields, type in all the information you
    want to provide for people trying to reach you. It is not necessary to

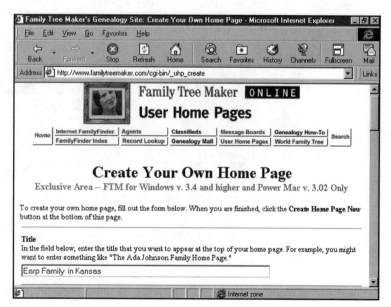

Figure 15-2

Create your home
page by filling out a
simple form.

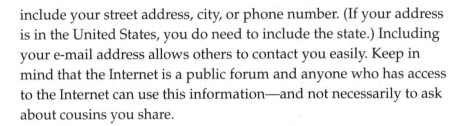

include your street address, city, or phone number. (If your address is in the United States, you do need to include the state.) Including your e-mail address allows others to contact you easily. Keep in mind that the Internet is a public forum and anyone who has access to the Internet can use this information—and not necessarily to ask about cousins you share.

✤ **NOTE** ✤   *Your information may already appear in these fields, transferred from your Family Tree Maker Online registration. You can delete some of the address and phone information if you choose.*

6. If you already have another home page somewhere else on the Internet, you can type the address and title of this page in the URL and Description fields.

7. In the Text field, type in the text that you want to appear on your home page. You might include highlights of your research interest, the main surnames you are researching, information about upcoming family reunions or association news, and even current news about your family (see Figure 15-3).

Figure 15-3

Type in the text you want to appear on your home page.

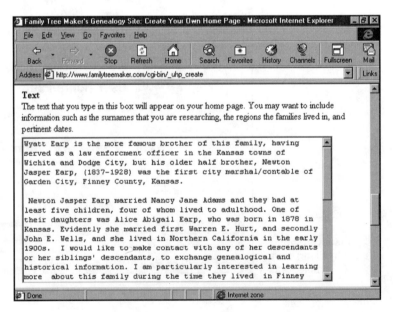

Figure 15-4

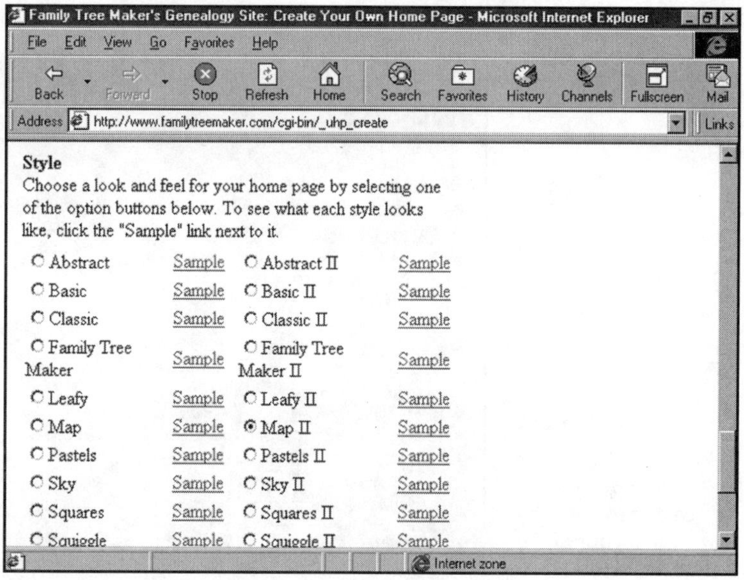

Pick the style for your home page by selecting from several options.

> Family Tree Maker's Genealogy Site: Create Your Own Home Page - Microsoft Internet Explorer
>
> File Edit View Go Favorites Help
>
> Back Forward Stop Refresh Home Search Favorites History Channels Fullscreen Mail
>
> Address http://www.familytreemaker.com/cgi-bin/_uhp_create   Links
>
> **Style**
> Choose a look and feel for your home page by selecting one of the option buttons below. To see what each style looks like, click the "Sample" link next to it.
>
> | | | | |
> |---|---|---|---|
> | ○ Abstract | Sample | ○ Abstract II | Sample |
> | ○ Basic | Sample | ○ Basic II | Sample |
> | ○ Classic | Sample | ○ Classic II | Sample |
> | ○ Family Tree Maker | Sample | ○ Family Tree Maker II | Sample |
> | ○ Leafy | Sample | ○ Leafy II | Sample |
> | ○ Map | Sample | ◉ Map II | Sample |
> | ○ Pastels | Sample | ○ Pastels II | Sample |
> | ○ Sky | Sample | ○ Sky II | Sample |
> | ○ Squares | Sample | ○ Squares II | Sample |
> | ○ Squiggle | Sample | ○ Squiggle II | Sample |
>
> Internet zone

8. In the Style list, select the option button for the layout format you want to use (see Figure 15-4). Click on the Sample link next to each option to view the various styles available.

    There are lots of choices, with names like Abstract, Basic, Classic, Leafy, Map, Pastels, Sky, Squares, and Squiggle. The hardest part of creating your family tree online may be choosing just the right style.

9. After you make all your choices, click on the Create Home Page Now button. Family Tree Maker Online will display a sample of your home page.

10. Review the information carefully (see Figure 15-5). You may discover that some typographical errors crept in and you will want to fix them. You can use your Web browser's Back button to return to the previous screen and make changes in the text box. When you are satisfied with the sample page, click on the Create Home Page Now button (again). Family Tree Maker Online will display a message indicating that your page is complete. It can take from a few minutes to several hours for the page to appear online.

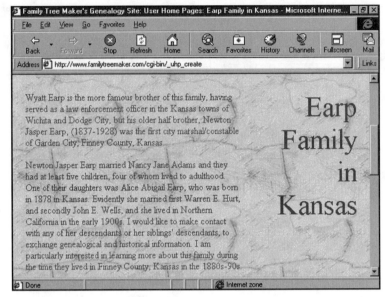

Figure 15-5

Typing errors can be corrected easily by editing your home page's text box.

Family Tree Maker Online congratulates you, tells you your page is done, and encourages you to create a bookmark for it. The URL for your home page will look similar to this, using *your* name of course: **http://www.familytreemaker.com/users/g/o/r/Myra-V-Gormley/**. Don't forget to write it down.

❄ **TIP** ❄ *Also, make a bookmark in your browser so that you can find your page again quickly. In Netscape Navigator, choose Bookmarks, Add Bookmark. In Microsoft Internet Explorer, choose Add To Favorites from the Favorites menu.*

After you create your home page, you can add a family tree or report from your Family File. Your home page can contain links for up to five reports, one Family Tree Maker book, and the trademarked box-style InterneTree. You can choose to present any amount of information, and it can be in one of several formats:

🏃 Outline Descendant trees

🏃 Custom reports

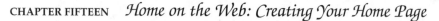
- Genealogy Reports (Register, NGS Quarterly, and Ahnentafel formats)
- Family Tree Maker Book
- InterneTree

ADDING REPORTS

Before you decide to add various reports to your home page, it is a good idea to do some pruning within those reports—to avoid posting information about living family members, for example. Genealogy enthusiasts often forget that the Internet is a public forum and that anyone with access can find this material—not always for benign purposes. Few of us can remember all the details we collect in our pursuit of learning about our ancestors, but some or possibly a lot of your genealogical reports may include information about living persons. Remember, your relatives have a right to their privacy, so don't post their birth dates and whatnot on the World Wide Web. If you decide to include a Genealogy Report that starts with your immigrant ancestor and comes down to your grandchildren, you should edit it before posting it on your Web page by excluding the more recent generations. A good rule of thumb is to exclude information about persons born after 1920, 1910, or even 1900, unless they are deceased. There are utilities, such as GEDClean (**http://members.aol.com/tomraynor2/gedclean.htm**), which will remove individuals from your database based on specified parameters. Family Tree Maker also allows you to select which individuals to include in reports and Outline Descendant Trees.

Additionally, double-check your reports to be sure you do not have any copyrighted material in them. Almost all material available on others' home pages is protected by copyright, whether or not the pages contain a copyright notice. Many people believe that a copyright notice must appear on publications to protect them and that everything on the Web is free for the grabbing—but both ideas are false. Moreover, if your generous cousins have supplied information about their families or contributed information to you on various lines, be sure it is OK with them for you to publish it on the Web.

To add a Family Tree Maker report to your home page, press Alt+Tab or use the Windows Taskbar to switch back to Family Tree Maker, and then follow these steps:

1. Open the Family File from which you want to create a report.

2. From the <u>V</u>iew menu in Family Tree Maker, select the view that you want to use (<u>R</u>eport, <u>G</u>enealogy Report, or <u>O</u>utline Descendant Tree).

3. Using any of the features available on the <u>C</u>ontents or Forma<u>t</u> menus, select the individuals you want to include and make formatting choices. The appearance of your report in Family Tree Maker is the same as it will have online.

4. From the <u>I</u>nternet menu, choose <u>P</u>ublish Report to the Internet. A message box appears, advising you to ensure you have established an online connection.

5. Click on OK. Family Tree Maker informs you of the uploading progress of your report (see Figure 15-6).

6. Click on OK. Family Tree Maker asks if you would like to contribute your Family File to the World Family Tree project. Click on No unless you have properly restricted the information you will be contributing. (You can answer Yes at another time when your Family File is ready.)

7. Switch to your browser and display your home page to see if the report link is there yet. You may need to click on your browser's Reload or Refresh button to update the page.

�֎ **TIP** �֎ *If your home page isn't already on the screen, use your bookmark to jump to your home page. If you forgot to bookmark it and lost track of where it is, you can look it up. See the section, "Searching for User Home Pages," later in this chapter.*

Figure 15-6

Uploading reports to
your home page is
easy with Family
Tree Maker.

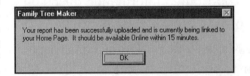

The link will appear on your home page in a Report Section created by Family Tree Maker Online. The type of report and your title for the report will be shown as an underlined link.

8. Click on the new report link on your home page. The report appears on a separate page. Be sure it looks the way you expect it to look.

9. End your Internet session by closing your browser and disconnecting from your ISP.

Depending on which report you have chosen to include in your home page, it may look something like "Descendants of Nicholas Porter Earp" (see Figure 15-7).

Figure 15-8 shows part of the report from Figure 5-7, starting with Nicholas Porter Earp (the father of Wyatt Earp). Figure 15-9 shows a portion of the sources used to compile this genealogy.

Figure 15-7

The start of a Genealogy Report in NGS Quarterly format on a home page.

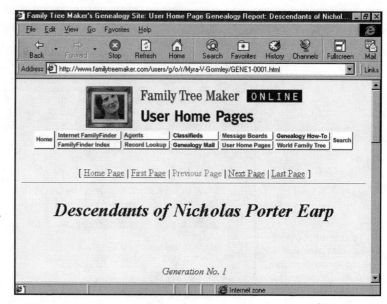

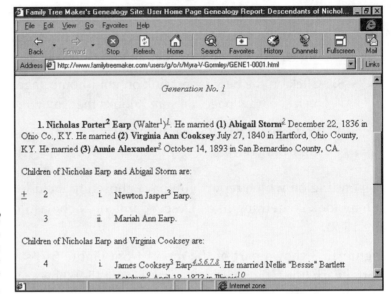

Figure 15-8

You can publish a genealogy of your family on your home page.

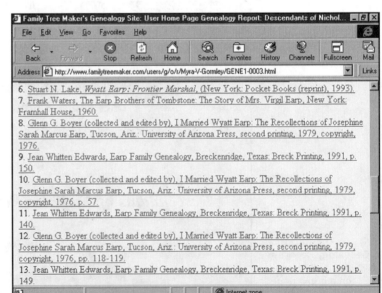

Figure 15-9

Footnotes showing sources used in the Earp genealogy also appear in the Genealogy Report published on the Web.

ADDING THE INTERNETREE

You can add a tree to your home page, but you don't create and customize a tree and upload it like you do with a report. Instead, Family Tree Maker Online uses InterneTree, a Java applet that lets you view box-style trees on Web pages. It displays a tree of individuals (you decide whom to include) with a person in the center, all of that person's ancestors to the right, and all of the descendants to the left. You can zoom in and out, click on any of the boxes to move through the tree, choose a new center person, and view details about the center person.

> ❊ **TIP** ❊   *It is best to have no more than 500 people in your InterneTree because slower computers may not be able to view it if it gets any larger.*

The family tree created by InterneTree will automatically show the following information for individuals you choose to include in the tree. (If you prefer not to share this information, you can edit a copy of your Family File to exclude it.)

- ❊ Names of individuals
- ❊ Birth date
- ❊ Death date

To add an InterneTree to your home page, follow these steps:

1. Open the Family File from which you want to create the tree, and display the Family Page. Don't switch to a tree view—the menu option for the next step won't be available if you do.

2. From the Internet menu, choose Publish Family Tree To The Internet. A message box appears, advising you to ensure that you have established an online connection.

3. Click on OK. The Include dialog box appears (see Figure 15-10).

4. Select the All Individuals option button to include everyone in your Family File, or choose the Selected Individuals option button and click on the Individuals To Include button to select the individuals from a list.

Figure 15-10

Decide which
individuals to include
on your InterneTree.

If you clicked on the Individuals To Include button, the Individuals To
Include dialog box appears. You're already familiar with selecting individuals from the Available Individuals list box on the left and
moving them to the Included Individuals list box on the right. Select
all the individuals you want to include in the InterneTree. Keep in
mind that birth and death information is included for each individual
you select. Click on OK to return to the Include dialog box.

5. Click on OK again. Family Tree Maker displays a status bar while
    the tree information is being uploaded, and informs you when it is
    complete.

6. Click on OK. Before the tree information is finished uploading, Fam-
    ily Tree Maker will probably ask if you would like to contribute your
    Family File to the World Family Tree project. Click on No unless you
    have properly restricted the information you will be contributing.
    (You can answer Yes at another time when your Family File is ready,
    and Family Tree Maker will lead you through the transfer.)

7. Switch to your home page to see if the tree link is there yet (it might
    take a few minutes to become available). You may need to click on
    your browser's Reload or Refresh button to update the page.

    The link will appear on your home page with the name InterneTree.
    It will be in the Report Section along with the reports you create (see
    Figure 15-11).

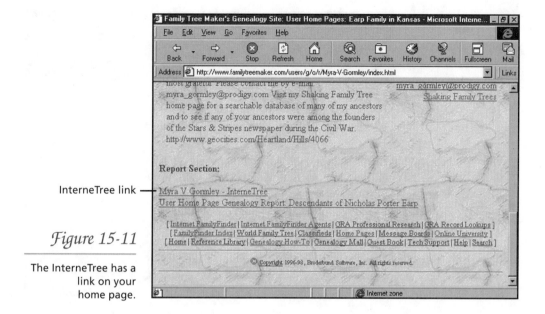

InterneTree link

Figure 15-11

The InterneTree has a
link on your
home page.

8. Click on the InterneTree link on your home page. The InterneTree appears on a separate page (see Figure 15-12). There are instructions and more information available on that page. Read them to learn how to navigate the InterneTree.

9. End your Internet session by closing your browser and disconnecting from your ISP.

ADDING A BOOK TO YOUR HOME PAGE

You learned how to create a Family History Book in Chapter Thirteen. Be sure your book is as polished as you would like it to be before you publish it on the Web for the whole world to see. Also, remember the usual privacy considerations, excluding information that should not be shared publicly.

Your home page can only contain one book; if you add a new one it will replace the previous one. Due to current limitations of the HTML used to display information on the Web, your book may look significantly different on the Web than it does in Family Tree Maker, and some of the formatting options,

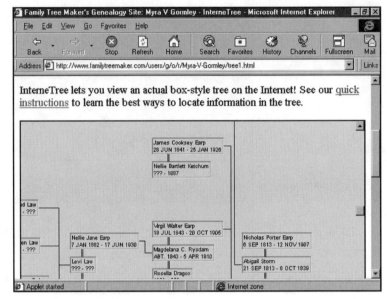

Figure 15-12

The InterneTree has instructions at the bottom of the page.

such as colors and borders, may not transfer to the Web at all. To publish a book from your Family File to your home page, use the following steps:

1. Click on the Books button on the toolbar, or from the View menu, choose Books. The Books window appears.

2. Open the book you want to publish.

3. From the Internet menu, choose Publish Book To The Internet. The Book Upload dialog box appears, telling you Family Tree Maker will prepare your book for publication on your home page.

4. Click on OK. Family Tree Maker displays a status bar while the book information is being uploaded, and informs you when it is complete.

5. Click on OK. Before the book information is finished uploading, Family Tree Maker will ask if you would like to contribute your Family File to the World Family Tree Project. Click on No unless you have properly restricted the information you will be contributing. (You can answer Yes at another time when your Family File is ready, and Family Tree Maker will lead you through the transfer.) The link with your book's title will appear on your home page in the Report Section along with your other reports and the InterneTree. You can click on the link to view your book.

6. End your Internet session by closing your browser and disconnecting from your ISP.

    ⚜ **NOTE** ⚜   *When you first upload your book, it may take anywhere from a few minutes to several hours for it to appear as a link on your home page. However, the length of time will be directly related to the size of the book. Trees will take the longest amount of time since each tree has to be converted into an InterneTree.*

Removing and Deleting Stuff

You can remove the book or any of the reports from your home page as well as delete your entire home page if you want. Go to the Family Tree Maker Online User Home Pages, located at **http://www.familytreemaker.com/users/ index.html**. (You can also access this page from the Family Tree Maker Online home page by scrolling down to the Genealogy Community heading in the left column and clicking on Home Pages.) Click on any of these options:

    🏃 Remove a Family Tree Maker report from your home page.

    🏃 Remove a Family Tree Maker book from your home page.

    🏃 Delete your home page.

If you choose to remove a Family Tree Maker report from your home page, you'll see a page listing the report names and the dates they were uploaded

Figure 15-13

Removing reports
from a home page
is simple.

(see Figure 15-13). If you created an InterneTree, it also appears on the list and can be deleted here. Click on the check box in the Delete column for the reports you want to delete. Then click on the Delete button. Family Tree Maker confirms your deletions.

> ➳ **CAUTION** ➳ *Remember that deleting your user home page will also delete all reports, books, and trees attached to that page.*

If you decide to permanently delete your home page and have clicked on the Delete Your Home Page link, simply click on the Delete Home Page button shown in Figure 15-14. If you change your mind, click on Keep Home Page. Family Tree Maker confirms that you deleted or kept your page.

Searching for User Home Pages

You will want to see what others have done and explore their home pages at Family Tree Maker Online by searching the User Home Pages. To do this, you can browse through home pages of people by surnames of the persons who created them (arranged in alphabetical order).

Figure 15-14

It's easy to delete a home page from Family Tree Maker Online.

From the Family Tree Maker Online User Home Pages page (**http://www.family treemaker.com/users/index.html**), scroll to the Look At Other Home Pages section, and click on the first letter of the last name of the person whose home page you want to view. Family Tree Maker will display either a list of additional letter choices or a list of people with home pages that begin with the letter you selected.

> ❋ **TIP** ❋   *The Internet FamilyFinder is a good tool to use if you are searching for names. It will show you some of the text in the pages matching your search to allow you to determine if you want to go see that information.*

Another way to find User Home Pages is to click on the Search option (located on the menu at the top or bottom of the page) and type in the name you want to find. The Search Family Tree Maker Online option allows you to search for information anywhere in the Family Tree Maker Online Web site, *except* the FamilyFinder Index. You can search for the following:

- ❊ Names on Family Archive CDs
- ❊ Names on the Internet

⚞ E-mail addresses on the Internet

⚞ Current phone numbers and addresses

Simply fill in the fields provided and click on the Search Now button. Family Tree Maker Online will search, and then show you a list of pages that contain all the information you entered. It will search any or all of the following (depending on the check boxes you select):

⚞ User Home Pages, message boards, classified ads, uploaded reports, as well as the Sons of Union Veterans of the Civil War (SUVCW) and Sons of Confederate Veterans (SCV) project pages.

⚞ Genealogy SiteFinder.

⚞ All other sections of Family Tree Maker Online, including genealogy articles, the Genealogy "How-To" Guide, Family Tree Maker product descriptions, the genealogy mall, and technical support.

You will have greater success if you take the time to read the Searching Instructions posted on this Web page, and then experiment with the various options to find your names. Web pages constantly change, and some of the hits—the sites the search engine finds for you—may be obsolete or not accessible (see Figure 15-15).

Building a home page with Family Tree Maker is easy, and you'll be surprised at how many cousins you will make connections with as a result. Enjoy your home on the Web—and update it often. See you online.

Figure 15-15

Searching for the surname of Earp turned up hits in 258 pages.

Glossary

Ahnentafel. German for *ancestor table* (a type of chart). The term also refers to a genealogical numbering system that makes it easy to identify the relationship between any individual listed on a chart of this type and the individual who is its primary subject.

Ancestor. Person from whom one is descended.

Ancestor Tree. A type of chart that starts with an individual and moves back through the generations of all his or her ancestors; also called a pedigree chart.

Annotated. Explanatory or critical notes and commentary for text. One of the options for Family Tree Maker's Bibliography Report is an Annotated Bibliography, which displays all the information you enter about your sources.

ASCII (pronounced Ask-key). American Standard Code for Information Interchange. The most widely used computer coding system in the world. Most word processing programs allow users to save and read documents in ASCII format.

Bibliography. A report that shows the sources of information used in compiling a genealogy. Family Tree Maker provides this option in standard and annotated styles—that is, with publication info only or with publication info plus commentary on the quality and content of the source.

BMP. Bitmap. A file format used for graphics such as Windows wallpaper.

Book. A complete chronicle of your family history with family trees, reports, stories, pictures, Table of Contents, Index, and more.

Bookmarks. Similar to a bookmark that is placed in a book, an electronic Bookmark is a Netscape Navigator browser feature that keeps track of a particular Web site's address and name so that users can easily return to the site. Microsoft's Internet Explorer browser calls the feature *Favorites*.

Browser. See *Web Browser*.

Case-Sensitive. Distinguishing between uppercase and lowercase characters.

Chart. A diagram of family relationships. Family Tree Maker uses the term *Tree* for this concept.

CD-ROM. Compact disc with read-only memory. A CD can hold approximately 650MB of data, or approximately 300,000 pages of text, or what it would take about 450 1.44MB floppy disks to hold.

Citation. The formal notation of the source of the information.

Cite. To record or call attention to the proof or source of a piece of information.

Clipboard. A memory feature that Windows uses to store the last information that a user copied or cut (but not deleted). It is useful when transferring information within a document or between documents. However, it can hold only one item at a time.

Collateral Line. Persons with whom you share a common ancestor, but who are not on your direct line of descent.

Contents Pages. These appear in the FamilyFinder Index and list all of the Family Archives that are referenced in it. All Family Archives have a contents page that shows you how the data on the CD is divided into sections and chapters and information about the material.

Descendant. One who lineally descends from another, through infinite generations.

Descendant Tree. Graphical chart that lists an individual down through generations that list the individual's children, grandchildren, and so on.

Download. To receive a file sent from another computer via modem. Download is synonymous with "receive," while upload is synonymous with "transmit."

E-mail. Electronic mail, which is typically sent over the Internet to a specified individual or group. Received messages can be stored in an inbox and kept, deleted, replied to, or forwarded.

Endnotes. Source citations and explanatory notes that appear at the end of a document. Similar to footnotes, only appearing at the end of the whole piece rather than at the bottom of each page of text. Compare to Inline Notes.

Export. To transfer data from one computer to another or from one application to another. See Import.

FACD. An abbreviation for one of Family Tree Maker's Family Archive CDs.

Family Group Sheet. A form used to display information on a family unit; often abbreviated as FGS.

FamilyFinder Index. A genealogical list with currently 170 million names included in Family Tree Maker's CDs.

Family History Library and Centers. Refers to the famous genealogical library of the Church of Jesus Christ of Latter-day Saints (Mormons) in Salt Lake City. Family History Centers are branches of this library and are located throughout the world.

Family Page. This is the main screen in Family Tree Maker where you enter information about individuals in a family. It is made up of a series of fields (where you type information) and labels that tell the purpose of each field.

Family Traditions. Stories handed down from generation to generation, usually orally.

Favorites. See *Bookmarks*.

Format. One of Family Tree Maker's options pertaining to the style and various options of reports and trees.

Gateway Ancestor. See *Immigrant Ancestor*.

Genealogy. The account or history of descent of a person, or the study of family history.

Genealogy Report. A detailed listing of family information displayed in narrative format, including basic facts about each family member, plus any biographical information that's been entered into the Family File. Family Tree Maker provides three styles for these reports: Register, NGS Quarterly, and Ahnentafel.

GEDCOM. Genealogical Data Communication. A standard file format designed by the Family History Department of the Church of Jesus Christ of Latter-day Saints used to transfer genealogical data between different genealogy software packages.

Generation. An average period of time between the birth of one group of individuals and the next, usually about 25 to 33 years.

GIF. Graphic Interchange Format. A bit-mapped color graphics file format that is widely used in HTML documents for images.

Given Name. First name (and middle name, where present) given to a child at birth or baptism. Also called a *Christian* name.

Holographic Will. A document, in this instance a will, wholly in the handwriting of the person whose signature it bears, but not witnessed (attested).

Home Page. The main page at a Web site.

Hourglass Tree. Diagram that shows both ancestors and descendants of a particular individual in a style resembling an hourglass, because it spreads out above and below the primary individual.

HTML. Hypertext Markup Language. The standard language used for creating and formatting World Wide Web pages. HTML documents are essentially text documents (as you would create in a word-processing program) that have tags embedded in them, which contain coding for text formatting, graphics, and hyperlinks.

Hyperlink. Something in one file that automatically brings up another location for viewing if a user clicks the mouse on it. These links are graphics or different colored text attached to HTML code that provides the actual connection to the other location, which may be part of the same file, another file on the same Web site, or a different Web site entirely.

Icon. A small graphical representation of an object or idea, used to represent a function on a program.

Ibid. Abbreviation for *ibidem*, a Latin term meaning in the same place; used especially in Register and NGS Quarterly System endnotes when referring to a work fully cited previously and immediately preceding the current note.

Immigrant. Person who comes to a country from another to establish permanent residence.

Immigrant Ancestor. First of a family line to arrive in the new country and establish a permanent residence there. Also called a *gateway ancestor*.

Import. To bring a file created in one application or system into another application or system. See *Export*.

Inline Notes. Sources that appear within the text rather than as endnotes or footnotes; an option offered in Family Tree Maker's Genealogy Reports.

Internet. A noncommercial, self-governing network devoted mostly to communication and research, with millions of users worldwide. The Internet is not a service and has no real central hub. Rather, it is a collection of tens of thousands of networks, online services, and single-user components.

Internet Service Provider (ISP). A company or organization that allows other computer users to dial in and connect to its Internet connection for a fee. Some ISPs provide other services, such as e-mail or chat areas.

Kinship. In genealogy, refers to relationships of any and all of one's relatives; Family Tree Maker has a Kinship Report that lists the names, relationships, and relationship degrees of the primary individual's blood relatives and their spouses, as well as the blood relatives of the primary individual's spouse or spouses.

Newsgroup. A group of messages about a single topic. On the Internet, newsgroups bring together people from around the world for discussions on topics of shared interest.

NUCMC. National Union Catalog of Manuscript Collections. Detailed descriptions of manuscript collections in public, private, and academic libraries are indexed and cross-referenced in this catalog, which has been published annually since 1962 by the Library of Congress.

JPEG. Joint Photographic Expert Group. Often used in discussing file format .JPG that uses a compression technique to reduce the size of a graphics file. This is the preferred file format to use when you want to put a photograph on a Web page.

Maternal Ancestor. An ancestor on the mother's side of the family.

MIDI. Musical Instrument Digital Interface. A file format indicated by MID, for digitally representing and transmitting sounds of electronic devices such as keyboards and sound cards. Provides a protocol for transforming music into data and vice versa.

NGSQ. An abbreviation for *National Genealogical Society Quarterly,* a periodical published by that society; also refers to the NGS Quarterly System of its descending genealogy used therein.

OLE. Object Linking and Embedding. A technology that enables you to create items in one program and place them in another. OLE objects are items such as video clips, still images, or pictures and text objects from a word processor, spreadsheet, or database.

Online. Refers to the successful connection with another computer via a modem, cable line, or through a network.

Online Service. A service that provides news, information, and discussion forums for users with modem-equipped PCs and the access software provided by the service.

Outline Descendant Tree. Diagram that shows an individual's children, grandchildren, great-grandchildren, and so on in an outline form rather than in boxes on a chart. Each individual's information is on a separate line, and each generation is indented slightly more than the one before it; each descendant's spouse is directly beneath him or her and is marked with a plus sign.

PAF. Personal Ancestral File. A genealogy software package produced by the Church of Jesus Christ of Latter-Day Saints.

Paternal Ancestor. An ancestor on the father's side of the family.

PCX. A graphics file format.

Pedigree Chart. Diagram that shows direct ancestors of an individual. See *Ancestor Tree*.

Preferred. A term Family Tree Maker uses in reference to parents and spouses, meaning the individuals you wish to see first or have displayed in Ancestor Trees or Family Pages.

Primary Individual. The main individual in any of the Family Tree Maker diagrams and reports.

Research Journal. Record used by genealogists to keep track of their research findings (negative and positive) and a place to note references and sources that need to be examined or explored further.

Reports. Any of the various standard and custom accounts in various formats that can be created by Family Tree Maker. These include standard, custom, and genealogy reports as well as Family Group Sheets.

Register. Refers both to a descending genealogy format used by the New England Historic Genealogical Society and its periodical of that name.

RTF. Rich Text Format. A cross-platform, cross-application text document format. It includes some, but not all, of the formatting information that is included in many word processor-created documents.

Scrapbooks. A term used by Family Tree Maker for collections of information, including photos and other scanned images, video, sound, text, and OLE objects, that can be stored for each individual and each marriage.

Search Engine. Software that resides on a Web server and allows you to search documents on the Web for specified keywords.

Siblings. Children of the same parents.

Source. The book, record, or interview from which specific information was obtained; this information is necessary in order to document a genealogy properly.

Spouse. The person to whom another person is married.

Surname. Family name or last name.

Tree. The term Family Tree Maker uses to refer to the various charts (diagrams) it produces. See *Ancestor Tree, Descendant Tree,* and *Outline Descendant Tree.*

Upload. To transfer a file from a local computer to a remote host. Upload is synonymous with "transmit," while download is synonymous with "receive." See *Download*.

URL. Uniform Resource Locator. A naming or addressing system that helps users locate Web sites on the Internet.

Vital Records. Records relating to birth, marriage, and death. Divorce records are often included in this category. These records may be civil, church, or personal ones. Literally, the term, which comes from the Latin *vita* (life), simply refers to the facts of a life—born, married, and died. The records may be official or unofficial.

WAV. Windows Audio Visual. Sound files that work with Media Player and Sound Recorder.

Web Browser. Software that lets you access and navigate the World Wide Web. Using a graphical interface that lets users click on buttons, icons, and menu options to access commands, browsers show Web pages as graphical rather than text-based documents. Browsers let users move between sites either by clicking on hyperlinks or by entering a Web page's URL. Netscape Navigator and Microsoft Internet Explorer are two popular browsers.

Web Page. A document on the World Wide Web that is formatted with Hypertext Markup Language (HTML), the standard format in which documents are exchanged on the Web. Web pages are found by addresses called URLs.

Web Site. A location managed by a single entity that provides information such as text, graphics, and audio files to users as well as connections (called hyperlinks) to other Web sites on the Internet. Every Web site has a home page, the initial document seen by users, which acts as a table of contents to other available offerings at the site. For example, the Family Tree Maker Web site is located at **http://www.familytreemaker.com/**.

Wildcard Characters. Symbols that replace one or more characters in a file name or other word; useful when searching for variant spellings of names. The two most common wildcard characters are the asterisk (also sometimes called a star) and the question mark. The asterisk replaces a group of characters while the question mark replaces only one.

World Family Tree (WFT) Project. A multivolume CD collection created by Brøderbund from genealogies submitted, electronically and on disk, by family history enthusiasts. Individuals in the World Family Tree Project are listed in the FamilyFinder Index.

World Wide Web. A graphical interface for the Internet that is composed of Internet servers providing access to documents, which in turn provide hyperlinks to other documents, multimedia files, and sites.

Index

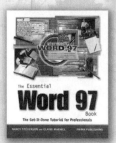

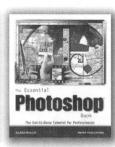